Land of Famished Beings

LAND OF FAMISHED BEINGS

West Papuan
Theories of Hunger

Sophie Chao

DUKE UNIVERSITY PRESS
Durham and London
2025

© 2025 DUKE UNIVERSITY PRESS
All rights reserved
Project Editor: Livia Tenzer
Designed by A. Mattson Gallagher
Typeset in Minion Pro and Source Sans 3
by Westchester Publishing Services

Library of Congress Cataloging-in-Publication Data
Names: Chao, Sophie author
Title: Land of famished beings : West Papuan theories of hunger /
Sophie Chao.
Other titles: West Papuan theories of hunger
Description: Durham : Duke University Press, 2025. | Includes
bibliographical references and index.
Identifiers: LCCN 2024055515 (print)
LCCN 2024055516 (ebook)
ISBN 9781478032038 paperback
ISBN 9781478028765 hardcover
ISBN 9781478060956 ebook
Subjects: LCSH: Food security—Indonesia—Papua Barat |
Marind (Indonesian people)—Food | Marind (Indonesian
people)—Nutrition | Hunger—Indonesia—Papua Barat | Food
supply—Indonesia—Papua Barat | Agriculture—Indonesia—
Papua Barat | Farm produce—Indonesia—Papua Barat | Crop
rotation—Indonesia—Papua Barat
Classification: LCC HD9016.I53 P378 2025 (print) |
LCC HD9016.I53 (ebook) | DDC 338.7/630899922—dc23/
eng/20250519
LC record available at https://lccn.loc.gov/2024055515
LC ebook record available at https://lccn.loc.gov/2024055516

Cover art: Dried betel nuts and slaked lime powder passed
around during a community meeting, rural Merauke, West
Papua, June 2019. Photograph by the author.

For Mina

CONTENTS

This work draws on fieldwork conducted in Bahasa Indonesia, the national idiom in the Republic of Indonesia, and *logat* Papua, a creole of Indonesian and the lingua franca across different Indigenous groups inhabiting the Indonesian-occupied region of West Papua. The Bian dialect of Marind is spoken fluently only by a few elderly villagers in the settlements of Mirav, Bayau, and Khalaoyam, where ethnographic research was undertaken. In this book, terms in Bahasa Indonesia and *logat* Papua are italicized, and terms in the Bian dialect of Marind are underlined. In both instances, terms are translated into English from the source language used by my interlocutors.

The name Merauke refers to the regency of Merauke (*kabupaten* Merauke) and Merauke City to the regency's capital city (*kota* Merauke). The name West Papua refers to the western half of the island of New Guinea, formerly known as Irian Barat and Irian Jaya. Under Indonesian jurisdiction, West Papua is divided into Papua province (*propinsi* Papua) and West Papua province (*propinsi* Papua Barat), with Merauke regency located in Papua province. Pseudonyms are used for all places except major cities, regencies, and provinces. Names of persons have been retained in the original where so requested by the individuals cited. In all other instances, pseudonyms and descriptive qualifiers were chosen by my companions. In line with my companions' wishes, I have not distinguished pseudonyms from actual names within the text.

All photos were selected for inclusion by the individuals and groups featured therein, by mothers in the case of children and infants, and by close relatives in the case of now-deceased community members.

ACKNOWLEDGMENTS

This book was crafted on the unceded lands of the Gadigal People of the Eora Nation in Australia. I pay my respects to Gadigal elders past, present, and emergent, and to Gadigal kin—human, vegetal, animal, and elemental. The lands of Gadigal, like those of Indigenous Peoples across the world, were taken without consent, treaty, or compensation. They are lands whose stories have historically been stolen, silenced, and sanitized. And they are lands of ongoing Indigenous survivance, continuance, and resurgence. Indigenous lands—always have been, always will be.

I thank the participants of an ultimate peer review held on September 15, 2015, for their rich and incisive feedback on an earlier version of this manuscript: Warwick Anderson, Philippa Barr, Mark Byron, Hannah Della Bosca, Laurens Ikinia, Aila Naderbagi, Natali Pearson, Robbie Peters, Hans Pols, Bill Pritchard, Gregoire Randin, David Schlosberg, and Lee Wallace. I extend gratitude to the Sydney Social Sciences and Humanities Advanced Research Centre at the University of Sydney for hosting this event and particularly to Craig Santos Perez for acting as expert authority in this ultimate peer review.

The analysis presented in this work was informed by generous comments received during guest lectures, conference papers, keynotes, and work-in-progress seminars hosted by the University of Wisconsin–Madison; Deakin

University; Carleton University; the School of Oriental and African Studies; the Sydney Environment Institute; the Sydney Center for Healthy Societies; the Charles Perkins Centre; the Sydney Southeast Asia Centre; the Australian Food, Society, and Culture Network; and the Australian Anthropological Society. I thank the organizers and participants of these events for their generative insights and questions, in particular Aida Arosaie, Danielle Celermajer, Teresa Davis, Ariane Defreine, Marion Durocher, Eloise Fetterplace, Michele Ford, Anthony Ryan Hatch, Lindsay Kelley, Christopher Mayes, Timothy Neale, Elspeth Probyn, David Raubenheimer, Alice Rudge, Angie Sassano, Nikita Simpson, Stephen Simpson, Jakelin Troy, Carina Truyts, Blanche Verlie, Christine Winter, and Genevieve Wright. I extend particular gratitude to the participants of the 2023 American Anthropological Association roundtable, "Metabolic (In)justice," for their insightful provocations: Ariana Ávila, Megan Carney, Sarah Elton, Terese Gagnon, Hanna Garth, Jessica Hardin, Pallavi Laxmikanth, Amy Moran-Thomas, Lupita Vazquez-Reyes, and Emily Yates-Doerr. I also thank my doctoral students for many deep conversations around questions of ethics, representation, and fieldwork that revolved around and informed both their and this project: Victoria Bonilla-Baez, Meherose Borthwick, Emily Crawford, Myles Oakey, Misty Shan-e-alam, and Samuel Widin.

I am grateful to the participants of the "Analytics of Vulnerability" advanced seminar, held on January 22–24, 2024, in Santa Fe, New Mexico, for helping me think through questions of violence and vulnerability within this book: Heather Howard, Don Kulick, Martin Lamotte, Norma Mendoza-Denton, Michel Naepels, Karen Nakamura, Timothy Pachirat, Sharon Rider, and Mary Weismantel. The following cited scholars responded generously to my queries regarding self-identification, for which I am deeply grateful: Louise Boscacci, Athia Choudhury, Elaine Coburn, Trisia Farrelly, Simon Foale, Paloma Gay y Blasco, Jessica Hardin, Melinda Hinkson, Noriko Ishiyama, Aya Kimura, Tamara Kneese, Camilo Leon-Quijano, Valérie Loichot, Michelle MacCarthy, Carole McGranahan, Kenna Neitch, Juno Salazar Parreñas, Elspeth Probyn, Parama Roy, Peter Rudiak-Gould, Felicity Amaya Schaeffer, Matthew Scobie, Will Smith, Alice Street, James Vernon, Anita von Poser, Suliasi Vunibola, Kyla Wazana Tompkins, and Erica Weiss.

Fieldwork toward this book was supported by grants and scholarships received from the Australian Ministry of Education and Training, the Wenner-Gren Foundation for Anthropological Research (Gr. 9942; Gr. EAG-136; Gr. 9196), the Australian Research Council (DE220100025), the Janet Dora Hines Postdoctoral Endowment, the Charles Perkins Centre, the Faculty of Arts and Social Sciences at the University of Sydney, and the Department of Anthropology at Macquarie University.

At Duke University Press, I thank Ken Wissoker for his invaluable editorial support and care in shepherding this work through the review and revision process. It has been a continued and sustained joy to think with and learn from you in bringing this second book to full fruition, Ken. I thank Kate Mullen for guiding me through the publication process and Susan Ecklund for her meticulous copyediting, as well as project editor Livia Tenzer and designer A. Mattson Gallagher. I extend deep gratitude to the two peer reviewers of this monograph for their immensely thoughtful and constructive contributions.

Much of the thinking in this work was directly nourished by constructive critiques of my first monograph, which also drew on long-term fieldwork conducted in rural West Papua. I thank the authors of published reviews of that first work for pushing and prodding me to revisit my ethnographic materials and conceptual analyses in ways that were generative of different and enriched insights for this second book: Warwick Anderson, Sebastian Antoine, Sally Babidge, Nicholas Bainton, Carter Beale, Sarah Besky, Kevin Burke, Tomas Cole, Camelia Dewan, Nathália Dothling, Rebecca Dudley, Shaila Seshia Galvin, Jamon Halvaksz, Isabelle Hermanns, Shweta Krishnan, Tania Murray Li, Nicholas Mahillon, Orven Mallari, Jennifer Marshman, Julia Morris, Sara Mejía Muñoz, Philippe Pataud Célerier, Sylvia Pergetti, Serina Rahman, Mardi Reardon-Smith, Jessica Richardson, Tyler Riordan, Alice Rudge, Danilyn Rutherford, Ainá Sant'Anna Fernandes, Pujo Semedi, Rupert Stasch, Marilyn Strathern, Sarah Thomson, Jakelin Troy, Irene van Oorschot, Rosa Cavalcanti Ribas Vieira, Eve Vincent, Kirsty Wissing, and Robert Wolfgramm.

I thank the Marind communities of West Papua for their immense hospitality and generosity throughout and beyond my fieldwork in rural Merauke. I extend particular gratitude to the individuals cited in this work for their intellectual companionship over the last decade, for their patience, and for their courage: Adriana, Alexandrina, Ana, Ariana, Aurelina, Bendita, Benedicta, Bernardina, Caritas, Carlotta, Carmelita, Cesarina, Circia, Cistina, Cosmina, Costanza, Eliana, Fenella, Florensia, Geraldina, Gilbertus, Jovi, Julia, Justina, Karola, Karolina, Katarina, Klara, Klaus, Kloella, Kosmina, Kristal, Marcelina, Marcella, Marcia, Marelina, Mariska, Matthias, Mina, Mirabela, Nora, Oktavia, Olivia, Paola, Paolina, Patricia, Paula, Paulina, Perpetua, Petra, Pia, Pius, Rafaela, Rubina, Selena, Serafina, Sofia, Stefania, Susana, Veronika, Vicentia, Virginia, and Yoanna. Of the many beings who made this research possible, yet who cannot be named for reasons of safety and security, I acknowledge and thank my sisters of the Kaize (cassowary) clan, my brothers of the Basik-Basik (pig) clan, and the women elders of the Walef (kangaroo) and Balagaize (crocodile) clans. I also thank Angky Samperante and Emil Ola Kleden at Yayasan Pusaka Bentala Rakyat and Father Amo Anselmus at the Secretariat for Justice and Peace for their support throughout my research and Albertus Vembrianto and various community members who wish to remain unnamed for the permission to use their photographs within this book. I also thank Geoffrey Wallace for permission to reproduce the map featured in this book. Last but not least, heartfelt gratitude goes to my parents, Dominique and Jacques, my brother, Emmanuel, and my partner, Jacob, for their unfailing support and nourishing presence over the years. All shortcomings in this book are mine.

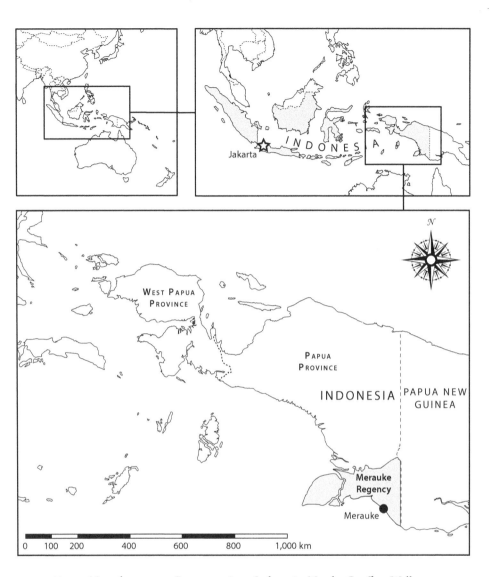

Map 1. Merauke regency, Papua province, Indonesia. Map by Geoffrey Wallace.

INTRODUCTION

Sitting cross-legged on the front porch of her hut in the West Papuan village of Bayau, Ana, an Indigenous Marind woman in her mid-twenties from the Kaize (cassowary) clan, watched the sun sink against the bleary sky. It was a torrid evening in late December 2016. The air quivered with swarms of mosquitoes. Their languorous buzzing mingled with the metallic rattle of chainsaws in a nearby oil palm plantation and the irregular breathing of Ana's two youngest children, Julius and Circia, who lay huddled on a cot of woven sago fibers, sleeping.[1] My companion slowly massaged her legs, then the lids of her eyes, and then her slightly protruding belly, where her sixth child was growing.[2] She said this child was weak and would likely not grow well—just like her five other children, who were not fed well. Only a few days prior, Ana's elder sister, Mikaela, had lost a second child in labor—a misfortune my friend attributed to Mikaela not eating enough sago and to Mikaela's husband not hunting enough game. Ana ran her fingers along the limbs of her slumbering children. She reached out for my hand, pulling it momentarily away from the small pile of papaya leaves we had collected in the forest earlier that day and that I was destalking in preparation for dinner. My companion murmured: "I worry for these children. I worry about their skin and their wetness. I worry about the world they will inherit. It is a world that will give them nothing good to eat and that will eat them. It is a world of new and different hungers." Then, Ana began to sing.

Ada lagu buat semuanya di tanah-tanah ini
There is a song for every being in this land
Lagu buat kasuari, lagu buat sagu, lagu buat pinang
A song for the cassowary, a song for the sago, a song for the betel nut
Lagu yang cerita hujan, lagu yang cerita tanah, lagu yang cerita keringat
A song that stories the rain, a song that stories the soil, a song that stories the sweat
Tapi setelah sawit datang, kitorang nyanyi lagu baru
But since oil palm arrived, new songs are being sung
Ada lagu tentang hutan, dusun sagu, dan sungai de beri makan
There are songs about being fed—from forests, sago groves, and rivers
Ada lagu tentang jalan, perkebunan, dan kota de makan kita
There are songs about being eaten—by roads, plantations, and cities

Sa nyanyi buat anak-anak, yang su lahir dan belum
I sing for all our children, the born and the unborn
Sa nyanyi buat pace-pace, de jual hutan kita
I sing for all the men, who sell away our forests
Sa nyanyi buat mace-mace, rahimnya su jadi kering
I sing for all the women, whose wombs have all dried out
Sa nyanyi lapar yang hantui, tanah lapar-lapar ini
I sing the haunting hungers of this land, this land of famished beings

Songs have long constituted a central mode of expression and exegesis among the Indigenous Marind People of Indonesian-occupied West Papua, whose experiences and theories of hunger constitute the central theme of this book. These inherited and improvised songs draw into their fold—or, in local parlance, "give voice to" (*kasih suara*)—an array of human and more-than-human beings who together animate the forests, savannas, and wetlands of the southern Papuan landscape.[3] In the last decade, "hunger songs" (*lagu kelaparan*) such as the one uttered by my companion Ana have become increasingly prevalent among those Marind living along the upper reaches of the Bian River in the West Papuan regency of Merauke. The emergence of this new genre coincides with an unprecedented intensification in deforestation and industrial oil palm expansion across Marind's customary lands and territories. Initiated and performed primarily by women, hunger songs juxtapose the storied origins, lives, and relations of Marind and their cherished plant and animal kin with the deleterious effects of waning traditional food environments on their collective well-being, bodies, and futures. They are performed across the public and private domains of homes and hearths, villages and groves, forests and plantations, and roadsides and riverways. Their lyrics conjure in poignant and poetic ways the transformation of nourishing, sentient forests into impoverished, extractive zones. They speak to the emergence of a discordant and disfigured landscape, haunted by a multitude of beings whose hungers are at once new, different, and insatiable.

Drawing on long-term fieldwork conducted in rural West Papua, this book explores how hunger is understood, theorized, and critiqued by Indigenous Marind inhabitants of an emergent plantation frontier. Its analysis revolves around four central questions: How do Marind sense and make sense of hunger? How does hunger multiply depending on its relative subjects and objects? How do Indigenous theories of hunger offer new ways of thinking about the relationship between the environment, food, and nourishment in an age of self-consuming capitalist growth? And when it comes to storying the violence of hunger, how do Indigenous critiques invite us to reimagine the ethics and politics of ethnographic writing and the responsibilities and compromises that shape anthropological commitments, in and beyond the field?

As Ana's lyrics intimate, hunger has become a matter of growing urgency among Marind of the Upper Bian, who have seen vast swaths of their lands and forests targeted for conversion to privatized agro-industrial monocrops since 2010. Implemented as part of a government program known initially as the Merauke Integrated Food and Energy Estate and later renamed the Food Estate Program, plantation expansion is driven by Indonesian food security policies seeking to achieve national self-sufficiency in staple commodities such as palm oil, sugar, and rice. At the time of writing, monocrops extended across over a million hectares in the regency of Merauke and were expanding at a relentless pace. These top-down developments were taking place without the free, prior, or informed consent of local communities, whose land rights were routinely violated and whose customary representational and decision-making institutions were often overlooked or superseded by state-sanctioned administrative bodies.[4] Local women in particular were frequently excluded from consultations surrounding land use and food systems—even as they self-identified as, and represented, primary providers of food at both household and village levels.

In my prior career as a human rights advocate, I collaborated closely with Marind activists, local nongovernmental organizations (NGOs), and transnational coalitions in documenting the adverse impacts of industrial oil palm expansion on Marind's rights to land, food, and environment. It was these activist collaborations, sustained through repeated field visits between 2011 and 2015, that allowed me to develop personal relationships with Marind communities and that lay the grounds for my subsequent long-term fieldwork in Merauke as a doctoral and postdoctoral researcher between 2016 and 2019. Over the course of joint investigative fieldwork, my partners and I gathered evidence of growing food insecurity and malnutrition across the villages of the Upper Bian, which correlated with intensifying rates of deforestation and agribusiness development in the region. Oil palm expansion was threatening the biodiverse ecosystems that Marind rely on for their subsistence, together with the intergenerationally transmitted practices of hunting, fishing, and gathering that forest foodways entail. With forest ecologies giving way to capitalist natures, villagers were becoming increasingly dependent on imported, processed foods such as instant noodles, canned meat, and rice that they received from agribusiness companies as part of corporate social responsibility programs or from the government as compensation for lands surrendered.

Rates of malnutrition, wasting, stunting, and low body weight had soared since the inception of oil palm developments, with particularly pronounced impacts among women, babies, and infants. Data my partners and I obtained from local clinics across the region revealed that malnutrition rates had doubled since 2011 and wasting occurrences had more than tripled over the same period. Of the dozens of children between the ages of four months and four years who passed away during the eighteen months I spent in the field, an overwhelming majority died of malnutrition-related musculoskeletal, gastrointestinal, and immune system ailments including diarrhea, anemia, tuberculosis, gastroenteritis, and bronchopneumonia. These disturbing local realities are symptomatic of a growing trend of rising malnutrition across West Papua, which, together with the eastern provinces of Nusa Tenggara Timur and Maluku, represents one of Indonesia's most food-insecure regions.[5] They also sit within a broader context of ongoing, egregious human rights abuses perpetrated against West Papuans since Indonesian occupation, and which include child killings, disappearances, torture, and the mass displacement of people without access to food, health care, and education facilities.[6]

Marind activists and allied NGOs I worked with deployed the language of "food insecurity" (*ketidakamanan pangan*) and "malnutrition" (*gizi buruk*) in the many reports, petitions, and statements they submitted to corporate sustainability standards and national and international human rights bodies.[7] The recognition of these terms in legal and scientific discourse, they claimed, would strengthen the visibility and validity of their cases and complaints before global audiences. It was only during ensuing long-term ethnographic fieldwork and participant observation in the Upper Bian, enabled in large part by my professional transition from advocacy ally to activist-researcher, that I came to grapple with the limits of these idioms in capturing and conveying what my companions were experiencing on the ground, and the reasons for their hesitancy to invoke such idioms outside legal and lobbying settings.

In everyday life in the villages, people did not talk about food insecurity or malnutrition. Rather, they spoke of living in a state of permanent and pervasive hunger (*kelaparan*)—a state in which people were not only going hungry themselves but also being eaten by multiple different hungry others. Centering hunger as an object of analysis in turn uncovered other kinds of entangled hesitancies among my interlocutors when it came to the question of how and whether to story violence and vulnerability across the realms of the lived and representational, and the descriptive and theoretical. Described in further detail later in the book, these hesitancies were never about Marind and their hungers alone, but rather were deeply revelatory of the risks and responsibilities that accompany anthropological endeavors and research more generally as the often non-innocent metabolization of others' words and worlds.

As the narrative that follows will uncover, Marind experiences and theories point to hunger as a condition that cannot be reduced to an individual, biophysical state defined purely in nutritional, quantitative, or even human terms. Rather, hunger traverses variably situated humans, animals, plants, institutions, infrastructures, spirits, sorcerers, and also anthropologists, who are bound with and against each other in more or less reciprocal relations of feeding and being fed. Across these diverse ecologies of hunger, different foods and associated metabolic processes serve different transformative purposes—some destructive, others generative, and all always dependent on, and diagnostic of, the intersubjective entanglements of consumers and consumed. When approached through the lens of Indigenous Marind philosophies, practices, and protocols, hunger thus reveals itself as a multiple, more-than-human, and morally imbued modality of being—one whose etiologies and effects are no less culturally crafted or contested than food and eating, and one that also raises vital, if troubling, questions around the ethical stakes of communicating hunger, for both those who experience it and those tasked with writing it.

In exploring how hunger reshapes Marind selves, bodies, and relations in Merauke, this book distinguishes itself from technoscientific accounts of food and diet that are anchored in the quantitative metrics of nutrients, food groups, and calories.[8] It offers a grassroots perspective on food insecurity and malnutrition that informs macroscalar, geopolitical analyses character- istic of political economy approaches and food policy discourses.[9] In both respects, the work responds to the call by the American anthropologists Nancy Scheper-Hughes and Kirsten Hastrup for a "critical medical anthro- pology" that recognizes how class, race, ethnicity, and gender intersect with geopolitical, historical, and capitalist world systems in ways that are often obscured by the technocratization and medicalization—and consequent depoliticization—of hunger within state and scientific discourses.[10] In par- ticular, the work pushes against the framing of hunger as a universal, stable, quantifiable, or scalable object or referent. Instead, it approaches hunger as an emergent ecology of situated and shifting meanings, narratives, practices, experiences, affects, spatialities, and temporalities, combined in particular material and discursive assemblages in particular places and at particular times.[11] This framing brings into the fold a range of life-forms, institutions, and infrastructures that are connected to one another through variably re- ciprocal processes of eating and being eaten. It points to hunger as a material and moral *relation* that both troubles and transcends local-global divides.

As Noriko Ishiyama, a Japanese geographer, and Kim TallBear, a Sisseton Wahpeton Oyate science and technology studies scholar, remind us, the fact that relations and relationality are constitutive of worlds does not mean that all relations are good.[12] Centering the violence of hunger as a relation does work on multiple, interrelated levels. It pushes against the straitjacketing of hunger within dominant discourses of food security or malnutrition—framings that, while recognized and deployed by Marind activists themselves in light of their strategic valences and intelligibility to formal policymaking and biomedical institutions, fail to capture in their apolitical, human-centric, and clinical dimensions the bodily, cultural, and affective ways in which hunger manifests and is signified. It identifies in the expansion of industrial food production systems and top-down rural devel- opment policies and projects the roots of intensified "nutritional structural violence," set against cumulative histories of colonial occupation, wherein resource extraction and land exploitation operate hand in hand with Indigenous displacement, dispossession, and disempowerment.[13] It calls for a critical interrogation of the possibility for Indigenous food sovereignty in settler-extractive frontiers like West Papua, where the twin forces of empire and capital exert a visceral grip on human and other-than-human modes of being, becoming, and belonging.[14]

This approach further allows for a reappraisal of hunger as a socially modulated condition and idiom through which distress and the structural violences that produce it and the metabolic injustices that mediate it are differentially experienced and expressed by Indigenous communities on the periphery of the capitalist world system.[15] It draws attention to colonization itself as a project driven by material and ideological forms of hunger, grounded in the protocapitalist logic of property, growth, and surplus, and fueled by the intensifying exploitation of privatized land, labor, and resources, to the benefit of some and the detriment of others.[16] It also raises broader and deeper questions for anthropologists around the politics of writing the violence of hunger through the non-innocent medium of ethnographic texts, as these are shaped by the authority of researchers, the heterogeneous perspectives of their interlocutors, and the equally diverse positionalities of their audiences.

Delving into the dispersed meanings and manifestations of hunger among Marind follows injunctions by the Indian anthropologist Veena Das and the American cultural theorist Kathleen Stewart to approach sociality and suffering through a descent into the ordinary affects, ontological conflicts, and social frictions of everyday life.[17] This approach brings me to attend to Marind's own deliberations and dilemmas over what hunger is, what it does, what can be done with it, why it exists, and why it persists. What emerges from these deliberations and dilemmas, as I trace them in the book, are concepts of hunger that vary in both kind and degree. Certain hungers are positively valued in that they testify to individuals' and groups' investment of labor, toil, skin, and sweat in daily activities that sustain both those individuals and groups and their wider social circles—for instance, hunting game, processing sago, walking the landscape, and providing for one's kin. Some hungers are seasonal and foreseeable, whereas others are protracted and punitive. Some are regulated through local protocols and customary etiquette, while others stem from external forces like government institutions, industrial plantations, road infrastructures, and corporate sorcerers that are difficult, if not impossible, to control. Different foodstuffs are said by Marind to satisfy different kinds of hungers, while other foodstuffs come with the promise of satiation but never deliver—or, at times, even exacerbate and amplify the hunger of those who consume them.

In each instance, Marind concepts of hunger vary in meaning and manifestation depending on the relationship between the feeder, the food, and the fed within an ecology of eating and being eaten that encompasses not only Marind people and places but also the broader capitalist system within which they are embedded and its unevenly distributed gendered, racial, political, and ecological dynamics. In these and many other respects, Marind conceptualizations identify in the condition of hunger a way of being *in* the world that is also a statement *about* that world and a reconfiguration *of* that world, enacted through different modes of narration, contestation, and interrogation. Hunger, in other words, exists to Marind as a multiple and active disposition rather than solely a passive experience of lack and deprivation— even as hunger also exerts at times viscerally diminishing effects on those who experience it, and even as it is frequently idiomatized by Marind as the result of others eating (in) their place.

Marind philosophies of hunger thus uncover how disparate gastrological regimes are differentially defined and evaluated depending on what foods are believed to satiate or undermine hunger, and depending on the material-semiotic valences of the places, persons, and practices associated with particular foods and particular hungers.[18] They reveal hunger to be a consequence of externally imposed gastrocolonial regimes *and* a site of contested internal gastropolitics among Indigenous Marind themselves.[19] In each instance, hunger comes to constitute a politically charged, phenomenological index for broader dynamics of consumption and production, health and disease, and becoming and belonging.[20] It conjures what the South Asian postcolonial studies scholar Parama Roy identifies as the centrality of the alimentary tract as a "corporeal, psychoaffective, and ethicopolitical contact zone" wherein dynamics of identification, desire, dissent, and difference are performed and debated.[21]

In framing hunger as a *more-than*-local condition and crisis, Marind critiques of the broader political, historical, and economic forces transforming their forests, foodways, and futures speak visceral—if unpalatable—truths about the capitalistic (il)logic of limitless resource and profit accumulation that dictates who must go hungry in order for whom to be fed. Specifically, they urge us to rethink capitalist modernity itself as a regime of excessive, rapacious, and insatiable hunger—one that banalizes the hunger of the dispossessed, neglects the lessons that hunger as a relation can teach us, and, in doing so, perpetuates what the Black American author and activist bell hooks describes as the violence of empire fueled by "eating the other."[22] In these and other respects, Marind theories of hunger raise vital and unsettling questions for us all around what it means to eat well in an epoch of ecological unraveling, when industrial activities and imperial logics undermine the possibility of nourishing futures at a planetary scale.

The theories of hunger I draw on in making these points are rooted in specific and situated sociocultural frameworks, gendered dynamics, lived experiences, geopolitical contexts, and settler-colonial histories of the Pacific region.[23] But as the materials that ensue will reveal, their scope and significance also extend well beyond the Papuan resource frontier. Far from limited to the geographies and communities wherein they gain ground and grow, Indigenous epistemologies of hunger in rural Merauke position Marind hungerscapes in relation to a range of implicated places, peoples, and practices. These include globally dispersed palm oil consumers and transnational supply chains, predatory state and corporate forces, but also foreign anthropologists and their readerships as equally, if differently, non-innocent mediators and consumers of hunger-as-violence across the realms of the real and the representational.[24]

The interconnection of responsible eating and responsible writing, as it is expressed by my companions in the field and discussed in this book, raised challenging yet critical questions surrounding my positionality as a young, Eurasian, female, middle-class anthropologist and author; my fluctuating and transient identity as "insider" and "outsider"; and my consequent obligations toward those who made my ethnographic research and subsequent scholarly outputs possible—including the one before you. Each of these dimensions has shaped the particular ways in which my role and responsibilities were understood by Marind. Each engages with questions of power, privilege, and vulnerability in the researcher-researched dynamic that are intrinsically linked to, and inform, the book's empirical inquiry, and that sit in turn within longer traditions of interrogating the ethics and politics of ethnographic writing in anthropology. Attending to these questions through their relationship to one another, and from the perspectives of Marind women themselves, illuminates the behind-the-scenes deliberations that took place as my companions and I were drawn into contentious spaces and non-innocent scripts, animated by differently shared harms and differently motivated hesitations, and making the crafting of this book necessary for some but problematic for others.

Centering these troubled ethics, as they were debated by my Marind companions, creates generative fissures in the often deceptively smooth veneer of well-polished ethnographies. It unearths possibilities for crafting more honest and humble narratives that insist on remaining creaky and cracked rather than comprehensive and coherent. It interrogates the forms of power, privilege, and positionality that "we" as anthropologists are willing to reckon with, become responsible for, and sometimes relinquish as we attempt, in the words of the queer diasporic Filipina scholar Juno Salazar Parreñas, to craft ethnography that prioritizes "pushing readers to think, feel, and act in different ways" over (or at least alongside) meeting the demands of what academia recognizes as meaningful knowledge production.[25] In holding on to the sense of being torn between conflicting demands from fields both literal and disciplinary, this approach invites what I call a praxis of hesitant anthropology—one that engages up front with the heterogeneity of perspectives, obligations, and at times, betrayals that are so much part of the experience of being there, and (not) writing it.

In centering Marind theories of hunger, this work further raises questions around how to take seriously the heterogeneous ways in which individuals and collectives on the ground understand and critique existing systems of being and knowing, alongside the hermeneutics of hesitancy, suspicion, uncertainty, and doubt, and the forms of situated and strategic discourses, that are equally important to Marind's ever-evolving, dynamic, and internally contested forms of knowledge production and (self-)representation. It also invites us to interrogate the pragmatic and political role that anthropologists can (and cannot) take as mediators of the different interpretive frameworks they are entrusted with in the field, at a time when the values, uses, and good of anthropology are increasingly being interrogated within and beyond the discipline.[26] It underscores how there is no singular or non-innocent move that allows us to escape the power dynamics and compromises inherent to the writerly form. It also draws attention to the perilous lure of presuming or claiming to convey "pure" theory (or ethnography) as a product of the field, and even more so when theory, much like the worlds it interprets and explains, is understood to be coproduced in intersubjective and intercorporeal relation to anthropologists' own presences, bodies, and responsibilities, and also in relation to the disparate audiences to whom ethnographic theory must at times be strategically—if also at times hesitatingly—(re)packaged and performed.

I write this book from the positionality of a Sino-French, female, middle-class anthropologist whose initial access to the field in 2011 was enabled by the support and assistance of both Marind customary representatives and allied local NGOs. My early encounters and interactions with communities in rural Merauke were shaped primarily by my role as a project officer for the nonprofit organization Forest Peoples Programme, in which capacity I was tasked with investigating human rights abuses in the palm oil sector in Indonesia, the world's top palm oil–producing country. The longer I spent living with and learning from Marind, however, the more uneasy and dissatisfied I became with the radical, if necessary, simplification of messy worlds and relations required for effective advocacy in the face of dominant state and corporate institutions. This unease was only further amplified in light of my Marind companions' own reservations and critiques regarding advocacy's at times reductionist way of framing lived realities. As noted earlier, such reductionisms manifest in terms like *food security* and *malnutrition* that, while recognized by international audiences, do not adequately encompass hunger's dispersed meaning, materiality, and morality for many of my interlocutors in the field—and particularly so among Marind women, whose knowledges and experiences of hunger lie at the core of this work.

It was the desire to understand Marind lifeworlds and conceptualizations of hunger through the lens of their own ecosocial epistemological frameworks that eventually brought me to move away from the formal realm of human rights activism and conduct long-term ethnographic fieldwork among the residents of three Marind villages, with whom I had established close relations of trust and rapport in the context of our prior joint investigative research and human rights lobbying, and with whose permission I was able to reside in rural Merauke for a total period of eighteen months.[27]

Retaining an applied or engaged edge to the research endeavor constituted for the vast majority of my Marind hosts a basic precondition for my subsequent anthropological investigations in the Upper Bian, including in the form of single or coauthored nonscholarly activist outputs such as op-eds, reports, documentaries, community petition translations, and media features. At the same time, long-term ethnographic fieldwork was understood by my companions to allow for a differently deep immersion in, and description of, everyday life events, experiences, encounters, interactions, and discourses around hunger that could not easily or usefully be accommodated within advocacy-focused initiatives and associated publications and their more instrumental telos. This included attention to the reflexive ways in which Marind villagers understood, assessed, and critiqued both activist and anthropological endeavors, and their respective ability to convey internally operative debates and disagreements around hunger's causes and effects, as these were shaped by gender, class, age, and other intersectional factors that generate the heterogeneous perspectives sustained by any single community, collective, or, indeed, individual. It further opened space for staying with, and problematizing, the question of how stories of hunger ought to be narrated for audiences that included but were but not limited to advocacy's usual primary targets—namely, the government and corporations. It was in these and other respects that my professional shift from activist to researcher was associated by my companions with different sets of expectations and possibilities to those afforded by advocacy-oriented activities alone.

In taking hunger as its central object of inquiry, the work before you converses with and extends findings presented in my first book, which examined how industrial plantation expansion in Merauke reconfigures Marind's sense of place, time, personhood, and dreams, and their relations to native and introduced plants and animals, generating a world that many of my companions describe as uncertain (*abu-abu*).[28] Central to this work was the ambivalent ontology of oil palm—an introduced cash crop that Marind resent and fear for its destructive effects but also pity for its own subjection to human control—and the practical and epistemic challenges faced by Marind activists in protecting their lands from state- and corporate-driven developments, in a world region where the theft of sovereignty over Indigenous lands, bodies, and futures is as much of the past as it is of the present.

Alongside its thematic focus on hunger, this book further distinguishes itself in attending specifically to the experiences, theories, and critiques of Marind *women*, whose presence and perspectives were often overshadowed by the male-dominated composition of the Marind anti–oil palm land rights movement that I focused on in my earlier activist work (see figure I.1). While gendered and generational distinctions both shape in different ways the gastropolitical terrains of the Upper Bian, it was first and foremost Marind women (and, in particular, mothers) who acted as my mentors in understanding what it meant to eat well in a more-than-human world, and whose knowledges have shaped the empirical, conceptual, methodological, and ethical insights presented in this book. It was also primarily Marind women who identified in my own professional shift from human rights advocate to anthropologist possibilities for a form of engagement and learning that could, in new and potentially more productive ways, be both *for* and *about* them.

Figure I.1. Women and children of the Upper Bian in rural Merauke, West Papua, 2013. Photograph by Serafina Basik-Basik.

This focus on women's experiences and perspectives is further reflective of the particular, lived contexts in which hunger came to matter during the process of fieldwork, many of which my companions affirmed could be meaningfully storied in an ethnographic work and in ways that advocacy-styled activist outputs like official reports and court cases did not easily allow. Many of these events, interactions, and discourses occurred in the presence of women only, or majoritarily—during foraging expeditions in the forest, family visits to the clinics and hospitals, meal preparations in the village, conversations with fellow female teachers at the primary school where I volunteered as an English instructor, and at the incantation of hunger songs for dead animals and uprooted trees along dusty roads and plantation boundaries. Many more were prompted by visceral manifestations of hunger in everyday life—the constant chewing of betel nut to quell grumbling stomachs between meager meals, the moaning of malnourished infants in their cots at night, the fainting of women exhausted by their labors in the grove, the miscarriages suffered by young mothers too weak to bring their children to term, and the troubling transformations that my companions read in their own and their relatives' bodies and behaviors. Unfolding on the sidelines of organized, large-scale, and largely male-dominated advocacy movements, these events unearthed what the Kānaka Maoli scholar and educator Noelani Goodyear-Kaʻōpua terms the centrality of "the personal and the familial" as potent political spaces for the articulation, disarticulation, and rearticulation of Indigenous women's theories and critiques.[29]

The need for a separate, ethnographic analysis of hunger, and from women's perspectives in particular, came strongly to the fore in August 2019, when I returned to the field to share my research findings with my host communities and jointly decided with them on the form and outlets in which they would be published.[30] During this workshop, women participants collectively and repeatedly emphasized that hunger demanded treatment in its own right, within a body of work distinct to all others. This work, they insisted, would not be limited to, but nonetheless would prioritize, the views and voices of Marind women, both in uncovering the experience and meanings of hunger *and* in considering the ethical and representational stakes of writing about hunger for differently positioned audiences. In this respect, too, anthropological narratives were often seen by my friends to extend far beyond what activist outputs alone could achieve in terms of reach and readership.

Aspirational audiences for this ethnographic work identified and invoked by my companions included the Indonesian government bodies and oil palm corporations that are stealing their lands and eating their forests, and the global communities of consumers whose everyday existences are sustained by plantation commodities like palm oil. But women also talked of writing this book for the men in their villages whose decisions and actions undermine intergenerational and ecological continuance. They spoke of stories that needed to be written to honor their children present and long gone, whose lives had to be remembered and retold. To deceased female kin and matriarchs, whose identities are commemorated in this work in the form of pseudonyms that recall and celebrate these women's names and their knowledges. To foreign anthropologists, academics, and students in West Papua, Indonesia, and beyond. To transnational human rights organizations and pan-Melanesia and pan-Pacific feminist grassroots movements. To ancestors, spirits, and the deceased. To withering sago palms. To fleeing cassowaries. To flattened roadkill.

This book interpellates these and other audiences by drawing attention to the distinctive effects of historical, cultural, social, and environmental change on Marind women's sense of self and relationality, as these are shaped by their divergent politics, interests, obligations, and concerns.[31] In doing so, it pushes against what Sarah Nickel, a Tk'emlúpsemc (Kamloops Secwepemc) historian, describes as the marginalization of women within scholarship on Indigenous politics resulting from "the depoliticization of women's work . . . and the collapsing of women's politics within the broader narrative of male-dominated political organizations [that render] women's activities invisible."[32] As such, it is the women of the Upper Bian, as engaged theorists and critics, who have made this book both possible and necessary.

Women in the field explained their particular interest in the question of hunger as intrinsically linked to their sense of identity and pride as food providers and mothers. But their investment in these questions also stemmed from other, more covert sentiments. On the one hand, speaking about hunger offered an avenue for women to condemn the attritive effects of histories of colonial racial capitalism on Indigenous Papuan lands and bodies—to "renarrate" themselves back into these histories and, in doing so, counter what the Kānaka Maoli Indigenous studies scholar Lisa Kahaleole Hall and others identify as the erasure of women's experiences and agencies under settler-colonial rule.[33]

On the other hand, speaking about hunger also enabled women to voice their frustrations, resentment, and anger toward Marind men *within* their communities, whose monopoly over decisions to surrender land to, or otherwise cooperate with, agribusiness corporations many saw as exacerbating food insecurity on the ground. Here, women's narratives served a cathartic function in communicating gendered power asymmetries that have been amplified in the context of intensifying land conversions and that are revelatory of a nascent or implicit Indigenous feminist consciousness around hunger—one that in turn acts as an internal critique and as the potential grounds for activism against the masculinism of both the colonial nation-state and the patriarchy of customary systems.

And yet, the cathartic or self-empowering function of hunger narratives as a mode of "speaking truth to power" was often accompanied by an equally strong sense of shame and culpability among those women who read in hunger a testament to their own failure to fulfill the needs of Marind generations present and to come.[34] This shame was compounded with uncertainties and hesitations that my female companions were widely reticent to convey in the context of formal food activism initiatives—for instance, uncertainties over who exactly was to blame for the emergence of new and different hungers, how the attribution of responsibility was distributed across gendered and racialized scales and subjects, and by whom these hungers ought to be storied for global audiences without reproducing what the Indian American feminist scholar Chandra Talpade Mohanty identifies as the colonial logics of Western feminist theories that present "a composite, singular 'third-world woman' image" and in doing so, replicate the "authorizing signature of western humanist discourse."[35]

I use the terms *feminism* and *feminist* with care and caution throughout this work. On the one hand, the materials I present are in direct conversation with, and richly informed by, Indigenous, Black, and new materialist/posthumanist feminist theories that in turn cannot be divorced from gender theory or from critiques of racial colonial capitalism, sharing as these currents do the common pursuit of critically analyzing relations of difference and inequality through the lens of gender roles and from the perspective of differently situated women. Much like Marind women's own interpretive frameworks, these scholarly theories are reflective of lived realities at the same time as they are political and discursive practices, driven and shaped by their specific intellectual and empirical origins and contexts.[36]

Bringing Marind women's theories into dialogue with Indigenous and critical race feminist scholarship draws attention to the importance of considering how gendered and situated identities, roles, and relations may differ from, and be incommensurable with, Western models and attendant trajectories of societal transformation, or contexts where feminist action must remain strategically implicit in order to achieve its ends.[37] While a few of my companions who had familiarized themselves with certain strands of feminism in the course of their studies in Merauke City (the capital of Merauke) or Jayapura (the capital of West Papua) recognized affinities between these currents and their own pursuit of justice, recognition, and participation in political life, they also often distanced themselves from Western concepts of equality and democracy and, in particular, the Western feminist pushback against assumed connections between women, land, and the domestic sphere, from which many Marind women derive a sense of pride rather than subordination.[38] Attention to situatedness is all the more important given that the views conveyed in this work do not represent those of all Marind women, nor are they exclusively held by Marind women alone.

Not all women in the villages where I conducted fieldwork were equally interested in questions of hunger—or, more specifically perhaps, in discussing these questions with me. Those who participated in this project did so for very different reasons. In particular, and resonating strongly with similar debates in the sphere of Pacific and Indigenous feminisms, disagreements abounded among women over the relative importance of, and mutually reinforcing or impeding relationship between, struggles for gender equality on the one hand and Indigenous sovereignty on the other. As such, and even as the women I worked with might not self-identify with or deploy the language of feminism themselves, their contentions over the relationship between gender, land, power, and inequality (in both real-world and representational terms) uncover their deeply nuanced understandings and critiques of the connections and intersections between the historical violence of settler colonialism and the gendered violence of heteropatriarchies and heteropaternalisms both internal *and* imposed.[39]

Attending to women and their situated experiences and knowledges of hunger illuminates new insights into the fraught relationship between gender, food, and ecology on the Papuan plantation frontier. It further allows me to return to previously examined themes in ways that are generative of distinctive and complementary analyses. These include the relationship that my female companions identify between diminishing forest foodways and growing structural inequalities between men and women, the threatening masculinity they attribute to occupying infrastructures and corporate sorcerers, and the gendered modes of historicity and causality that inflect their understanding of the etiologies of hungers past, present, and to come. These findings amplify the opacity (*abu-abu*) of the Marind lifeworld by revealing the diverse and disputed ways in which my female companions grapple with their dual marginalization at the intersections of custom and colonialism—at times rooting their theories of change in their positionality as women, at others in their positionality as Marind, and at others yet at the oft-awkward interstices of gender and Indigeneity.[40]

In tandem with guiding its thematic trajectories, Marind women's experiences and knowledges also shape the narrative terrain and tenor of this work, which were determined together with the individuals whose stories this book attempts to do justice to, and in conversation also with their responses to the generous feedback and queries received from the book's reviewers, which I shared with my companions in translated form.[41] For instance, incorporating particular hunger songs in each chapter, which were recorded, translated, and selected by those who created and crafted them, was deemed critical by women in honoring the songs' communicative and poetic potencies and also in interrupting, inflecting, and informing the text's shifting rhythms and refrains. Alongside particular terms and expressions, translations of selected key quotes were included in full in their source language where so requested by those cited. Primacy has been given to the flow of Marind's own stories and experiences within the body text, with comparative ethnographic examples from across Melanesia and beyond and theoretical debates unfolding in anthropology and consonant fields strategically positioned in detailed endnotes. Together with translations, songs, and endnotes, the broader chapter structure and narrative arc of the work before you were also developed through a collaborative approach to storytelling. Each chapter opens with a fleshy account of a particular moment in the field that embodies what the American anthropologist Sally Falk Moore terms a "diagnostic event," or a specific instance captured in the stream of time that my companions and I agreed to be especially revealing of hunger's form and effects, either in situ or in retrospect.[42]

For instance, thick descriptions of forest foodways presented in the opening chapter serve to introduce the reader to the intimate bodily and affective pleasures of multispecies commensalities but also to the inherent violence and vulnerabilities that more-than-human relations of eating, being eaten, and not eating entail. These violences and vulnerabilities find heightened expression in subsequent chapters that uncover not only the injuries inflicted by colonial-capitalist regimes on gendered bodies and occupied landscapes but also, and just as importantly, the forms of epistemic sovereignty that Marind women practice in questioning and challenging these injuries and their causes, as they unfold within and across different subjects of hunger, victimhood, and complicity. The stakes of acknowledging these modes of epistemic sovereignty are tackled head-on in the final chapter, which considers in a reflexive mode the non-innocences entailed in the craft and consumption of ethnographic narratives as a particular way of representing and narrating the violence of hunger.

Attending to the non-innocence of ethnographic writing, as it is articulated by Marind women, brings me to pair the ambiguous (*abu-abu*) dynamics of life on extractive resource frontiers with the *abu-abu* nature of anthropological practice itself and the contested forms of responsibility and refusal that ethnographically representing one's own and others' lives entail. Ethical concerns, conundrums, and critiques among Marind women surrounding ethnographic writing were central to the production of this work—from field to press, and likely beyond—and operate as a shadow argument throughout the book, with their full force examined in detail in the final segment. These concerns uncover the importance of disclosing the consequential whys, whos, whens, and hows that matter to the people who make our research and writing possible. They problematize what anthropology can do in pragmatic terms, for and with the places and peoples it describes and theorizes. They bring to fore the methodological challenges that arise in storying hunger as violence through the craft and consumption of ethnography as a non-innocent practice, anchored as much in principles of responsibility and reciprocity as in realities of compromise and complicity.

In examining these questions through the heterogeneous perspectives and critiques of my companions in the field, and their broader implications for anthropology as a discipline and academia as an institution, the book unveils a multiplicity of "hidden transcripts" through which Marind women push against and problematize dominant ideologies across different yet interrelated scales, subjects, and struggles.[43]

The stakes outlined above have shaped the choice and craft of the narratives this book recounts, and that I invite the reader to engage with through a practice of "slow reading" wherein one allows oneself to be pulled into ethical proximity with the events described, while considering carefully the strategic reasons why and to what ends these events may be storied the way they are.[44] In particular, I invite you to consider descriptions and interpretations that might appear to veer toward romanticization within this work—whether in the form of seemingly idealized Indigenous lifeworlds or singularized capitalist violence—through what Elaine Coburn, a white Canadian settler and international studies scholar, and her Indigenous colleagues term a "contrapuntal" reading, or a reading that situates Indigenous experiences and theories against the context of ongoing colonization as a form of resistance to centuries of stigmatization of Indigenous ways of being and knowing.[45]

A similar invitation to the reader applies in the context of the visual elements that accompany this work's textual core. Some of these photographs were taken by me, others by my Marind companions, and yet others by a Papua-based Indonesian documentary photographer, freelance photojournalist, and local activist ally, Albertus Vembrianto, who has dedicated much of his career to documenting and giving voice to Papuan people and landscapes through the medium of pictures, op-eds, documentaries, and books.[46] Selecting these photographs jointly with Marind women involved an often difficult balance between conveying people, interactions, and places in a vivid and visceral way, on the one hand, and avoiding, on the other, the kind of voyeuristic and objectifying gaze that has so long plagued not only the discipline of anthropology but also the media representation of crises in general and of extreme hunger or famine in particular.

Captured at a specific moment in time and within a particular visual frame, the images retained in this work offer what the Colombian anthropologist and photographer Camilo Leon-Quijano describes as "a socially experienced picture that is inevitably incomplete, uncertain, sometimes inconsistent, and contradictory"—not just in relation to their actual contents and contexts of production but also in relation to the many *other* images with which *these* images are in dialogue, but that were ultimately and deliberately excluded in light of the representational risks I have just outlined.[47] For instance, many images depicting bodies (especially those of children) suffering from malnutrition were included in earlier iterations of the text but later removed so as not to perpetuate the colonial and racializing othering of non-Western bodies. These absences, operating across visual-textual terrains in the form of intentionally omitted photographs and stories, are, in different ways and for different reasons, necessary. But many continue to sit uneasily with my Marind friends, speaking through their conscious erasure to the non-innocences and hesitancies that have shaped both the intersubjective relations of the field and its partial representation within this book.[48]

Finally, a word on theory. In opening this account with a hunger song, crafted and performed by a Marind woman and friend from West Papua, I foreground a key aim of this work—namely, to center the experiential and speculative forms of theorization produced by Indigenous People who persist in the teeth of colonial racial capitalism.[49] Following Linda Tuhiwai Smith, a Māori education studies scholar, I understand "theory" in the broadest sense to encompass the diverse ways in which people interpret the world and, in doing so, make a claim in and about the world.[50] To acknowledge Marind women as theorists, alongside other intellectuals, practitioners, and activists cited in this work, counters what the Fijian sociologist Simione Durutalo and the I-Kiribati and African American scholar and activist Teresia Teaiwa call the "elimination of innovation" in representations of Pacific peoples that fail to "account for changes in [I]ndigenous ways of knowing and being."[51] It challenges what David Welchman Gegeo, a Solomon Islands anthropologist, identifies as the (often hierarchical) positioning of theory as opposite to, and distinct from, everyday practice, activist engagement, and grassroots discourse.[52] It further responds to the invitation by the Fijian and Ngāi Tahu interdisciplinary scholars Suliasi Vunibola and Matthew Scobie to attend to the creative, critical, and innovative ways in which Pacific peoples articulate their worlds "within-and-against, and beyond" the colonial-capitalist relation.[53]

Marind women in rural Merauke have crafted their theories through their bodily, affective, and historical encounters with the forces of colonization, capitalism, plantation modernity, development, and globalization. These theories, as such, are not so much "learned" by Marind from other academic theorists through transnational flows of scholarly concepts or ideological currents as they are generated internally from (often, indeed, with) the grass roots, across rural and urban divides, between men and women, youth and elders, and at times in creative response to the effects of external forces on local places, people, and bodies—the state, corporations, imperial powers, NGOs, anthropologists, and more. On the one hand, the ecosocial ruptures that Marind (and Papuans more generally) have experienced over two consecutive periods of colonization (Dutch and then Indonesian) have been generative of new kinds of theorizing and new communities of theorists, as people strive to interpret a rapidly changing world and, in doing so, articulate "claims that stick and words that matter," both in and about this world and their own place within it.[54] These theories often take hold and are expressed in everyday life as people encounter the material infrastructures through which the forces of colonial capitalism become palpably present—roads, cities, plantations, and more. But theorizing among Marind also vastly predates the incursion of capitalism and colonialism. It is a collective practice that is birthed in spaces that have long been objects of local observation, immersion, analysis, and interpretation—from forests and swamps to sago groves and savannas. It is in these intimate and more-than-human realms, as much as in those infrastructures introduced and imposed by imperial-industrial regimes, that Marind concepts and philosophies of relationality, violence, and vulnerability find root.

More generally, then, I hope to invite the reader with this framing to interrogate, rather than take for granted, the dynamics of voice and visibility that determine when and why theory becomes Theory, what theory does, how it is distributed and cross-pollinated, who gets to decide what lies within and beyond its ambit and aura, and how theory comes to matter as something not only written and read but also storied and sung.[55] The intention here is to unsettle, enrich, and expand what the British Australian feminist theorist Sara Ahmed calls the "citational chain" of academic theorizing that determines and delimits whom we see ourselves in theoretical conversation with.[56] To adopt this framing pushes against the (white) intellectual monopoly and ownership over theory as a particular and privileged mode of knowledge production and academic capital wherein colonized and silenced "others," as the Kahnawà:ke Mohawk anthropologist Audra Simpson and the American feminist scholar Andrea Smith note, are positioned as "those who can be theorized about, but not those who can theorize."[57] Instead, it recognizes the complex, transforming, and praxis-based interpretive frameworks through which our field interlocutors, in the role of active knowledge producers, understand, explain, and evaluate the nature of, and relationship between, local realities and global forces, as these arise through their identification of meaningful connections, resonances, gaps, hesitations, and contradictions—some lived and remembered, others imagined and speculative.

Chapter 1 examines the meanings of satiety and hunger in the forest in light of Marind ethnonutritional frameworks and the principles and practices undergirding the procuration, preparation, consumption, and exchange of traditional forest foods. Both hunger and satiety find expression in the appearance and abundance of people's skin and wetness, generating an energy that is distributed across humans, plants, animals, and elements, and that is enhanced by the affordances of kindred organisms from which forest foods derive. Eating in and from the forest is associated by Marind with peace, liveliness, knowledge, freedom, and the complementarity of gendered and intergenerational forms of labor. In the forest, Marind themselves become good food that satiates the hunger of others by transmitting their sweat, blood, and flesh to animals, plants, and soils through tactile encounters in life and bodily decomposition after death. The ecosocial significance of satiety in the forest in turn shapes the multiple meanings of hunger as a diagnostic of individuals' moral and material relations to human and other-than-human beings.

Chapter 2 examines the transformation of Marind into subjects of new and different kinds of hunger that find root in longer histories of settler-colonial occupation and that have been exacerbated by the recent expansion of industrial oil palm concessions and the subsequent disappearance of food-providing forests. Marind's hunger for forest foods speaks to the devastating consequences of plantation proliferation on the mutually sustaining relations of humans and other life-forms. The hunger for imported, processed goods, in contrast, speaks to a desire for a modern and globalized way of life that nonetheless fails to satiate, and even intensifies, the hunger of those who experience it. A third form of hunger is the hunger for money and human flesh that many Marind women attribute to those male villagers who collude with the agribusiness sector and further their individual interests to the detriment of human and more-than-human communities of life. Together, these emergent ecologies of hungers entail destructive and unilateral, rather than generative and reciprocal, forms of consumption. Insatiable and multiplying, they literally and figuratively eat away at the bodies, environments, and futures of Marind and their other-than-human kin.

Chapter 3 examines the transformation of Marind into objects of hungers that are attributed to an array of invasive, foreign, and masculinized entities—roads, cities, the government, and corporations. The effects of these hungers manifest in the depletion of victims' bodily skin and wetness but can also take more ambiguous, indirect, and non-innocent forms—the mysterious disappearance of kin and friends on the roads and in the cities, the vulnerability of women to sexually transmitted diseases and sexual abuse, and the susceptibility of Marind men to sorcery-induced mental manipulation, among others. Far from being restricted to human subjects and objects alone, hunger becomes a defining trait of diverse infrastructural and institutional forces that operate across different sites and scales, and that together consume Marind and the nourishing ecologies they depend on to survive and thrive.

Chapter 4 examines how Marind explain and rationalize the causes of hunger. Some women understand hunger as a punishment meted out by ancestral spirits on their male relatives for their failure to protect the forest and its animal and plant dwellers from death and destruction. Other women identify hunger's roots in the ongoing colonization of West Papua and the multiple forms of dispossession that have accompanied settler occupation. Yet other Marind women interpret hunger as a necessary and altruistic sacrifice in achieving a greater good—namely, feeding the nation and feeding the world. This etiology speaks to religious notions of martyrdom and sacrifice instilled through historical processes of Christian missionization and conversion. It also expresses an acute, if troubling, awareness and acknowledgment among Marind women of the unequal resource distribution dynamics underlying the neoliberal capitalist system—one in which some people must go hungry in order for others to be satiated.

Chapter 5 considers the ethical conundrums that arose in the course of my ethnographic research on hunger among Marind communities and the conflicting expectations of Marind women pertaining to the disclosure (or withholding thereof) of the findings documented in this work. These conflicting demands on the part of my variably situated hosts draw reflexive attention to how the nature and negotiation of power, privilege, and precarity within community-researcher relations can at once transform, transcend, and trouble the layered meanings and matterings of hunger, in and beyond ethnographic terrains. They invite a practice of hesitant anthropology that acknowledges the force of uncertainty and doubt in shaping the worlds we study, while at the same time reckoning with the non-innocence of ethnographic writing as a compromised and compromising exercise in responsibility and reciprocity.

I conclude by drawing on Marind theories of hunger to reflect on the conceptual, political, and practical implications of reframing hunger as a culturally modulated, historically situated, and morally imbued phenomenon, in an epoch of ever-intensifying capitalistic extraction and anthropogenic activity. I identify avenues for future research that takes hunger as a starting point for reimagining struggles for social, environmental, racial, and multi-species justice as mediated and moved by the pursuit of metabolic justice. I leave the last words to Mina, a child from the village of Mirav, whose hunger song first sparked this foray through the land of famished beings, and to whom this book is dedicated.

SATIATION AND HUNGER
IN THE FOREST

Crouched ankle-deep in the mud, Marcella, a Marind woman in her late thirties from the Ndiken (white stork) clan and a resident of Mirav village, was teaching me how to cook sago. With her callused yet nimble hands, she patted the freshly leached sago starch into round, even-sized clumps and slid them into chopped bamboo stalks, alternating sago with shredded coconut flesh, destemmed papaya leaves, slivers of possum meat, and the plump, writhing sago grubs that I had earlier been tasked to gather by Marcella and her sisters. Then, Marcella carefully aligned the bamboo stalks atop a small fire of dried juniper twigs and interleaved sago fronds, where they would steam until cooked through. Marcella's three-year-old son, Fransiskus, sat beside us, giggling. He was entertained by the sight of giant red ants scrambling erratically around the fire, competing over stray crumbs of sago pith and coconut flesh. The air was alive with the sounds of birds and wind and river. Children laughed and splashed in the muddy waters of the grove. Villagers were pounding sago and chanting nearby, their songs and lyrics reaching my ears in sporadic fragments.

Sagu, sagu, kau tumbuh, beri makan, beri makan
Sago, sago, you flourish, giving us food, giving us food
Disini ketemu kebebasan, disini ketemu ilmu
Here, freedom is found, here, knowledge is found

Dari nenek moyang yang kasih kitorang arah
From the ancestors who guide us
Dari dunia hutan yang membesarkan kita
And the forest world that grows us

Igid, dubadub, igid, dubadub
Skin, wetness, skin, wetness
Bersama kita makan, bersama kita dimakan
Together we eat, together we are eaten

Keringat kita, kulit kita, air liur kita, darah kita
Our sweat, our skin, our saliva, our blood
Daging kamu, getah kamu, minyak kamu, pucuk kamu
Your flesh, your sap, your grease, your shoots

Tanah, sungai, dusun, rawa
Land, river, grove, and swamp
Dengan semangatnya amai dan anim
With the spirit of plant and animals and of humans

Dengan semangatnya pace dan mace
With the spirit of our fellow men and women

Satu bersama hutan, hilanglah kelaparan
One with the forest, may hunger disappear
Satu bersama hutan, hutan yang beri kitorang makan
One with the forest, the forest that feeds us

Marcella let out a sharp hand whistle. The bamboo stalks had cracked and split under the heat. The sago was ready to eat. One by one, Marcella's companions made their way to the fire—some bearing bows, arrows, machetes, and knives, others fruit, betel nuts, and tubers. Marcella distributed the bamboo stalks among us, pulling the charred strands apart to release the steaming contents. She took a bite, chewed it, then spit it out and placed one shred first into her daughter Viktorina's mouth, and then into mine. Her companions proceeded to do the same for each other—for their wives, uncles, nephews, and grandmothers. The first bite, Marcella told me, is about sharing skin and wetness. She herself would not eat just yet. Preparing the sago and watching her friends and family eat it had already made her feel full. Her sweat had mingled with the sago. Now, it mingled with the bodies of her kin. This, she said, was how people shared skin and wetness with the forest, with the food, and with one another.

As people ate, they began to talk and sing—about their mothers, the forest, their plant and animal siblings, and the ancestral spirits inhabiting the grove. Singing and storying, they told me, enhanced the flavor of the foods consumed. It reminded people of how these foods came into being and how people themselves become good food for others as their blood, grease, sweat, tears, and flesh continue in the bodies of organisms that will consume them in the future. "In the forest," Marcella explained between two bites of sago, "we eat and we are eaten. We feed the forest and it feeds us. We are all food for each other." Suddenly, a shrill shriek reverberated in the grove. Marcella's son Fransiskus has just noticed a black leech hanging off his calf, already plump from the blood it had sucked from its unwitting host. The child ran into my arms, and I helped him remove the feasting leech the way his mother had taught me—palm placed flat on the flesh, followed by rapid and repeated circular movements that disorient the worm, causing it to lose its grip and its suckers to detach. Marcella watched and smiled. The multispecies feeding had begun.

This chapter explores the ecosocial significance of forest foods among Marind of the Upper Bian and the forms of satiation and hunger that forest food practices, systems, and environments create. I open with these themes because even as traditional hunting, fishing, and gathering practices are now rapidly declining as a result of ongoing deforestation and monocrop expansion across the region, forest foodways remain a crucial starting point in many women's reflections about hunger. As Marcella, my companion in the grove, reminded me time and again, "If you want to understand hunger in the village, you must first understand satiation in the forest."[1] Storying the pleasures of satiation in the forest further aligned with the wishes of those interlocutors who were deeply hesitant to offer a damage- or suffering-centered narrative alone within this work. Just as important, uncovering hunger's multiple meanings in the context of forest foodways was deemed central in positioning more recent manifestations of hunger against preexisting moral economies of hunger. These moral economies of hunger point to violence and vulnerability as integral to relations of eating and being eaten. In doing so, they temper the idealization or romanticization of Indigenous food systems and relations as always or necessarily life-sustaining for all parties involved.

Participating in foraging expeditions such as the one described earlier acted as the primary avenue for understanding Marind notions of satiety and hunger in the context of forest foodways. These collective expeditions constitute a central part of everyday life among Marind communities, who have traditionally relied on forests, swamps, and groves for their daily subsistence and other material needs. They take place on average every two months and last between one and twelve weeks. Participants range from eight to over thirty and include nuclear family members and members of extended families and clans. Children and infants are also brought along, as foraging trips are seen as central to their enculturation as fully fledged members of Marind society.

Sago groves visited during expeditions to the forest provide villagers with their staple starch, sago flour, which is manually extracted from the felled trunks of sago palms prior to flowering when their starch content is at its highest, with the inedible pith then separated from the edible flour through a process of repeated rasping, beating, and leaching. Sago flour is cooked as dakh kakiva, a mixture of sago, coconut meat, sago grubs, or pig or cassowary meat, steamed inside bamboo stalks over a wood fire. It can also be prepared as dakh sep, where ingredients are wrapped in banana or coconut leaves and cooked over hot stones underground. In its most basic form, the flour is fashioned into balls the size of a fist and cooked directly over the flame.[2] Taro and yam supplement carbohydrates obtained from sago starch, while proteins are derived from fish and game such as deer, lorises, possums, cassowaries, fowl, tree kangaroos, crocodiles, and pigs. Fruits, including rambutans, papayas, bananas, golden apples, traditional mangoes, figs, watery rose apples, langsat, kedondong, jackfruit, and coconuts, are also gathered in the forest, alongside roots, barks, and saps that serve to make medicinal brews.

This chapter begins by examining how freedom and knowledge crystallize in Marind practices of eating with and from the forest ecology, and the more-than-human exchanges of skin and wetness that imbue forest foods with their life-sustaining qualities. It then considers the relationship between affect, alimentation, and labor shaping forest foodways, and the experiences of liveliness, peace, and memories shared by men, women, children, and elders through their different and complementary roles in food procuration and preparation. The ensuing sections attend to the different forms of hunger that Marind associate with eating and being eaten in the forest, together with the customary protocols and moral codes that govern the distribution of hunger across human and nonhuman beings. Central to this discussion is an analysis of how violence and vulnerability participate in the process of Marind bodies "becoming good food for others," in an environment where the positionalities of predator and prey and eater and eaten are neither static nor species-bound but rather in perpetual and often contingent flux.

Freedom and Knowledge

Forest foodways are associated by Marind men and women alike with the condition of "satiety" (*kekenyangan*). This satiety is said to stem in large part from the vitality of the living organisms from which forest foods are derived. Referred to by my companions in the Bian dialect of Marind as "grandparents" (amai) or "siblings" (namek), plants and animals share kinship through common descent with different Marind clans (boan) from ancestral spirits (dema).[3] Included also within this kinship system are various abiotic elements and forces—the sun, rivers, soil, rain, lightning, and dew—that, together with biotic life-forms, animate and sustain the sentient ecology of the forest. These ancestral forms of relatedness find expression in a highly elaborate taxonomy of clans, moieties, and phratries, which in turn serves to identify the groups primarily responsible for the care and protection of particular forest beings.[4] For instance, the Basik-Basik (pig) clan is primarily responsible for the everyday protection and ritualized reenactment during village ceremonies of the pig (basik-basik), followed by the batna tree, thunder, lightning, the rainbow, the black cockatoo, the betel nut, the nar yam, the mumu mussel, the breadfruit, the echidna, the possum, the white gull, the scrub hen, and the suraki banana. The Mahuze (dog) clan, meanwhile, is entrusted with the protection and ritualized reenactment of the dog (mahu), followed by the shark, the sami snake, the keke hawk, the bower bird, and the open savanna plains.

Procuring, preparing, and consuming forest foods involves an array of ritual codes that commemorate and celebrate Marind's more-than-human kinships. These include the incantation of spells prior to and during hunting, the ritualized handling of foods when gathered and cooked, and the recitation of songs and origin stories when food is distributed and consumed. Food restrictions, too, are often explained as expressions of respect toward plants and animals. These restrictions encompass prohibitions on hunting juvenile or gestating animals, capturing animals during the mating season, and gathering plants at the early stages of maturation. They also include taboos on hunting or harvesting plant and animal species with whom community members have recently entertained meaningful encounters in the forest. Instances where such proscriptions came into play during foraging expeditions I participated in included a cassowary that was tracked down but not captured because its feathered markings resembled the birthmark of the hunter who came upon it. On another occasion, villagers decided that a group of wild pigs we encountered would not be hunted down and instead were allowed to wallow in peace in a sago grove. This was because the animals reminded my companions of a group of children from a nearby village who had recently lost their way in the forest and who had followed pigs of similar appearance and also traveled in a similar pack formation to find their way safely back to their families. Abiding by these restrictions demonstrates Marind's ability to notice and respond to the meaningful beings and doings of the forest environment at the same time as it enables Marind to make respectful use of forest resources without leading to their depletion.

Within Marind ethnonutritional systems, the people with whom one eats are just as important as the foods that one consumes.[5] This was conveyed to me by Kosmina, a woman in her early twenties from the Kaize (cassowary) clan who hosted me during my fieldwork in her home village of Bayau. Echoing Marcella's words, Kosmina explained that satiety derives from sharing food with those who obtained and prepared it, but also with whom one traveled to the forest and with whom one entertains relations of kinship through descent, marriage, or adoption. Participating in the sharing of food was also central to my own socialization as an outsider, alongside the careful and daily enskillment I received from my companions in the arts of collective foraging, fishing, sago processing, and cooking.

This sharing of food would occur informally throughout the course of subsistence activities in the forest, but particularly at the end of the foraging day, when villagers congregated around the fire to sing, story, and eat. In addition to affirming and creating social ties, the collective consumption and procurement of forest foods acted as an important means through which animus or otherwise conflictual relations can be harmonized and overcome. Indeed, the resolution of interpersonal disputes in Marind society often entails gathering and bringing the individuals concerned, along with their relatives, to the forest to prepare and eat sago together. As Marcella's elder sister, Yoanna, described to me over a meal of dakh kakiva shared in her clan's ancestral sago grove, "When enemies eat from the forest together, they remember their roots. They remember their pasts. They forget their anger because their stomachs, ears, and eyes are satiated by the sounds and smells and tastes of their shared home. When enemies eat from the forest together, they remember what it means to be Marind."

Knowledge (*ilmu*) and freedom (*kebebasan*) further enhance the satiation that Marind associate with forest foods. Resonating with the forms of emplaced "intelligence" and Indigenous "sacredscience" described by the Michi Saagiig Nishnaabeg scholar Leanne Betasamosake Simpson and the Xicana feminist scholar Felicity Schaeffer, respectively, "knowledge" (*ilmu*) enfolds a range of practices, interactions, skills, and affects that together reanimate connections with ancestors and sustain the intricate web of entanglements that nourish humans and their forest kin.[6] It encompasses the origin stories, ecosystemic relations, and uses of plants and animals created by dema in time immemorial, as these vary according to species, locality, and clan. It is anchored in the enmeshment of landscape, life-forms, spirits, and environments, or what the Tongan-Fijian anthropologist Epeli Hau'ofa describes as the indivisibility of people and land, wherein land constitutes not only a source of livelihood but also the root of people's knowledge, history, and identity.[7]

Instilled into children as soon as they are able to walk and speak, *ilmu* entails a meticulous apprenticeship in which forest trails to follow during food procurement activities; which ones to avoid; how these decisions vary depending on age, gender, and clan affiliation; and what meaningful signs or signals to consider along the way. Arts of *ilmu* passed on to me by Marcella and her sisters in the forest included learning to detect and interpret the color, flow, and level of the river; the relative brightness or cloudiness of the sky; the voice of a kindred bird alternately inviting human presence or cautioning people of imminent danger; and the guiding "breath" (*nafas*) of dema animating the canopy overhead. Knowing the forest also entailed undertaking activities that make the environment more conducive to plants' and animals' own sympoietic thriving. During our foraging expeditions, for instance, my companions taught me how to clear pathways for pigs and deer to facilitate their travel to water catchments; scatter nuts, seeds, and fruit for cassowaries to feed on; and transplant sago suckers to enhance their access to water, sun, and nutrients. Passed on from one generation to the next in the form of stories, songs, and skills, these activities imbue forest foods with meanings and memories that are at once bodily and affective, individual and collective, and human and more-than-human. They point to the organic interconnectedness of knowledge and practice within Marind onto-epistemological frameworks that are rooted in lived experiences and nurtured relations with the land as sentient ecology and nourishing presence.[8]

Figure 1.1. A Marind mother processes sago pith with her toddler, 2015. Marind affirm that forest foods are most satiating when eaten in the forest itself. Photograph by the author.

Marind affirm that forest foods are most satiating when eaten in the forest itself. In this environment, full-bodied sensory, auditory, olfactory, and kinesthetic immersion, together with acute attention to and observation of one's surrounds, is said to enhance the gustatory attributes and nourishing qualities of the foods consumed. In the forest, for instance, community members paid close attention to the rippling of meandering rivers, the gentle swaying of sago fronds, and the fleeting movements of insects and birds. Every so often, they noticed and commented on the patterned bark and foliage of nearby vegetation, and the footprints left by itinerant packs of boars and cassowaries. As we rasped and pounded sago, my companions sporadically invited me to pause and inhale with deep breaths the rich scent of what they identified as burning juniper twigs, petrichor, and damar resins (see figure 1.1). During breaks in between activities, my companions would occasionally run their fingers along the pubescent leaves of shrubs and bushes, and deep into the rotting sago stumps where plump sago grubs and larvae incubate. Eating, working, and feeling blended as taste and touch mingled with the dispersed sounds, smells, and sights of the forest as nourishing milieu.[9]

Marind often describe traveling the forest in the company of their kin, and encountering the abundance of foods within it, as a form of "freedom" (*kebebasan*). During these expeditions, travelers frequently talked of the pleasure of being able to choose where and when they moved across the landscape, how long they spent in the forest, what they consumed there, and with and from whom. Foods obtained in the forest, Marcella stressed, do not require money or access to a kiosk or market. Rather, they are freely available to those who possess the *ilmu* required to properly identify, procure, and prepare them.

In line with the more-than-human ethos undergirding forest foodways, freedom is understood by Marind not only as a human affordance but also as an attribute of plants and animals from which forest foods derive. Indeed, my companions often invoked the importance of "freedom" for their non-human kin, or <u>amai</u>, in explaining their reluctance to engage in intensive or sustained plant cultivation or animal domestication. These practices are seen as forms of human control and manipulation that do violence to living organisms by depriving them of their capacity to grow, interact, and propagate autonomously.[10] Instead, forest organisms are said to become good food when they travel the forest at their own will and with their own kin, and when they mature, reproduce, and eventually age and die at their own respective pace and rhythm. "Free beings," Marcella's younger sister Rafaela explained, "make free food. Forest foods taste of freedom. And nothing tastes as good as freedom."

Skin and Wetness

As Marcella imparted during our meal of sago in the grove, forest foodways are satiating because they require and enable the sharing of skin (<u>igid</u>) and wetness (<u>dubadub</u>).[11] Central to Marind conceptualizations of the body, skin and wetness express the state of health of the individual and their social and cosmological relations.[12] Skin refers to the exterior and visible surface of the body. Expressions of skin identified to me by my companions during our foraging expeditions in the forest included the physical skin of their own bodies and of fellow human beings but also the bark of trees, the coats of mammals, the laminae of leaves, the carapace of beetles, the cuticle of larvae, the topographic relief of the land, and the sleek or rippled surface of rivers and streams.

Wetness, as the counterpart to skin, refers to the various fluids that animate the bodies of sentient life-forms. In humans and animals, wetness takes the form of blood, grease, muscle, sweat, saliva, and tears. It also includes sexual, maternal, and postdigestive substances such as breast milk, vaginal excretions, semen, urine, and feces. In reptiles and amphibians, wetness manifests in the mucilaginous integument of frogs, toads, newts, and salamanders and in the gluey scutes and scales of snakes, lizards, and crocodiles. In vegetal organisms, wetness is found in resin, sap, pith, and nectar and in the water-carrying xylem of roots, stems, and shoots. Rivers, mangroves, swamps, mudflats, and clouds, too, are imbued with dispersed life-sustaining wetness that nourishes the landscape's terrestrial, subterrestrial, aquatic, and aerial milieus.

Skin and wetness in Marind onto-epistemologies exist differently, but are also shared, between transcorporeally connected life-forms and landscapes.[13] These connective substances are not static but rather malleable. They change over time and across bodies in contact. They are not limited to biological entities but rather are inclusive of elemental beings—the soils, rivers, and clouds—and also of invisible entities such as spirits, ancestors, and the dead.[14] Importantly, the sharedness of skin and wetness is not one that demands overcoming in order to become autonomous but rather one that sustains the individual, in and through their palpable connections to others.[15] It is precisely through these iterative, more-than-human, bodily sharings that freedom (*kebebasan*) is actualized.

Knowing how to "share skin" (aatna igid) produces bodies that are glossy, shiny, and robust, all of which are indicators of good health and reveal strong social ties within a community of life that encompasses both human and nonhuman beings. These physical traits are enhanced by, and embody, the experiences and traces of morally valued and sustained activities in the forest—hunting, processing sago, fishing, foraging, walking, and more. They are considered key markers of beauty and health among Marind and are subject to everyday scrutiny, evaluation, and cultivation. Men renowned for their hunting skills, for instance, were often praised for their sinewy bodies and bulging calves, women recognized as experts in sago processing for their sturdy arms and callused palms, and children adept at collecting forest tubers and nuts for their silken, dark skin and gleaming locks of curly black hair. In plants and animals, health and beauty were identified in the alternately smooth or scabrous bark of different tree species; the thick or matted fur of animals; the glaucous or glabrous texture of foliage; the anthracite or translucent exoskeleton of insects; the soft, pulpous flesh of grubs; and the vibrant and lustrous plumage of birds, all of which my companions reveled in noticing and describing as we walked the forest, worked the sago, and observed our surrounds during occasional moments of rest and conversation.

Each of these valued bodily attributes testifies to the organism's ability to sustain life-generating symbiotic relations with other organisms in the forest, as both feeder and fed. Each in turn gives rise to plants' and animals' aesthetic, gustatory, and nourishing qualities as food for humans. For instance,

Figure 1.2. A Marind woman stands beside a sago-processing structure, 2014. Palms growing in the wetness of swamps produce nourishing sago starch. Photograph by the author.

the meat of cassowaries that grow in close contact with the skin of primary forests, drink the wetness of their rivers, and consume their abundant berries, nuts, and snails, is chewy, salty, and intricately patterned with blood-rich capillaries. The flesh of fish nourished by the flesh of juicy algae, shrimps, and worms is compact and firm to the touch but exquisitely melting in the mouth. Similarly, sago starch is most dense and moist when obtained from palms that flourish in the abundant moisture of mangroves and swamps (see figure 1.2).

Forest foods in turn beautify and replenish the skin and wetness of Marind by imparting on them the life-sustaining flesh and fluids of the kindred plants and animals from which they derive. These transfers of vitality begin long before food itself is ingested. For instance, as we journeyed across the landscape on foot during hunting, fishing, and foraging expeditions, people spoke of taking in the skin and wetness of the forest by imbibing the moisture of the soil beneath their feet, the dew hanging in the morning air, and the droplets of rain falling from overhead. Wetness was produced and passed on as we participated in food procurement and preparation activities in the grove—felling sago palms, rasping their boles, leaching their pith, and cooking their starch. Skin, meanwhile, was strengthened through bodily and kinesthetic interactions with the forest environment—as when Marcella instructed me to run my palms along the meandering trails left by insects on the ribbed bark of trees, caress the fur and feathers of captured birds and possums, or dig my fingers deep into the fertile muds of the grove. Matter and meaning crystallized in the forest as a more-than-human, tactile contact zone, inscribed in and deciphered through the storied textures of the landscape and its nourishing beings.

Resonating with the American anthropologist Paige West's characterization of Maimafu foodways in Papua New Guinea as rooted in "dialectical transactive relationships that produce [Maimafu] as persons, animals as active agents, and forests as living social arenas," the more-than-human socialities that Marind affirm imbue forest foods with their satiating qualities are in turn enhanced through practices of commensality that enable the transfer of skin and wetness between and beyond humans.[16] For instance, Marind children who eat sago ingest the wetness of the adults who procured and cooked it, together with the moisture of the palm and the wetness of the rivers, soils, and species that enabled its growth. Women who consume pig or cassowary meat absorb the perspiration of the men who tracked and hunted the animal, together with the animal's fat, blood, and sweat. Similarly, forest foods consumed by pregnant women penetrate the body of their infants, enabling them to develop skin and wetness in the womb and to familiarize themselves with the world of the forest before birth.[17]

More-than-human consubstantialities achieved through exchanges of skin and wetness manifest most vividly in the practice of premastication, wherein community members chew food prepared by them or for them by others, spit it out into their hands, and respectfully offer it to their loved ones, as Marcella did with her daughter Viktorina and then with me in the grove, and as I then learned to practice for those in the community with whom I had developed particularly strong friendships. Undertaken by men and women alike, these intimate transcorporeal exchanges enable people to bestow on their companions not only the vitality of the foods consumed but also a literal part of their own self in the form of cells, sweat, and saliva, in what is considered by villagers to be one of the most tangible testaments of care and kinship.[18]

Eating in and from the forest, in the companionship of human and other-than-human beings, produces a sensation in the body that my companions call *semangat*. This sensation, which can be translated as "vitality," "energy," or "spirit," begins to make itself felt when people walk the forest in search of food. It increases the longer they spend in the forest, and the more they eat forest foods. *Semangat*, Marcella explained, arises first in the stomach, manifesting as a soft rumble or dull vibration. As people's appetite increases, *semangat* works its way outward from the viscera into the muscle, bones, veins, and finally the skin. At this point, a pleasant tingling spreads within and across the surface of the individual and beyond, permeating the flesh of fellow community members who are hunting, fishing, gathering, or cooking nearby. The feeling reaches its apogee when people finally sit down together and ingest foods imbued with the fleshly *semangat* of forest organisms. Singing and storying, which often accompany the act of eating in the forest, further communicate and enhance people's collective experience of *semangat*, as do the sounds and smells of the living environments in which eating takes place.

Semangat, then, constitutes a central cultural, culinary, and corporeal idiom for the vitality generated by the work of food procurement and the satiation achieved through the shared consumption of forest foods. Echoing the ethos of "empathetic foodways" identified by the German-Serbian anthropologist Anita von Poser among the Bosmun in Daiden, Papua New Guinea, the collective nature of *semangat* means it can arise even in the absence of direct food consumption, and instead through the act of witnessing others achieve satiation from eating foods one has procured for them.[19] As Marcella explained when I questioned her abstinence from the meal her relatives and I shared in the grove, "People need *semangat* to obtain food—to walk, hunt, fish, and forage. Eating forest foods generates *semangat*—when we take in the wetness of the sago or the skin of the pig. Seeing friends and kin eat our food, too, makes us *semangat*. Finding food, eating food, and providing food for others to enjoy—these all produce *semangat*."

Affect and Alimentation

Liveliness, peace, and memory constitute the affective counterparts to skin, wetness, and vitality in the more-than-human phenomenology of Marind foodways. Together, these dispositions foreground how the nourishment derived from forest foods arises not only from the material qualities of the species and substances consumed but also from the affective context and experience of eating, including the corporeally mediated feelings and emotions these contexts and experiences generate.

Ramai, meaning "lively" or "busy," encompasses the various movements, actions, and interactions that take place in the forest and that render forest foods flavorsome. It finds expression in the collective pounding and leaching of sago pith by groups of women, the pitter-patter of children's feet as they scurry around the grove in search of fruit and nuts, and the syncopated singing and laughing of villagers as they weave rattan fronds and filaments into intricate bags (<u>noken</u>) beside the fire. *Ramai* manifests also in joking, teasing, and storytelling that accompany the preparation and consumption of food under the welcoming shade of coconut, sago, and nipa palms. It speaks to the shared feelings of excitement, eagerness, and pleasure that community members experience as they discover new sources of food in the forest, encounter overgrown sites where their deceased kin once foraged or hunted, detect fresh suckers burgeoning at the base of sago palms, inhale the smell of sago flour cooking, and anticipate the tastes and textures of the meal to come.

Equated by many of my companions with a sense of shared "elation" (*kesenangan bersama*), *ramai*, as Marcella explained to me in the grove, is something experienced differently but collectively by different people, at different times, and in different places—from the thrill felt by hunters when they successfully track and capture game, to the delight of young children who return to their parents proudly bearing an abundance of ripe tubers and legumes. *Ramai* also extends beyond the human realm to encompass the hustle and bustle of Marind's diverse companion species in the grove—the birds squawking and ruffling their feathers in the canopy, the tree kangaroos creeping cautiously up and down tangled lianas and buttress roots, and the pigs splashing and wallowing in shallow mud pools. The wind, too, participates in *ramai* as it sweeps across the forest, rippling the surface of streams and swaying the foliage in a glimmering dance of light and movement. Villagers experience *ramai* in these moments as an intense and delightful tingling sensation on their skin, comparable to the gentle tickle of a feather, that intensifies to the point that they feel their skin might burst from within. Marcella's adolescent daughter, Petra, described this sensation to me during a fishing expedition down the Bian River, during which she pointed out the multiple manifestations of *ramai* happening in and around us. Gesturing to the landscape as we paddled down the waterway, she said: "If you pay attention, you can hear the voice [*suara*] of the river singing, the wind whispering—also the fish flapping and the trees creaking. You can feel the warmth of the sun above and the shade of the clouds. You know their wetness is moving and mixing, and your own is wetness moving and mixing. In these moments, there is so much beauty and movement around us that it's hard to keep it all within one single skin. You want to share *ramai* with others. You want to keep moving, working, and singing, at one with the forest."

Punctuating lively moments of *ramai* are introspective moments of *damai*, a term that translates as "peace" and that Marind characterize as a sense of inner calm, quietude, happiness, serenity, and harmonious unity with the forest. Achieving this state of quietude requires taking pause from

Figure 1.3. A father and son rest by the Bian River, 2015. Villagers interrupt fishing, hunting, leaching, or cooking to go and find *damai* (peace). Photograph by the author.

one's labors in the grove and creating moments of silence (*diam*). For instance, villagers whom I accompanied to the forest regularly interrupted their fishing, hunting, leaching, or cooking activities to "go and find *damai*" (*pigi cari damai*). Leaving their implements behind, they would walk to sit by the riverbank or on a nearby sago stump, often bringing with them a close friend, young child, or other relative (see figure 1.3). Here, they would do nothing other than observe their surrounds for extended periods, without moving or speaking. Remaining silent in these moments of pause, as I was taught to do, enables people to better notice the movements of animals and insects around them, the oscillating fronds above them, and the softness of the soil beneath them. Occasionally, villagers would point out to me and describe in half whispers the attributes or particularities of the landscape, the weather, the light, and the heat, or remark on the sounds that enlivened the air—the chirping of birds, buzzing of flies, and gurgle of rivers.

Resonating with the Fijian education scholar Unaisi Nabobo-Baba's description of silence as an epistemology and pedagogy of respectful engagement with and reverent attunement to one's living environment and its diverse dwellers, *damai* among Marind constitutes a cultivated praxis of wonder that is at once in, about, and with the forest—a realm animated by myriad alterities in perpetual flux and flow who together shape Marind's own sense of ecorelational being, becoming, and belonging.[20] To experience this wonder demands a hiatus in human activity that enables people to reckon in bodily and affective ways with everything else that is, always and everywhere, going on. These shared moments of reflective meditation, Petra explained, are just as much about finding peace and creating silence as they are about listening to the forest and celebrating the nourishing foods that it has and continues to bestow on its human and more-than-human dwellers.

As intimated by Marcella's companions in the grove, memories (*ingatan*) constitute another important facet in the phenomenology of being and eating in the grove. Consuming forest foods, according to Klaus, Marcella's husband and a member of the Basik-Basik clan, reminds people of their ancient kinships to the plants and animals from which these foods derive, in a form of embodied memory that is at once transspecies and transgenerational.[21] During meals shared in the forest, for instance, villagers often recounted how ancestral spirits (dema) had fashioned the organisms they were eating from a primordial mud at the beginning of time, bestowing on each of them the bodily and behavioral capacities they require to survive and thrive. They described in great detail notable events, encounters, and interactions that had taken place between particular organisms and particular humans, in living and collective memory. It was through the sharing of *ingatan*, for instance, that I came to learn on one foraging journey about the slippery struggle of an aged widow and a stubborn eel at the third bend of the Bian River. On another forest expedition, I heard stories of the shared peregrinations of a mythical hunter named Getum in the company of a lone male cassowary that he befriended at the eastern boundary of the Gebze (banana) clan. Later during that same journey, Marcella storied for us the silky clusters of reeds that sheltered a group of errant children during a storm whipped up by the wrathful dema Kimbiri. The fall of dark in the patch of forest where we bivouacked that night brought with it other villagers' memories, including those of a cunning mottled brown frog that once lured the mythical hero Sosom to its damp and dark burrow, lulled him to sleep with its croak, and then cunningly stole Sosom's human voice, making it its own distinctive call from that day onward.

During food expeditions, villagers delved in *ingatan* as they recalled with fondness the journeys of their living and deceased relatives across the landscape, together with the places they rested, ate, and danced along the way. They sang about the creeks and clearings where their babies were born, or the sacred groves where their parents and grandparents are buried. They remembered in jest the many accidents, injuries, and mishaps they suffered as children and adolescents in their first, clumsy attempts to learn how to eat from the forest—how to hunt pigs, fashion bows, leach sago, capture fish, or carefully detach with the tip of their front teeth the sharp mandibles of live edible beetles in order to access their nutritious inner flesh. Often indistinct or overlapping in their temporalities, memories intertwined as people read more-than-human pasts in the materiality of the forest—the relief of a mound or watershed where <u>dema</u> once battled, the curve of a stream where clans once made peace, or the dense foliage of a sago grove where long-departed kin once shared skin and wetness.

Walking and eating in the forest generates new memories at the same time as it triggers the collective remembrance of meaningful past events. Long after we had returned to the village, for instance, foraging expeditions were extensively and repeatedly recounted to those who had stayed back to care for children too young to participate, or because of their age or ailments. Telling these stories in minute and intricate detail was said to allow others to experience the liveliness and peace of the forest as they consumed forest foods brought back to the village. Sessions that I was invited to participate in usually took place at the fall of night and lasted for several hours, and sometimes until dawn. Community members would gather by the hearth or on the front porch and describe the organisms they encountered in the forest, the labors they undertook, the sounds they heard and their provenance, and the tastes of the foods they ate. *Ramai* animated these lively discussions as individuals interrupted or elaborated on each other's anecdotes, shared their own reflections, praised each other's activities, fleshed out their own interpretation of particular happenings and circumstances, and invited others including myself to join in the recounting of events experienced individually or collectively, at the time or long prior. Much like *semangat*, which energizes those who procure food for others, the sharing of memories enables foods from the forest to retain their original flavor and sustain the bodies of those who consume them in the village. As Marcella put it, "Memories and stories fill the foods we eat with nourishing tastes, smells, and sounds. These memories are in our skin, our wetness, and our food. By sharing stories and memories with others, we bring *ramai*, *damai*, and *semangat* back from the forest, and home to the village."

Gender and Generation

Both gendered and generational differences shape the division of labor involved in procuring and preparing forest foods. Marind men who joined in on foraging expeditions were primarily responsible for the hunting of small and large game, including cassowaries, pigs, and tree kangaroos. Parties of two to six male individuals would often travel to the forest ahead of the group in order to capture birds, mammals, and reptiles when they approach water sources at dawn and at dusk. Men were also charged with collecting betel nuts, setting traps for possums and birds, and felling and rasping sago palms. They fashioned spears, bows, arrows, and harpoons and built the wooden canoes that Marind use to travel up and down the river. Another key responsibility of male community members was to ensure the safety of the group when in the forest—for instance, by standing guard at the outer rim of the clearings where they bivouac, shooing away packs of approaching wild pigs or lone male cassowaries, or keeping track of weather fluctuations such as billowing clouds and rising winds that signal the approach of storms and showers.

Sago processing and cooking during these expeditions were the primary chores of women, alongside minding young children and attending to the needs of the elderly group members. In groups of three to four, women began by building the sekuka, a canoe-like construction made of sago fronds that is erected close to a water source or dug-out waterhole. Sago pith rasped from freshly felled palms was added to the top of the sekuka along with abundant quantities of water and then beaten vigorously with wooden rods by the women. This leaching process separates the inedible pith from the edible starch, which, together with the water, flow down the sekuka funnel into a trough and are separated by a handwoven filter fashioned from thin sago filaments. Meanwhile, other female group members took charge of skinning and piecing the game brought back by the men, lighting fires, and grilling sago balls together with grubs, vegetables, and tubers foraged by their children. In between or during these activities, women breastfed or cradled infants and toddlers to sleep, tended to children's wounds and grazes with resins and saps, and kept the elderly entertained with the latest stories, gossip, and events from their own and neighboring villages.

Children from the age of five onward, too, had an important part to play in food procurement activities. For instance, boys and girls were tasked with carrying water back to their mothers and aunts to leach the sago starch, collecting grubs from the rotting stumps of sago palms, and finding mature fruit and edible mushrooms in the forest undergrowth. They also gathered twigs and branches throughout the day to feed the fire and trimmed the bamboo stalks in which the sago is steamed. Boys learned from their male relatives how to identify the right kinds of wood to make flexible yet sturdy hunting bows, the best resins to bind arrow shafts to the tip and fletching, and the most elastic vines to fashion lassos from and capture pigs with. Girls, meanwhile, were taught by their mothers, aunts, and elder sisters how to weave sago strands into bags of different shapes and sizes, which can then be used to transport food, tools, and infants. They also learned how to make sago frond skirts and ornaments, stuff sago flour and other condiments into bamboo stalks without breaking them, and descale and eviscerate fish freshly captured from the river by their parents.

Elders (*orang tua*), including grandparents and unmarried community members over fifty years of age, played the most significant role in children's enculturation and apprenticeship in the arts of forest foodways. These individuals were minimally involved in food procurement and preparation activities and instead were tasked with transmitting knowledge (*ilmu*) to the young. In the forest, elders educated children in the origin stories of different organisms encountered; their relations to ancestral spirits; and the plants, animals, and ecosystems they rely on to survive and thrive. They taught children the rituals, songs, and incantations that must be performed when animals are captured and killed, when sago palms are felled, and when food is consumed and distributed among community members and with the forest.

Elders also encouraged children to exercise respect, care, and caution in and for the forest by pointing out to them organisms that should not be hunted or consumed during their gestational periods, or those that are poisonous or otherwise inedible. They further cultivated children's attentiveness to the landscape and its life-forms by encouraging them to observe their surrounds as they walk the forest; to notice the sounds, sights, and smells around them; and to recognize the vegetal and animal beings with which they share kinships and pasts. In the process, children learned to recognize the bodily and affective sensations of *damai*, *ramai*, and *semangat* and how these sensations find expression in the condition of their own and others' skin and wetness.

The distribution of affective, pedagogical, and physical labors in the grove across men, women, children, and elders brought many of my female companions to describe forest foodways as a rare and valued space of egalitarianism across genders and generations. This equal distribution of labor is further accompanied by activities that are open to collective participation and are not seen as the prerogative of any particular subgroup. For instance, while hunting for game is practiced only by men, fishing activities I participated in were often shared among men and women, with men spearing the fish and women casting the nets. Boys and men together fashioned and set traps in the mangroves to capture possums and rodents. The foraging of edible nuts, fruit, and tubers was carried out by anyone who happened to come across them as they walked the forest. The rasping of sago pith, too, was often undertaken by men with the aid of adolescents and young women. Similarly, everyone eventually participated in the chains of singing, storytelling, and incantations initiated by elders.

Food procurement activities in the forest, then, are not ranked in importance or value; instead, they complement each other in ways that reflect the respective strengths, skills, and knowledges of different group members. This distributed labor in turn enhances the satiation offered by forest foods. Marcia, a young woman from the Gebze clan and a resident of Khalaoyam village, explained this to me during a moment of rest between bouts of sago pounding with her sisters in the grove. "When there are many different foods to eat," Marcia commented, "we know everyone has shared skin and wetness with each other and with the forest. Some have hunted, others fished. Some have processed sago, others collected fruit. Some have shared *ilmu* and others shared *ramai*. The food will be nourishing because it will taste of every single person's hard work." As Marcia intimates, the diversity of foodstuffs consumed in the forest condenses the diverse and complementary forms of work, effort, and care enacted by different individuals who together make reciprocal relations of feeding and being fed possible and pleasurable. Diverse human labors enable the procurement of diverse foodstuffs, that in turn reflect the diversity of the living forest ecology itself.

This layered diversity is often invoked by community members in explaining why the best meal is one that features an array of different food types. Sago flour, for instance, usually represents the largest portion of any forest meal, in terms of both quantity and calories. But, as Klaus often emphasized to me, "Sago does not grow alone in the forest. Therefore, sago should not be eaten alone either."[22] As people consume sago in the environments where it is procured, Klaus continued, they are reminded of the multispecies story (*cerita*) of sago—where it came from, how it made its way to the mangroves, and where and when it first yielded its nourishing pith. Tracing sago's ancestral lifeway in turn invokes to villagers the many *other* organisms that entertain symbiotic relations with the sago palm, and which Marind sometimes call "sago's friends" (*sagu pu kawan*). One among these is the sago palm weevil (<u>dakh mira</u>), a type of snout beetle that incubates in rotting sago trunks and can be consumed in either grub or adult form. The creamy, fatty texture of steamed or grilled weevil grubs in turn finds a succulent complement in the bitterness of young papaya leaves and the sweetness of gelatinous coconut flesh or ripe bananas—three other kindred species that tend to thrive in close proximity to sago in the swamps and groves, and that first sprouted from the soil together with sago in time immemorial.

The consumption of sago, as well as the stories and memories surrounding it, also brings to community members' minds the diverse animals that roost, nest, or feed in the sago grove canopy (possums, tree kangaroos, and bats) or in the undergrowth (cassowaries, pigs, and anteaters). Consuming the salty flesh of these animals adds yet another layer to the gustatory diversity of the forest meal. As my own palate was enskilled to appreciate by Marcella and her sisters, this meaty saltiness is best counterbalanced by the consumption of sticky-sweet seasonal forest fruit such as rambutans, mangoes, and guavas and the chewing of bitter sireh leaf mixed with tobacco, slaked lime, and areca nut. In these and other instances, the tastes and textures of one particular food whet people's appetite for a range of other, complementary foods at the same time as they draw in the range of different people who will labor to obtain and prepare them. Taken together, these foods and labors, along with the stories that accompany them, come to embody an alimentary microcosm of the feeding forest ecology and its constitutive, sympoietic relations.

Becoming Good Food for Others

The satiation that Marind associate with the consumption of forest food arises from the richly multisensory, bodily, and affective meanings and materialities that these foods and their environments evoke. But human satiation is only one part of the story of forest foodways. Just as important as the nourishment obtained by Marind from the forest is the nourishment that Marind themselves provide for their plant and animal forest kin. Being Marind, in Marcella's words, means becoming "good food for others" (*jadi makanan enak buat lain*).

Transfers of bodily fluids are one way in which Marind become good food for others. For instance, the sweat of community members sustains the growth of vegetation when it comes into contact with branches, leaves, fruit, flowers, and twigs as people walk the forest (see figure 1.4). Villagers enhance this transfer of wetness by intentionally rubbing their hands, forearms, and calves against the trunks, shoots, and adventitious roots they encounter along the way. Sweat infiltrates the soil as people labor in the grove, nourishing a mixed community of insects and gastropods, including centipedes, ants, snails, and grubs, and also feeding the root systems of nearby shrubs, bushes, and grasses. Human blood becomes fodder for hematophagous critters such as the leech that surreptitiously crept up young Fransiskus's leg during our visit to the grove, and the mosquitoes that swarm the forest during the monsoon season. Women who were breastfeeding during forest

Figure 1.4. A Marind peels a forest flower, 2015. The sweat of community members sustains the growth of vegetation. Photograph by the author.

expeditions would nourish the forest by smearing droplets of colostrum— the thick, golden fluid produced in the first few days after childbirth—on the trunks and shoots of nearby sago palms to encourage vegetative reproduction in the form of suckers and stolons. Some, like Petra and Marcella, spoke of having once buried their placentas in the forest to feed the soil and sustain the growth of native grasses, trees, and palms.

Other, more indirect transfers of fluid are enabled through the ritualized etiquette that accompanies food procurement, preparation, consumption, and disposal in the forest. Hunters, for instance, often imparted their sweat on the small portions of fruit, nuts, and sago flour that they left at the sites where they had captured and killed game, in exchange for the life of the animal taken and as a sign of respect toward its kin. Similar, tactically mediated food offerings were regularly made when people encountered juvenile or gestating animals and birds in the forest, and which were left near their nests or burrows. When food was being cooked, villagers would invite me to partake in scattering sago flour around the fire for maleo fowl and pigs to consume. A share equivalent to an adult male's intake, and often including a portion of premasticated food, was always saved for forest animals and usually placed atop a mound of soil or wrapped in layered banana leaves. Formulaic songs and incantations were then performed to entice animals to consume this food and to find nourishment in the human sweat and saliva that had mingled with and fortified it.

Marind continue to become good food for their plant and animal kin long after their death. While burial in the village cemetery is now widely practiced, many of my companions affirmed that they wished to be interred in the forest so that their bodies would become "useful" (*berguna*) to others. In this traditional mode of burial, which has waned with the advent of Catholicism but that I witnessed on a few rare occasions, corpses were wrapped in dried sago fronds and placed a meter or so underground, then covered with earth, on which a young nipa or other palm shoot genus is planted. As the body decomposes, human flesh and fluids seep into the ground, where they are ingested or otherwise absorbed by subterranean earthworms, beetles, and millipedes. Larger mammals, reptiles, and birds that prey on these organisms take in the skin and wetness of the deceased, passing it on to their own progenies through reproduction and eventually returning it to the forest when they die or are consumed. The flourishing of the plant atop the burial site, too, is enhanced by the diverse community of critters that feed off the flesh and fluids of human bodies, and also by the nutrient-enriched soil that this decomposition produces.

For Marind, then, eating well matters not only for the health and well-being of the consumer but also because it enables the consumer to become good food for others beyond their individual life course. As an expression of more-than-human metabolic justice, nourishing others thus comes to constitute what Kim TallBear might describe as "acting in good relation."[23] It is a way of remaining responsible toward the more-than-human communities of life that make human existence possible, and with which humans are bound in intimate, mutual, and transformative entanglements of eating and being eaten.[24] This is a stance that positions human death not outside or above the food chain but rather, in the Australian ecophilosopher Val Plumwood's terms, as "part of the feast in a chain of reciprocity" with the earth. In embracing the positionality of prey, Marind thus counter dominant exceptionalisms that identify humans as "the eaters of others who are never themselves eaten."[25] Instead, they reframe care for the self as care for the many other beings whose bodily skin, wetness, and vitality constantly disperse, cycle, and recycle within the metabolic flows of the forest as "nourishing terrain."[26]

Just as the collective care of feeding other humans is recognized anatomically in the condition of bodily skin and wetness, so too the collective care of nourishing the environment is concretized in the perceived health, diversity, and fertility of the landscape itself. Here, the state of the body affects that of the environment and vice versa, within what Candace Fujikane, a Japanese American English studies scholar, describes as a mutual "cultivation of abundance," distributed across human and other-than-human beings, living and dead, and past and future.²⁷ This intimate and reciprocal relationship between nourishing lives and nourishing deaths was captured poetically by Kloella, a woman in her late eighties from the Uabarek (coconut) clan and a resident of Bayau village, a few weeks prior to her passing. As we sat in a patch of forest together boiling freshly picked papaya leaves, she commented: "Soon, my body will be eaten by plants and animals. My body will transform into birds and rivers and soil. It will feed the forest that fed me. If my body is strong in skin and wetness, then it will strengthen the skin and wetness of the forest. In doing so, my body will also feed many forests to come, that will then feed many Marind to come. By feeding and being fed, everyone lives on [*makan, dimakan, semua hidup terus*]."

Hungers in the Forest

While Marind widely associate traditional foodways with satiation and nourishment, my companions often stressed that experiences of hunger are equally important to the moral economy that undergirds relations of eating and being eaten in the forest. The availability of forest foods has always varied according to seasonality, animal migration patterns, plant growth and senescence cycles, and fluctuating weather conditions such as drought or monsoon. Knowing which foods are accessible, where, and when, and what foods serve to compensate for the absence of others, are central elements in the vast body of knowledge that Marind call *ilmu*. They complement other adaptive coping strategies adopted in times of food scarcity, including the communal pooling of resources across clans and settlements, the selective rationing of particular foodstuffs, and the temporary uptake of informal employment by men and women in peri-urban and urban areas.²⁸

However, many of my companions affirm that periods of generalized food scarcity in the past were episodic rather than protracted. Extended periods of hunger—or chronic hunger—were interpreted primarily as punishments meted out by <u>dema</u> against community members for failing to respect their forest kin. Such violations included killing juvenile or gestating animals, felling or damaging immature sago palms and other vegetation, and neglecting to utter the requisite incantations during hunting and foraging. In line with customary law, a range of different rituals, ceremonies, and dietary restrictions helped ensure that food supplies were replenished over time, the fertility of the soils and waters of the forest maintained, and the violations of food procurement protocols remedied or redressed.

A complex taxonomy serves to distinguish different hungers in the forest. Marelina, a woman in her late seventies from the Mahuze clan and one of a handful of villagers still fluent in the Bian dialect of Marind, explained to me that Marind distinguish "drought hunger" (*kelaparan kemarau*), which occurs during the dry season, from "monsoon hunger" (*kelaparan angin musim*), which occurs during the rainy season. Marind also distinguish hunger depending on what foods are hungered after—for instance, "hunger for cassowary" (*kelaparan kasuari*) and "hunger for crocodile" (*kelaparan buaya*). Before Indonesian colonization, Marelina continued, when Marind of the Upper Bian were fully conversant in their native tongue, there existed over fifty different Marind words for hunger. The conjugation of these words depended on a number of factors, their semantic net encompassing the clan-based relationship between the eater and the eaten; the eater's gender and age; the setting when and where the hunger was experienced; its perceived pervasiveness or rarity, duration, and intensity; and its attributed cause and anticipated effects.

With *logat* Papua having now largely replaced Marind as the primary language spoken among Upper Bian inhabitants, many of these complex taxonomies of hunger have been forgotten by all but the most elderly of villagers like Marelina, whose own memory of the exact terms had become foggy and distant. Still prevalent among Marind today, however, is the classification of hungers as either "good" or "bad"—a moral distinction that in turn speaks to the actions and relations of hunger's relative objects and subjects.[29]

Hungers provoked by walking the forest, foraging and hunting for extensive periods, tending to children and elders, or processing sago starch are referred to as *kelaparan baik*, meaning "good hunger," or, somewhat paradoxically, as *kelaparan enak*, "tasty hunger." Closely linked to the sensation of *semangat*, or the notion of appetite, good hungers are positively valued because they demonstrate that one has invested one's energies in procuring food and caring for one's kin. These hungers are generated by, and therefore testament to, people's sustained and collective interactions and labors. They are openly spoken about and celebrated, both by those who experience them and those who satiate them.

Bad hungers, or *kelaparan buruk*, on the other hand, act as informal sanctions against behaviors that are seen to contravene the principles of relationality and reciprocity. Resonating with the concept of *loka* among the Massim of Papua New Guinea, which refers to a kind of hunger resulting from antisocial human actions, bad hungers among Marind are both punitive and remedial.[30] For instance, individuals or groups may experience bad hunger if they commit actions that displease or offend their relatives and fellow community members, who will intentionally refrain from sharing food or participating in foraging expeditions with them. Indeed, and as I learned on the many occasions when I committed cultural faux pas during my time in the field, withholding food over sustained periods constitutes a central means through which Marind communicate their discontent toward others. Conversely, individuals who find themselves excluded from food-sharing activities are usually quick to seek clarification on, and remedy for, the underlying conflict, dispute, or misunderstanding. Bad hungers, then, testify and respond to a perceived attrition of broader kinship values and social norms, as these are expressed through acts of eating and sharing. They are rarely spoken about publicly and instead are subject to gossip behind closed doors among those who witness or provoke them.

Other protocols are at play in the socio-logic of eating and hunger. For instance, refusing food on account of not being hungry is deemed highly offensive to those who have prepared or procured it. Conversely, consuming food ravenously is described as "bad hunger" because it is seen as selfish and inconsiderate, as are eating alone or in private and failing to share food with those whom one is related to, or otherwise on good terms with. Both the lack of hunger and constant hunger are also subject to moral evaluation. Echoing comparable associations identified among the Kalauna, Massim, and Yagwoia-Angan peoples of Papua New Guinea, these conditions are said to be symptomatic of physical illnesses that in turn are often explained as the result of a sorcery attack (kambara).[31]

Bad hungers and associated forms of behavior in turn manifest in the thinness or fatness of individuals' bodies. Excessive thinness suggests that food is being withheld from the individual by their family and friends, or that they have become subject to a kambara attack, as a result of an unresolved wrong on their part. Excessive fatness, meanwhile, suggests that the individual is consuming inordinately large amounts of food and thereby depriving others of their fair share. Both excessive thinness and excessive fatness are further said to result from insufficient physical labor in the forest, including collective food procurement and preparation, which generate strong and muscly bodies through the production and exchange of skin and wetness.

In line with this socio-logic, a central component of children's enculturation into Marind foodways entails learning to eat at a respectable pace and with due regard for others' share. Equally important is the need for children to learn to hunger for different kinds of forest foods, rather than any single one among them. An imbalance in foods hungered after is dangerous as it undermines the development of the child's skin and wetness and therefore predisposes it to illness and injury. Such an imbalance also prevents the child from acquiring the variety of aptitudes associated with different forest creatures—for instance, the sharp eyesight of the bird of paradise, the speed and agility of tree kangaroos, and the mellifluous vocals of male boatbills.

While a diverse diet allows children to take on the attributes of different plants and animals in equal and commensurate measure, a disproportional diet puts children at risk of becoming too much like the organisms they consume, and thereby threatens their processual development and social integration.[32] Overconsuming cassowary flesh, for instance, causes children to become solitary and violent, while overconsuming boar meat turns their skin tough and hairy. Overconsuming bamboo shoots, meanwhile, causes children to grow thin and wispy, and overconsuming papaya fruit turns their flesh flaccid and prone to bruising. The pursuit of a balanced diet, composed of multiple different food types, is thus of central importance to children's healthy maturation. It also buttresses the range of food protocols practiced by mothers and fathers, whose own diets are said to shape the skin and wetness of the child throughout the period of pregnancy and for up to two years postpartum.[33]

Eating in and from the forest, as such, is life-sustaining and meaning-producing—but it is never devoid of risk or danger. Misreading the skin of poisonous plants or fungi, for instance, can result in illness and even death if these organisms are collected and consumed. Not knowing how to decipher the skin or wetness of clouds or waterways can result in injury, hunger, and thirst if one fails to detect arriving storms, floods, or drought. Wrongly reading the morphology or behavior of plants and animals that are juvenile, mating, or gestating can result in punishment from ancestral spirits if these organisms are hunted or harvested. The skin of larger birds, reptiles, and mammals, such as cassowaries, crocodiles, and boars, may be good to eat, but encountering, trapping, and killing them is a hazardous endeavor, wherein human predators can all too easily become prey for hungry animals. Similarly, allowing one's skin to become good food for insects might satiate them and sustain their existences—but it also means exposing oneself to prevalent diseases, including malaria and dengue fever, as well as equally common parasitic gut infections and skin irritations, as people are reminded of their vulnerabilities to the hunger of other Others.[34]

In her reflections on Indigenous knowledges, practices, and responsibilities with kin, the Pairrebeenne Trawlwoolway geographer Lauren Tynan notes that while Indigenous understandings of relationality center the intimate connection of land and people, "connection to Country is not always rosy either."[35] In a similar vein, the pleasures that Marind derive from more-than-human (sk)intimacies in the forest sit alongside the perils they identify as inherent to traditional food environments and foodways, challenging the representation of Indigenous interspecies relations as necessarily or purely benign, giving, and life-sustaining. These contingent relations conjure bodily permeability and porosity as alternatively lively or lethal attributes of the fluid boundaries between one's own flesh and the flesh of the world one inhabits. Porosity is what allows beings to flourish—breathing air, metabolizing nutrients, absorbing fluids—but as the American philosopher Nancy Tuana reminds us, porosity "does not discriminate against that which can kill us."[36]

The dangers of eating and being eaten in the forest thus draw attention to the differential vulnerabilities that both precede and are (re)shaped by the act of being drawn together in more-than-human and often non-innocent encounters.[37] Becoming a source of food for blood-hungry leeches and mosquitoes, suffering potentially deadly injuries from the kicks of male cassowaries whose territory one infringes upon on the way to the sago grove, or finding oneself the target of a charging pack of wild boars during hunting expeditions is not the type of experience my companions actively seek out or derive particular pleasure from. Rather, these realities are understood as a condition and compromise that is inherent to more-than-human coexistence—as something that emerges from an active involvement in ecologies of mutual obligation with significant others across distributed temporalities and spatialities, even if it might come at a cost to one's own bodily well-being in the here and the now.[38] Less-than-benign encounters and their bodily consequences, as such, are anchored in a recognition of the responsibilities of care that sustaining a community of life demands *and* of the exposures and vulnerabilities that any form of consumption and commensality entail.

In this light, what counts as "good" or "bad" satiety and hunger for Marind is relative and contextual, shaped by both degree and kind. This distinction is determined as much by what foods are desired as by the identity of those who experience particular hungers, in what settings, and for what reasons. In these respects, hunger goes well beyond a biophysical condition defined purely by the absence or lack of "food" defined in generic terms. Rather, hunger expresses important truths about a person's social standing and their relationships to humans and other-than-humans, within what Cash Ahenakew, a member of the Ahtahkakoop Cree Nation and an Indigenous education and health scholar, describes as "a collective metabolism involving the land/earth and beyond."[39] Like its counterparts of satiation and nourishment, hunger's materiality and morality arise within a more-than-human spectrum of life wherein the trope of balance in social and environmental relations is given moral and metabolic expression, and wherein collective continuance depends on the willingness and ability of every organism to inhabit and shift across multiple and interlinked subjectivities—as feeder, as fed, and as food.

2

HUNGERS THAT NEVER GO AWAY

Dusk was falling over Khalaoyam village. A group of residents had gathered at the entrance of the settlement to greet their kith and kin who had been fishing in the forest since the break of dawn. Children dozed in the arms of their mothers and fathers. Chatter filled the air as clove cigarettes and betel nuts passed from lap to lap, hand to hand, and lip to lip. Paola, a young woman from the Samkakai (wallaby) clan and a newly trained nurse at the Khalaoyam clinic, was sitting beside me and scrolling through my phone, looking at the photographs we had taken that day during a visit to her sister-in-law in the neighboring village of Bayau.

At one point, her brother Klemensius drew our attention away from the screen and toward a dark shadow forming on the horizon. My friends perked their ears, awaiting with bated breath the song that would indicate a bountiful catch. As the shadow loomed closer, a sad, slow wail echoed through the muggy air. My companions bowed their heads. Paola sighed. She knew this wailing all too well. It signaled that her kin had, once again, returned from the forest empty-handed and hungry.

Mirabela, the middle-aged woman who had led the fishing expedition, collapsed at the foot of a nearby rambutan tree and flung her fishing spear and nets aside. She appeared pale and tired. Faint remnants of white paint, smeared by Mirabela's sisters prior to the journey for good luck and protection, dotted her furrowed brow. A baby whimpered. Gazes erred. The atmosphere was tense. Eventually, Mirabela spoke.

The group had spent the day fishing at the third bend of the Manaira tributary near the sacred grove of Akhaim. They had been guided there by the ancestral spirit of Mirabela's clan, the Kaize (cassowary) clan, who had appeared to her in a dream the previous night. The group had cast their nets far and wide but caught nothing. The river was gray and oily with toxic effluents released by the nearby palm oil–processing mill. Dead fish floated to the surface by the hundreds. When I asked why, Mirabela explained the fish had been poisoned by the mill's chemicals. They were unsafe to eat. Abandoning the fishing expedition, Mirabela's elder brother Carlos had then tried to track down deer and possums in the forest, but bulldozers hashing through the vegetation had caused the animals to flee to higher ground. One villager had encountered a young tree kangaroo, sheltering under a wizened nipa palm. Its leg appeared to be broken, and its mother was nowhere in sight. Reluctant to break customary law by capturing and killing a juvenile orphan, the young man had left the animal where he had found it.

Mirabela went silent. Her six-year-old son, Petrus, climbed into her arms, holding an empty instant noodle wrapper in his fist. Mirabela wiped dried noodle crumbs from his face. This child, she told me, was like the fish in the river. His skin was weak and his wetness was lacking. Like the fish that were poisoned by chemicals, Petrus was being eaten by rice and instant noodles. He did not know the skin or the taste of the forest. Mirabela spit out a bright red stain of betel nut juice. She reached out for Petrus's hand and held it to her chest, her body rocking side to side and her eyes lifted to the clouds gathering overhead. Mirabela's elder sister, Costanza, placed her hand on Mirabela's shoulder and whispered gently, "Sing it, sister. Sing your pain. Sing your anger. Sing a hunger song."

> *Hari ini lagi kitorang tidak dapat makan dari hutan*
> Today once again, we found nothing to eat in the forest
> *Dari Manaira di sebelah utara terus sampe Akhaim di sebelah selatan*
> From Manaira in the north to Akhaim in the south
> *Dari Kekok di sebelah timur terus sampe Dizil di sebelah barat*
> From Kekok in the east to Dizil in the west

Hanya kenal lapar
All we found was hunger

Setelah sawit datang hutan de su hilang, sungai sedang mati
Since oil palm arrived, the forests, they have vanished, the rivers,
    they are dying
Kitorang suku Marind, lapar macam-macam
As for Marind People, we face all kinds of hunger
Lapar untuk sagu, lapar untuk plastik, lapar untuk uang
Hunger for sago, hunger for plastic, hunger for money

Kelaparan-kelaparan ini, semuanya de baru, semuanya de beda
These hungers, they are different and they are new
Kelaparan-kelaparan ini, de muncul terus, de tidak berhenti
These hungers, they keep growing, they never go away

This chapter explores the new and different hungers that Marind have become subject to following the proliferation of oil palm plantations across
their customary lands and territories. Over the last decade, the inhabitants of
Khalaoyam and neighboring villages have seen some two hundred thousand
hectares of their forests converted to monocrop concessions by domestic
and foreign agro-industrial corporations. Deforestation and agribusiness
expansion have radically undermined Marind's access to forest-derived
foods, which are now increasingly substituted with processed or imported
commodities that Marind purchase from settler-owned kiosks in the village, obtain at subsidized rates from government agencies, or receive from
oil palm corporations as part of social welfare schemes or as compensation
for lands surrendered. The shift from a nutritionally diverse diet composed
of forest game, fish, vegetables, fruits, and tubers to a nutritionally impoverished diet composed of rice, instant noodles, canned meats, and biscuits,
compounded with the contamination of forest ecologies and food resources
by plantation fertilizers, pesticides, and effluents, has resulted in widespread
protein and micronutrient deficiencies, malnutrition, and food poisoning
across the villages of the Upper Bian.

The association invoked in Mirabela's song between the destruction of
the forest, the arrival of monocrops, and the rise of pervasive and constant
hunger represented a recurring and prevalent motif within the discourses
of many women in rural Merauke. This stands in stark contrast to the previously described association of forest foodways with nourishment and sati-

ation, which was articulated by Marind men and women alike. Just as forest foodways are never just about food, my female companions explained, so too the new and different hungers afflicting villagers today act as markers of relationality within a more-than-human cosmos. However, these hungers diverge significantly in their respective origins and moralities, as well as their relative subjects and objects. Their significance is embedded within and produced by violent histories of colonial racial capitalism that have long undermined Marind's food systems, bodies, and well-being, and that manifest today in the relentless proliferation of industrial oil palm plantations. At the same time, their meanings are inflected by the ambivalent role and responsibility of Marind themselves—and especially, of Marind men—in the production and proliferation of hunger. The new and different hungers I trace in this chapter thus speak both to the attritive effects of colonial occupation on Marind collectives *and* to the splintering of gendered relations within these collectives that, if not entirely new, have now become newly prominent. In the process, the relative importance or influence of these two factors on the production of hunger in turn reveals itself as an object of widespread hesitation and debate among my female companions.

The chapter begins by situating the rise of new hungers in the last decade within Marind women's understanding of historicity and of the temporal ruptures that have over time undermined forest foodways in rural Merauke. I then examine how available statistics on malnutrition provided by clinics and hospitals in the region fail to encompass hunger's qualitative, cultural, and more-than-human dimensions while also not accounting for the practical impediments that limit Marind's access to biomedical institutions and the sense of shame and culpability that brings many women to avoid visiting these establishments in the first instance. The chapter further uncovers how emergent forms of hunger in the Upper Bian in the form of hunger for sago, hunger for plastic foods, and hunger for money and human flesh come to signify a broader ecosocial breakdown in relations of eating and being eaten within and across species lines. Taken together, these emergent hungers conjure the attrition of morally valued forest foodways prompted by industrial landscape transformations, the deleterious effects of increasingly consumed imported and processed commodities on Marind bodies and relations, and what many women describe—if never without hesitation—as the complicity of Marind men themselves in furthering intergenerational and interspecies violence through their involvement with the oil palm sector as landowners and plantation laborers.

Just as Marind understand hunger as shaped by its specific spatial, ecological, and cultural contexts, so too hunger accrues significance for communities in light of its particular (and particularly prominent) relationship to local conceptualizations of time. Hunger's temporal situatedness sits in turn within a broader understanding among Marind of the present condition as produced through a series of episodic ruptures that together have provoked a generalized breakdown in social, material, and moral relations.[1] While this view was commonly expressed by both men and women, the centrality of hunger within Marind senses of historicity was especially pronounced among my female companions. During conversations that took place in the absence of village men, for instance, women frequently characterized and remembered the past through a sequence of consecutive, differential, and cumulative hungers that were in turn connected to historically specific events, encounters, and processes.[2] Embodying what the British historian James Vernon calls differential "regimes of hunger," it is these events, encounters, and processes that imbue the new and different hungers proliferating across rural Merauke today with their distinctive political, social, moral, and gendered valences.[3]

The first "new hunger" (*kelaparan baru*) to spread across the Upper Bian was prompted by the plume trade of the early 1900s, which saw an unprecedented surge in demand for exotic birds that traditionally had constituted an important part of Marind's diet but in this period became the targets of a lucrative wildlife trade, their feathers supplying trimmings, hats, and ornaments for the middle and upper echelons of European and North American society. This time was described to me in detail by Caritas, a Gebze (banana) clan elder, resident of Khalaoyam, and grandmother of seven, during one of the many evenings we spent weaving sago bags together on the front porch of her hut. As we spun the fibers and barks side by side, Caritas spoke of an era when bird <u>amai</u> (plant and animal kin, in the Bian dialect of Marind) that had long been regarded and cherished as family and food by Marind became subject to the deadly and indiscriminate violence of gun-wielding foreign hunters. Marind men were complicit in this killing because they were often the ones to organize and lead bird-hunting expeditions in exchange for monetary compensation.

The rampage continued until the mid-1920s, when the plume trade was banned in most of Dutch New Guinea. By then, Caritas noted, bird of paradise populations had dwindled dramatically across Marind territories and beyond, their song only rarely heard by those who traveled the forest or visited the sago groves. Among the primary victims of the bird trade identified by my companion were the maroon- and yellow-crowned greater and lesser birds of paradise, the velvet black and golden twelve-wired bird of paradise, the metallic oil-green rifle bird of paradise, the crimson-bodied and green-tipped king bird of paradise, and the dark-breasted, orange-winged magnificent bird of paradise. Community members refrained from consuming these species for several years afterward to give the birds a chance to replenish their numbers and escape total extinction. The active exclusion of bird of paradise from local diets contributed to an imbalance in foods hungered after and consumed in the villages, which in turn undermined the ethos of distributed and diverse food sources described in the previous chapter. But, as Caritas explained, "We did this in the hope that <u>dema</u> would forgive our men for the killing and hunting. We did this so that the birds would multiply once again. We did this so that our <u>amai</u>'s song would once again make the forest *ramai*."

The establishment of a formal government post in Merauke City in 1902 and the arrival of Christian missionaries in the Upper Bian in the early 1930s led to a number of social and environmental transformations that were seen to be both beneficial and detrimental by many Marind women. On the one hand, missionization led to the abolishment of customary practices that were condemned as backward and violent by some of my female friends. These practices, they stressed, were led and enacted primarily by men, including headhunting and homosexual and heterosexual fertility and initiation rites.[4] Missionization, Caritas added, also brought new knowledge and education for both men and women, who were considered equal before God. Employment opportunities in mission-established clinics and school did not discriminate between men and women, nor did participation and leadership in religious activities, including catechism and charity work. The arrival of Christianity thus offered to women, in Caritas's words, a greater "voice" (*kasih suara*) and greater space (*kasih ruang*) to contribute to and shape religious, economic, and educational life in the villages.

But Dutch colonization also brought new hungers to the stage. During this period, Caritas explained, Marind along the coastline and in the hinterland were subject to sedenterization policies that entailed the clustering of previously temporary settlements and their mobile populations into concentrated, fixed villages. Traditional foraging and hunting activities were discouraged by the Dutch administration and substituted with small-scale horticultural and animal-breeding projects. Marind villagers, and in particular women, were reluctant to participate in these projects of domestication because they violated the ethos of restrained care that Marind had traditionally entertained with wild animals and plants in the forest. The foods these projects produced were consequently deemed weak, bland, lacking in skin and wetness, and unable to satisfy or satiate the hunger for forest foods that Marind had traditionally procured. Meanwhile, communal feasts, ceremonial food exchanges, and collective foraging expeditions that had once sustained the relationships between clans, phratries, amai, and dema declined as Marind were encouraged to convert to Christianity and abandon their primitive traditions.

In tandem with the deprecation of traditional forest foodways and associated cultural practices was the subjection of Marind themselves to lethal viruses and bacteria that were unintentionally introduced into New Guinea by colonial agents. In 1919 and then again in 1937–38, a viral influenza epidemic reportedly killed off some 21 percent of the inland Marind population. This was compounded by the deadly effects of donovanosis, a bacterial venereal disease first diagnosed in Merauke in 1916 that reportedly affected more than 25 percent of Upper Bian Marind and particularly the women, who suffered from unprecedently high infertility rates during this period. Even after the donovanosis crisis was brought under control in 1922, Marind populations in the interior continued to decline until at least 1948.[5] Often characterized by my companions as "hungry," the diseases of donovanosis and influenza, in Caritas's words, "ate" (*makan*) the bodies of their vulnerable victims, causing them to lose body weight, appetite, and vitality; destroying their skin; contaminating their wetness; and limiting their ability to participate in food procurement activities in the village and forest. The generalized weakness, apathy, and lethargy provoked by these hungry viruses and bacteria further testified to their deleterious effects on the energy (*semangat*) of the infected and dying.

The takeover of the former Dutch territory of New Guinea by Indonesia in 1961 marked the rise of yet more destructive and pervasive hungers across the Upper Bian. The unlawful and systematic appropriation of customary lands by the state, military, corporations, and settlers hailing from the Indonesian provinces of Java, Makassar, Nusa Tenggara, and Maluku, together with the erasure of traditional tenurial rights and boundaries under formal legal administration, radically restricted Marind's access to the forest and to forest-derived foods. Capitalistic ventures, including mining, logging, and plantations, were enabled by the privatization of land in the hands of corporate actors who, my female companions often emphasized, were predominantly composed of men. The male demographic associated with Indonesian colonization was also central to how women characterized representatives of the Indonesian government, together with the male-dominated, incoming plantation labor force, the military troops garrisoned across West Papua, and the government-instituted, male village heads (*kepala kampung*) who came to replace former male and female customary clan leaders. As Caritas put it, "Indonesian colonization brought many men to our lands—foreign men, dangerous men. Men with weapons. Men with insatiable appetites. Men who hungered after the forest. Even today, men continue to control the government and the plantations. Settler men, but also Papuan men. Women and their voices are even more silenced than before."

Meanwhile, Marind's traditional foodways, together with their animist beliefs and dark skin, rendered them targets of racial and cultural discrimination on the part of incoming Indonesians—a dynamic that continues to plague the increasingly settler-dominated region of West Papua.[6] In tandem, foods introduced and promoted as "civilized" (*maju*) by non-Papuan settlers, including rice and instant noodles, started to replace the game, fruit, fish, and vegetables that had once composed the Marind diet and that were recast as backward, primitive, and uncultured. Amai, too, suffered from the processes of urbanization, infrastructural development, and species introductions that accompanied Indonesian occupation. The construction of roads, military garrisons, towns, and cities, for instance, caused animal and bird populations to flee to distant territories, dislocating them from their native homes and food sources and undermining the success of hunting expeditions for Marind themselves. At the same time, plants and animals that accompanied the arrival of settlers began to compete with amai over food, land, and water, resulting in competing hungers across species lines and posing a threat to native beings' survival and thriving. Species identified as introduced and now overpopulous by my female companions during encounters with these organisms in the forest or at the village outskirts included the climbing perch, a fish originating from Southeast Asia; the spiked pepper, a rapidly growing shrub native to the West Indies; and the Javan rusa, a deer whose natural range encompasses Java, Bali, and East Timor.

The influx of Indonesian settlers under state-endorsed and spontaneous migration schemes also marked the beginnings of an illegal trade in forest resources that further jeopardized amai's collective survival and subsistence. Targets of this illicit yet prolific industry included the communities of birds of paradise that had been driven to near extinction some forty years earlier, but also cassowaries that were sought out for their lustrous feathers, crocodiles that were stripped of their skins and teeth, and precious woods such as agarwood, New Guinea striped ebony, and New Guinea rosewood that were felled indiscriminately for the manufacture of furniture, essential oils, and decorative ornaments. Comparing these processes to the plume trade of the early twentieth century, Caritas noted, "This time, it wasn't just the bird of paradise that was threatened. All kinds of amai were threatened—their lives, their relationships to their forest kin, their homes, and their sources of food. All kinds of amai were killed and went hungry."

Then, the Merauke Integrated Food and Energy Estate (MIFEE) happened. Inaugurated by the Indonesian government in 2010 and exemplifying a broader trend in large-scale land acquisitions prompted by the food, fuel, and finance crisis of 2008, this project, costing $6 billion, aimed to transform Marind's home regency into a "rice barn" (lumbung padi) that would feed Indonesia and the world while also accelerating economic development in West Papua.[7] As my companions discovered from official pamphlets in Merauke City and corporate brochures distributed in the villages, ambitious targets were set by the government for the production of rice, corn, soybeans, sugar, and palm oil across an area spanning some two million hectares of former forest, savanna, peatlands, and grass plains in Merauke and in the neighboring regencies of Mappi and Boven Digoel.[8]

At the time of writing, land clearing for agricultural development was advancing at an unprecedented pace across the Upper Bian—a region that, due to its remoteness, had been spared the brunt of large-scale agricultural land conversions under earlier periods of Dutch and Indonesian occupation. Participatory mapping I conducted during my fieldwork with local communities using GPS and drones revealed that a third of their customary territories had been converted to monocrops in the last decade, with remnant patches of forest located far away from their settlements (see figure 2.1).[9] Today, Caritas described, foraging expeditions to the forest take place only two or three times a year. Community members often have to travel across privatized oil palm concessions to reach the forest, rendering them subject to interrogations, harassment, fines, and sometimes incarceration on the part of military patrols and security guards. While national food security prerogatives continue to legitimate the expansion of agribusiness plantations across the region, local food insecurity plagues the inhabitants of an increasingly disfigured socioecological landscape, or what my companion Ana in the opening of this book described in her hunger song as "a land of famished beings."

Figure 2.1. Oil palm seedling, 2012. Over a third of the Upper Bian has been converted to monocrops since 2011. Photograph by Vembrianto Waluyas.

The Stories behind Statistics

The erosion of forest foodways prompted by agribusiness expansion, compounded with the growing dependence of Marind on imported commodities such as rice and instant noodles, has resulted in unprecedented rates of wasting, stunting, and low body weight across all fourteen districts of the Upper Bian. Data I obtained during interviews with employees at the community health clinic (Puskesmas) in the township of Timase—the closest medical center to the villages of the Upper Bian—indicated that malnutrition rates in the area had almost doubled since 2014 to over 700 documented occurrences as of January 2019. Wasting occurrences had more than tripled over the same period to 533. Cases of stunting in infants and children, too, had risen across the region, and most markedly so in the villages of Khalaoyam, Mirav, and Bayau, which are within closest proximity to newly established oil palm plantations. In Khalaoyam, stunting rates more than doubled from 2018 to 2019, to just under 80 percent, and in Mirav, to just over 70 percent. Over 60 percent of deaths among children between the age of four months and four years were caused by malnutrition or related diseases, including diarrhea (35.7 percent), tuberculosis (35.7 percent), gastroenteritis (20.3 percent), and bronchopneumonia (18.97 percent).

The loss of game, meanwhile, has provoked widespread cases of chronic protein energy malnutrition (PEM) among local inhabitants. As was explained to me by Puskesmas staff, this condition causes poor muscular and skeletal growth and immunodeficiencies that in turn render PEM sufferers vulnerable to diseases, including pneumonia, measles, diarrhea, respiratory infections, parasitism, skin inflammations, and bronchitis. Among adults, PEM has also been linked to premature birth, miscarriages, liver disease, umbilical bleeding, and anemia and goiters caused by iron and iodine deficiencies, respectively. Babies born from malnourished women are now increasingly predisposed to developing sepsis neonatorum, harelip and cleft palate, and tetanus neonatorum. Importantly, comparisons between the aggregated number of PEM, malnutrition, wasting, and stunting occurrences and the aggregated area of forest loss during the years 2014 to 2021 indicate a strong to very strong positive correlation between the two. Cases documented outside deforested areas, meanwhile, tend to be predominantly located in villages downstream, where mill effluents and contaminants travel from upstream mills and refineries. In sum, where forest loss occurs, higher rates of malnutrition and associated health conditions tend to follow.[10]

And yet, rising rates of malnutrition in rural Merauke were routinely downplayed or dismissed by government representatives from the Indonesian Ministry of Health whom I interviewed over the course of my fieldwork. Instead, officials I spoke to in the ministry's headquarters in Jayapura, Merauke City, and across various districts within Merauke regency often attributed diet-related illnesses to Marind's forest-based, "backward" (*terlantar*) mode of subsistence and the incapacity of women in particular to manage (*mengelola*) their own health and that of their children. The idea that environmental degradation might be part of the story of hunger was often rejected in light of the fact that Marind now had access to modern, nutritious foods, like biofortified powdered milk, rice, instant noodles, cookies, and canned meat, all of which, my interviewees would stress, were brought to and made available to Papuans following the region's incorporation into the Republic of Indonesia in the 1960s.[11] As one representative from the Ministry of Health whom I interviewed in Merauke City exclaimed: "They should be getting fatter and healthier! If they still suffer from malnutrition, it must be because they are not choosing to eat right. It must be because Papuan women do not know how to feed their children well. And that's a problem of education [*masalah pendidikan*]."

The responsibility—and, by extension, the blame—often placed by government officials on Papuan women for instances of malnutrition was a source of immense frustration and anger among my female companions. Many perceived this representation and its moral implications as a devious distortion of their traditionally valued roles as mothers and food providers and as a deceptive cover-up for power asymmetries operating at two distinct yet interconnected levels. One such woman was Jovi, a mother of two from the Kaize clan and a resident of Mirav village, to whom I communicated the response of the official, mentioned earlier, during a shared meal in her hut following my return to the village from Merauke City. Clasping her hands in rage above her head, Jovi sighed in desperation and retorted:

> These officials—they use our own values to undermine us and conceal the reality. Of course, Marind women like me are proud to be mothers—to feed our children and families. But now that pride is being eaten up because the forests we rely on are dying and people are hungry. We cannot provide. We cannot feed. We cannot even stop the forest from dying because the government is in control, and will only listen to our men, who are also in control. This is not a problem of education—it is a problem of power and of voice. It is a result of colonization and oppression of all kinds.

As Jovi suggests, and as will be explored in greater detail later in this work, government discourses in West Papua neglect the uneven voice and power of Marind men and women at an internal level when it comes to land use, food security, and intergenerational well-being. Male villagers, in my companion's words, tend to be "in control" of such decisions. In tandem, women's pride and ability to perform their duties of care as mothers and child-rearers is undermined by a government that "will only listen to our men." At the same time, government discourses also obscure the structural factors provoking hunger among Marind collectively by reframing them as the consequence of local women's own purported inadequacy, ineptitude, and ignorance or by dismissing them as baseless fabrications. Such discourses found further legitimation in the form of a public statement made in July 2018 by then regent of Merauke, Frederikus Gebze, who outrightly denied that child malnutrition instances reported to him by Marind women's collectives were a significant problem in the regency and instead dismissed the statistics as "exaggerated" (*dibesar-besarkan*).[12] Meanwhile, figures published in local media around the same period that suggested a fall in malnutrition rates were viewed with suspicion by local women, who noted it was unclear whether the purported decline was the result of patient recovery or patient death.

There are, however, other reasons why statistics represent just one small part of the story of hunger in the Upper Bian. For starters, these figures represent only those cases that have been brought to the clinic at Timase township, which is located some 250 kilometers away from the closest Marind settlement and therefore is too costly for most villagers to travel to. Practical impediments in terms of physical and financial access to medical facilities are compounded by a widespread reticence among many rural Marind to visit medical establishments in the first instance. While this reticence predates the rise of hunger prompted by recent large-scale landscape conversions and attendant dietary changes in the Upper Bian, it bears direct implications for how hungers experienced by Marind today are (in)visibilized in state and biomedical discourses and data. Specifically, it stems from a prevalent perception among villagers, and particularly among women, of hospitals or clinics as spaces of heightened risk of contagion rather than of guaranteed promises of cure. This was explained to me by Fenella, a young woman from the Mahuze (dog) clan and a primary school teacher from Khalaoyam, who warned me time and again during my time in the field that

> the clinic is not a safe place. People go to the clinic with a cold and come out with pneumonia. People go to the hospital with a small cut and come out with an infection. Then, they have to go back to the hospital and they catch all kinds of other illnesses, from all kinds of other people—Papuans, but also Indonesians, Javanese, Sumatrans. I see this happen all the time. The clinic is where little diseases become big diseases. People go in there with pain and come out with more pain—and also with shame [*masuk bawa sakit, keluar bawa sakit tambahan, tambah lagi malu*].

The association made by Fenella and other villagers between medical institutions and heightened contagion is compounded by a profound discomfort with the one-on-one dynamic of patient-doctor interactions within biomedical settings, which further discourages villagers from seeking professional help for their physical and nutritional ailments. Described by my companions as "frightening" (*menakutkan*), "unpleasant" (*kurang enak*), "lonely" (*kesepian*), or "strange" (*aneh*), one-on-one interactions separate the patient from family members and friends whose knowledge of the patient Marind deem critical to their diagnosis and recovery. They also heighten the prevalent sense of inferiority and ignorance that patients experience in their interactions with medical practitioners. This diminishing experience of separation from one's kin was recounted to me by Geraldina, a mother of four from the Samkakai clan and a resident of Mirav village, who suffered from chronic bouts of pneumonia and whom I often accompanied to the clinic, together with her sisters and daughters: "Just like it is important to travel the forest with my kin, so too it is important for my family to be present during the consultation, because they know me well. They may have something to say that might help the doctor diagnose me. They can help me understand the doctor's questions when I don't have the knowledge, when the doctor doesn't explain things, or when I just don't understand. Having family there makes me feel safe. It helps me get better. It takes away the shame [*kasih keluar malu*]."

As Geraldina and Fenella suggest, many women invoke sentiments of shame (*rasa malu*) in describing their encounters with hospitals and the negative evaluation of the self that they experience under the "clinical gaze" of biomedical practitioners.[13] For instance, several of my companions reported having been treated in a condescending manner (*direndahkan*) by the primarily non-Papuan personnel of clinics and hospitals, including being blamed for their illnesses and those of their children, and in some cases being asked to keep physical distance from clinical staff because of the smell of their dark skin. Others had witnessed doctors hastily donning gloves and masks during consultations, even though no physical examination was undertaken or necessary. Yet others reported that their consultations had been conditional on their willingness to undertake a test for HIV—one of the most rapidly spreading and stigmatized sexually transmitted diseases in West Papua and one often attributed in biomedical and government discourse to the sexual promiscuity of Papuan peoples.[14] Some women, meanwhile, had noticed nurses assiduously spraying the seats, benches, and examination tables with antiseptic spray as soon as they had left the consultation room, alongside any other surface that the patient had come into contact with. One among them was Julia, a member of the Balagaize (crocodile) clan and the mother of two from Bayau village, who exclaimed in anger following a routine health checkup at the clinic: "It's as though Papuans and everything Papuans touch becomes polluted. I say 'Papuans' because I have been to the hospital many times and I have noticed that the doctors and nurses only do this kind of thing when the patient is Papuan—never when the patient is Indonesian. Maybe it is because we are black-skinned and curly-haired. Maybe it is because we eat from the forest. Maybe it is both. When the forest disappears, we become sick with hunger. When we go to the hospital, we become sick with shame."

Other villagers simply refuse to go to the hospital because their ailments have previously been dismissed by doctors as inconsequential. One such individual was Circia, Julia's forty-year-old cousin, who recalled her experience of seeking treatment for her anemia and developing goiter:

> A friend who studies nursing in Merauke City told me I had a problem with iron and iodine, and that I should go to see a doctor in Timase. I didn't want to, but she said my blood was sick and it would only get worse. The doctor took one look at me and told me I wasn't sick. I was just . . . hungry [*lapar sudah*]. Then, he sent me away with some candy and a few packets of instant noodles for the kids. After that, I never went back to the hospital. I was humiliated and angry. Yes, I was hungry then—but afterward, I also became ill with shame. That's why I'll never return to the hospital—even if it means the pain of hunger becomes worse.

Official statistics, as such, do not account for the many cases of malnutrition in rural Merauke that go unreported and why, nor the ways in which health and communicative injustices compound to exacerbate Marind's vulnerability when it comes to the diagnosis, treatment, and representation of disease and illness. Where available and if reliable, these statistics tell the story of hunger in primarily numerical terms. For many of my companions, this logic is epitomized in the very language of "malnutrition," or *gizi buruk* in Indonesian. Referring to quantitatively measured deficiencies or excesses in nutrient intake, imbalance of essential nutrients, or impaired nutrient utilization, the term *malnutrition* is often deployed by government agencies, corporate bodies, and biomedical practitioners in describing food insecurity and associated health effects, with "food insecurity" itself also measured in terms of quantity of food and food availability rather than quality of food and food accessibility. Both idioms fall markedly short of capturing the expansive significance of what Marind and their forest kin experience as "hunger" (*kelaparan*).

The statistical reductionism inherent to state and biomedical discourses surrounding malnutrition works hand in hand with what Olivia, a young woman from the Mahuze clan and a resident of Khalaoyam, described during a women's meeting on the outskirts of her village as a form of anthropocentrism. "Malnutrition," Olivia commented, "is about calories, and things like minerals and vitamins, that are unknown to Marind. But malnutrition leaves out many things—the land, the <u>amai</u>, the liveliness, the peace, the energy, the freedom, and so much more. Malnutrition only applies to humans, not plants, or animals, or the land—even though, they, too, are going hungry. Malnutrition is a government word. It is a doctor's word. It is not a Marind word. It is not the way we Marind feel or understand hunger, or how our amai [plant and animal kin] feel hunger."

Echoing a critique by the American anthropologist Emily Yates-Doerr of "nutritional black-boxing," or the consolidation of nourishment and dietary practices into seemingly unproblematic scientific categories, malnutrition discourses and statistics in Merauke thus obscure and occlude the culturally modulated ways in which Marind experience and evaluate foods and hungers familiar and emergent, and good and bad, the moralities and meanings of which, in the words of the Muscogee (Creek) legal scholar Sarah Deer and her colleagues, are rendered "statistically unreportable within dominant accountings."[15] These discourses and statistics are anchored in what the Asian diasporic feminist theorist Athia Choudhury calls the "scientification" of hunger, or the reduction of hunger from lived experience to quantifiable data.[16] As noted earlier, and while less prominent than my companions' critiques of the term *malnutrition*, a similar reductionism was also identified by some women in the language of "food insecurity" (*keamanan pangan*) deployed by state, corporate, and NGO institutions. Resonating with comparable pushback stemming from grassroots food sovereignty movements worldwide, these women criticized the prevalent focus in official food security discourses on achieving levels of food availability and quantity that meet purely physiological needs, the privileging of industrialized and export-oriented food production to the neglect of local communities' autonomous and self-sufficient modes of subsistence, and the generalized attrition of villagers' self-determined and democratic participation in decisions around food-related land use, management, and ownership.[17]

Importantly, the frames of both malnutrition and food insecurity render hunger a singular, measurable, and therefore universal (albeit human-only) phenomenon, eliding in the process how hunger in Marind onto-epistemologies multiplies depending on its relative and often more-than-human object and subject—in other words, how hunger is inflected by who is experiencing hunger, and what one hungers for. Hunger's concomitantly intersubjective and interobjective attributes undergird not only the meanings of those hungers long known and experienced in the forest, as described in the previous chapter, but also the ambiguous moralities of what my companion Ana described as the "new and different hungers" spreading across the Upper Bian today. Prominent among these new and different hungers are the hunger for sago, for plastic, for money, and for human flesh. Together, these conditions distinguish themselves through their primarily adverse effects on the bodily and behavioral dispositions of those who experience and witness them. Expressive of what the French sociologist Claude Fischler terms "gastro-anomie," they manifest in corporeal and cultural terms the attrition of traditional food systems wrought by histories of extractive colonial-capitalist incursion, together with the ecosocial relations that these waning food systems depend on and enable.[18]

Hunger for Sago

Hunger for sago (*lapar sagu*) takes as its object the diverse array of traditionally valued foods that villagers in the Upper Bian derive from the forest environment. This diverse diet finds synecdochic expression in the invocation of sago, the staple starch component and core of all forest meals.[19] As with satiety (*kekenyangan*), hunger for sago is experienced in both bodily and affective ways and is often described through its observable, physical manifestations in one's body and that of others. For instance, my companions often identified the effects of this hunger in the dull color of their own arms, legs, and faces, or the peeling elbows and knees of their young children whose bodies did not grow well or strong because they had not been nourished by the flesh and fluids of their forest kin. They would gesture to the patches of discolored skin along the backs and napes of kith and kin that were once taut and glossy but that had become parched and rough to the touch. Mothers would run their fingers over the shriveled skin of newborns and infants, plucking the tender flesh and feeling the frail bones beneath. The hunger for sago, according to Marcella, grips the gut and weakens the legs. It causes anger and grief among those who are no longer able to walk the forest, encounter plants and animals, and recount their lively stories and pasts.

The dryness of the skin provoked by hunger for sago is in turn linked to a generalized loss of wetness in people's bodies, as their grease, blood, muscle, and other corporeal fluids become depleted from the growing absence of nourishing forest foods.[20] This depletion is exacerbated by a decrease in activities that once enabled reciprocal transfers of life-sustaining fluids across species lines, such as walking the forest, traveling down rivers, and visiting sago groves, and that have become increasingly difficult to sustain since the advent of industrial oil palm plantations. In humans, the loss of wetness manifests in the shrinking biceps and calves of men, the sagging breasts and sallow cheeks of women, and the sunken eyes and decreased skin turgor of the skin of babies, infants, and children. The desiccated bodies of the hungry thus comes to replicate the growing dryness and disfigured terrain of the landscape itself as customary lands are privatized, biodiverse ecosystems converted to homogeneous monocrops, and watercourses diverted for irrigation and contaminated with toxic chemicals.

Parched, peeling skins, compounded with depleted bodily wetness, undermine the capacity of individuals to experience vitality (*semangat*). Children and adults who suffer from a loss in *semangat* are identified by their slow, lethargic gait, dangling arms, uncoordinated step, and absent gaze. Lacking the energy to hunt, forage, fish, or travel the forest, these individuals spend most of their time in their huts and sleep unusually often and for protracted periods. Their breath is heavy, slow, and rasping, and their voices hoarse, gravelly, or toneless. Just as *semangat* transfers and multiplies cumulatively from one individual to another when experienced in the forest, so too the lack of energy of one individual is said to be contagious to those in their presence. These individuals may begin to feel their own bodies weaken, their concentration fall, and their desire to move and interact decrease.

Resonating with the moral ontology of pain among Yapese of Micronesia, which constitutes a transformational experience for both the sufferer and those who witness suffering, hunger among Marind is thus less a private, individualized, or internalized phenomenon than one that is signified by and distributed across the broader collective, in a form of transcorporeal and affective transference.[21] Hunger, in other words, is not just a metabolic condition but also a *communicable* disease. As Marcella's aunt, Kristal, explained to me, "When people lose *semangat*, they make other people lose *semangat* too. It's like an illness. Even if you have eaten food, you lose your strength when you see others without *semangat*, because you feel their pain."

As Kristal suggests, the transbodily symptoms of hunger for sago are accompanied by affective responses that differ radically from the liveliness (*ramai*) and harmony (*damai*) associated with food procurement, preparation, and consumption in the forest. *Ramai* is preempted when villagers find themselves cut off from the bustling sensorium of forest, grove, and swamp; no longer partake in collective work such as sago pounding, game hunting, and fruit gathering; nor anticipate the fruits of their toil while storying and singing together. Instead, community members now spend most of their time in the village—a space that is associated by many villagers with enforced sedenterization policies instituted under both Dutch and Indonesian occupation—which is often described as "silent" (*diam*) or "lonely" (*sepi*) because it is devoid of the lively sounds and species of the forest, and that is therefore not conducive to valued social interactions in the form of shared labor, physical contact, and commensality, in and with the sentient environment.

In this regard, the silence and solitude of the village differ markedly from the reflective and meditative moments of *damai*, or peace, that villagers intentionally seek out in the forest. These affective dispositions are often accompanied by feelings of sadness (*sedih*), pain (*sakit*), and the hardship (*susah*) of not knowing when one will be able to obtain forest foods or provide them for one's kin. Marcella expressed these feelings to me one evening as we sat on the front porch of her hut in Mirav, waiting for her children to return from school. "In the village, we have houses made of concrete—sometimes a bit of electricity, sometimes a bit of signal," she noted. "But in the village, we cannot hear the voices of the forest. We cannot share skin and wetness with our amai [plant and animal kin]. We cannot make memories together. We spend our time inside our houses, hidden away from sight. We do not tell stories or jokes in the village, because there is no *ramai* or *damai*. We have nothing to offer others to eat. So, we all hide our hunger in our homes."

The hunger for sago thus exemplifies what the American anthropologist Jon Holtzman terms "gustatory nostalgia" in that it is shaped by a profound sense of displacement and disconnection from one's past and one's human and other-than-human kin.[22] Resonating with the notion of *anaingi* or *air-iski* among the Baining of New Britain Island, this hunger manifests as both a physical state and a set of emotions prompted by the severance of people from intimate and ancestral relations of feeding and being fed, and to the detriment of both Marind and their forest kin.[23] Indeed, and exemplifying the prevalent signification of human experience through its analogous relationship to that of plants and animals within Marind epistemologies, my companions often affirm that they are not the only ones who experience hunger for forest foods.[24] Amai, too, struggle to survive as groves, swamps, and grasslands give way to industrial monocrops, where little food is to be found and where plants and animals are vulnerable to chemical pesticide contamination, illegal wildlife poaching, precious wood logging, and introduced and invasive parasitic species. Much as Marind can no longer satiate themselves with forest foods, so too forest organisms lose the habitats vital to their well-being, reproduction, and growth. The bodies of these creatures are no longer fed by the blood and sweat of their Marind kin, or the direct and indirect actions that Marind undertake to enhance their environment. Their fur and feathers turn dull and scraggly, and their flesh tough and sinewy.

Hunger for forest foods, then, speaks to the growing incapacity of Marind to be nourished by the forest and to nourish the forest through kinesthetic and transubstantial exchanges of skin and wetness. This distributed hunger in turn points to the indissociability within Marind worldviews of food justice from multispecies and metabolic justice, as these manifest in the profound interdependence of human and other-than-human nourishment. In this light, and as Olivia intimated earlier, malnutrition statistics produced by state and biomedical institutions do not only fail to represent the complex bodily and affective phenomenology of hunger as it is experienced by Marind. They also fail to account for the *more-than-human* dimensions of hungers provoked by the severance of morally valued relations of feeding and being fed across species lines.

This point was poignantly invoked by my companion Circia, who once compared the dismissive treatment of her own anemia and goiter to the neglect of hunger's impacts on native plants and animals. Perusing the Excel spreadsheet that I had obtained from the Timase clinic and that detailed the latest statistics for stunting and wasting across Merauke, Circia commented, "These numbers, graphs, percentages—they tell us a lot about human hunger. But there are also plants, animals, and birds who are going hungry since oil palm arrived." And yet, Circia continued, "these are not the kinds of hunger that doctors care about. They do not see the connection between the hunger of the forest and the hunger of Marind. The forest can no longer give us good food, and we can no longer become good food for the forest. The doctors cannot understand that. That is why they cannot understand or heal our hunger."

Hunger for Plastic Foods

While hunger for sago is intimately tied to the erosion of native ecosystems and foodways, hunger for plastic foods (*lapar makanan plastik*) speaks to the substitution of forest-derived subsistence with processed or imported commodities. These commodities, which include rice, instant noodles, biscuits, canned meats, and fizzy drinks, now represent over three-quarters of Marind's daily caloric intake (see figure 2.2). Their characterization as "plastic" positions them alongside other objects, practices, and people that villagers associate with "development" (*perkembangan*), "progress" (*kemajuan*), and the "modern world" (*dunia modern*).

Central to the concept of "plastic" are the traits of proliferation and deception.[25] Patricia, a young woman from the Balagaize clan and a mother of

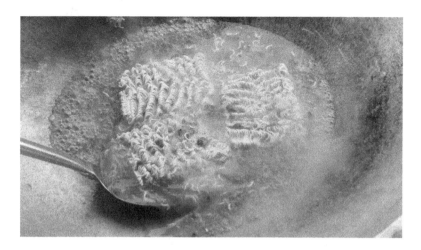

Figure 2.2. A pot of boiling instant noodles, 2013. Plastic foods such as these are said to fuel the sensation of hunger. Photograph by the author.

two, explained these attributes to me one afternoon, when we were walking back from the grove to her home in Mirav village. As we passed the local primary school, she pointed with disapproval to the dozens of crumpled candy, instant noodle, and biscuit wrappers littering the front yard of the school. My companion noted that these "plastic foods" were now arriving in the villages of the Upper Bian on a daily basis, and by the truckload. They come wrapped in glossy, plastic packaging and printed with colorful words, ingredients, logos, and illustrations that make them appear novel and enticing—and yet they invariably fail to satiate those who purchase, share, and consume them. As Patricia put it, "Plastic foods looks nice on the outside because of their shiny skins, but they hold no wetness on the inside. They do not nourish or satiate your hunger—they only deceive and make you even more hungry."

For women like Patricia, whose male kin had in the last few years surrendered vast swaths of her clan's customary territories for agribusiness development, the ubiquity of plastic foods and the forms of nonbiodegradable and highly visible waste they tend to leave in their trail constitute painful, everyday reminders of the unfulfilled promises of monetary compensation, education, and employment once made to their husbands, brothers, and uncles by plantation operators in exchange for their lands, and for which plastic foods often end up acting as paltry substitutes. Instead of jobs, cash, or degrees, villagers who cede territories to oil palm companies often receive in lieu of promised benefits cartons of instant noodles, sacks of broken rice, and boxes of cheap biscuits and soft drink powders that are sent to the villages as part of corporate social responsibility schemes, whose monetary value falls blatantly below that of the territories ceded, and whose nutritional, ecological, and cultural significance also pale in comparison to that of forest foods.

For opponents of the oil palm industry, in contrast, the imposition of plastic foods manifests in alimentary form the violence of the corporate and state organs relentlessly grabbing their lands, polluting their rivers, and replacing their forests with oil palm—even as these same foods are routinely framed in government and corporate discourses as instrumental to Marind's incorporation and advancement within the modern world. Within these discourses, the social judgment of taste operates along a distinctly racialized colonized-colonizer divide.[26] Papuan villagers in rural Merauke, as Patricia described, are often told by Indonesian government and company representatives that cultivating an appetite for and regularly consuming rice and instant noodles is a form of "progress" (kemajuan).[27] It will enable Marind communities to become "civilized" (berbudaya), "leave their forest-based lifestyles behind" (melepaskan diri dari hutan), and "integrate themselves" (mengintegrasikan diri) within an archipelago-wide Indonesian food community and culture. It will allow Marind, in the words of one government official whom I interviewed, to "educate themselves" (mendidik diri) in the preparation and consumption of modern foods that are "vastly more nutritious" (jauh lebih bergizi) and "refined" (jauh lebih halus) than sago-based foodways, and that will make it possible for "Papuan tribes to never go hungry in the forest again" (biar suku Papua tidak pernah rasa lapar lagi di tengah-tengah hutan).[28]

Exemplifying what the CHamoru poet and environmental humanities scholar Craig Santos Perez terms "gastro-colonialism," or the perpetuation of colonial racial violence through the medium of food, the abjectification of Marind's traditional forest food systems and environments thus works hand in hand with the objectification of Marind themselves as backward and primitive.[29] The racialized dimensions of Marind's gastrocultural transformation into civilized members of the Indonesian nation-state were captured by the government official quoted earlier, who confided to me in private: "Papuans are Black. It's very unfortunate, but that's just the way it is. We can't do anything about the color of their skin. But we can uplift them into the modern world by bringing them modern foods. Progress, for Papuans, begins not in the skin, but in the gut."[30]

Just as demeaning to Marind as the racializing discourses surrounding plastic foods are the means through which these foods are procured. As noted earlier, many villagers see themselves as having been duped (*dibo-hong*), tricked (*ditipu*), or forced (*terpaksa*) into accepting processed, com-modified foods by state and corporate actors within a broader landscape of shady land contracts and paternalistic civilizational projects. Getting hold of these commodities, too, is often described as a "humiliating" (*memalu-kan*) experience—one that is not radically dissimilar to Marind's demeaning encounters with biomedical infrastructures and practitioners, as described previously. As I witnessed on several occasions, villagers seeking to obtain corporate handouts at times when food supplies in the household had be-come urgently scarce had to queue at the entrance of plantation headquarters at the break of dawn, bearing tickets identifying them by name, age, profes-sion, and residence. Squatting on the ground and shrouded in the choking dust raised by passing trucks and bulldozers, these individuals and groups often waited for several hours to be seen by the community relations team. Upon receiving their goods, villagers had their wrists ink-stamped with the logo of the corporation and an identifying serial number to ensure that no allocations are duplicated. Those who presented themselves barefoot were dismissed and told to return the next day in proper attire.

The degrading treatment of villagers seeking food handouts was vividly captured by Karola, a young woman from the Ndiken (white stork) clan and a resident of Bayau village, who often spoke of being made to feel like a "beggar" (*pengemis*) and a "prisoner" (*tawanan*) during these interactions. On our return from one such trip together, she commented:

> You've seen it for yourself. They tell us we must arrive at the first light of dawn if we want to receive food. But then, they make us wait, and wait, and wait for hours—sometimes until the sun is high up in the sky above us, burning through our skin, making the hunger worse. All the while, we can see them in the mess, eating breakfast, sipping coffee, or smoking cigarettes, and laughing. Then, they stamp us with their logo and numbers, as if they own not just our stomachs but our whole bodies. My children are all grown up now. They could easily help me carry the boxes of plastic food back to the village. I have a bad back and arthritis. But I would never bring my children along. I do not want them to see their mother becoming a beggar and a prisoner.

For Karola's seventeen-year-old younger sister, Carmelita, who had also accompanied us on the visit that day to the company headquarters, the be-littlement experienced by villagers whose hunger has driven them to seek food supplies from plantation operators is exacerbated by the tenor of the verbal exchanges that take place with corporate employees. "They tell us this food is a gift [*hadiah*] from the companies and a blessing [*anugerah*] from the companies," Carmelita interjected as we walked back to the village. "They tell us we should say thank you and be grateful—even though we gave them all our land and they never gave us the money or jobs or scholarships we asked for. When we arrive in torn shirts and without shoes, we are sent away. Yet still, they want us to be grateful. Still, they want us to think that their rice and instant noodles are worth as much as our forest."

No less disparaging for many women than the experience of seeking food handouts from corporations is that of purchasing plastic foods from kiosks in the village. These kiosks are predominantly owned and managed by non-Papuan settlers who were widely described by my companions as "arrogant" (*sombong*), "rude" (*kasar*), and "racist" (*rasis*). Carmelita, for instance, spoke of kiosk owners pretending not to understand her "coarse Indonesian" (*bahasa kasar*) and making her repeat herself several times before handing over the requested goods. Karola reported that kiosk owners often claimed that particular items were out of stock that then made their way into the hands of non-Papuans. Patricia, meanwhile, affirmed that kiosk owners concealed a large portion of their goods in storage, prioritizing the quelling of the hunger of their own families and friends over that of native Marind inhabitants.

The material infrastructure of local kiosks amplified the stigma that some of my companions associate with these sites. One such individual was Madelina, an adolescent girl and cousin twice removed of Karola, who was always deeply reticent to purchase food from the kiosk in her home village of Khalaoyam and often asked me to do so in her stead. What Madelina resented most about the kiosk was its barbed wire screen that separates customers from the goods and owners of the shop, and the small hole in the wire through which commodities and payments are exchanged. "The settlers [*pendatang*] already look down on us because of our dark skin and forest livelihoods," Madelina explained. "When we visit their kiosks, we are separated from them by thick wires—as though they need to protect themselves and their goods from us. Maybe they are worried we are going to steal their goods. Or attack them. Maybe even just touch them. When we queue for food at the company offices, we feel like hungry beggars. When we queue for food at the kiosks, we feel like dishonest thieves."

As my companion Patricia intimated when we walked past the primary school in Mirav, and as Madelina's words further amplify, the hunger for plastic foods and the infrastructures of provision and distribution associated with these foods are understood by many women to be at once alienating, demeaning, and imposed. In addition, this hunger was often characterized by my companions as one that plastic foods stimulate but cannot themselves adequately satiate or satisfy. On one level, there is nutritional truth to this statement. The high content of refined carbohydrates, oil, sugar, and salt in imported commodities like instant noodles, biscuits, and fizzy drinks tends to stimulate rather than satisfy feelings of hunger. At another level, plastic foods also fail to quell the appetites of those who consume them because they are devoid of the cultural, social, moral, and ecological meanings that imbue forest foods with their nourishing properties—properties that, as I explored earlier, arise from the intimate and ancestral kinships of humans, plants, animals, and landscapes bound in mutual relations of feeding and being fed.[31]

In marked contrast to the intergenerationally transmitted stories of native organisms that are told and retold among kin in the intimate and familiar space of the forest, plastic foods are known to Marind through their extensive and often cryptic lists of codified and labeled ingredients—additives, preservatives, artificial colorings, and other enigmatic nomenclatures. It is unclear to my companions who is involved in their procuration and preparation; which lands, soils, and waters they have grown in and from; where they have traveled to and through before reaching the villages; and whose skin and wetness have mingled with them along the way. The consumption of these foods is not accompanied by rituals, singing, or storying. Rather than collectively obtained and shared in the forest, plastic foods, as Marcella noted, tend to be eaten in the lonely "silence" of the village, enclosed within and concealed behind the concrete walls of individual huts and homes.

For these reasons, the hunger for plastic foods neither conjures nor creates the kinds of memories (*ingatan*) that Marind associate with forest foodscapes and their more-than-human chains of commensality. Unlike forest foods, which invite the consumption of a range of substances in the image of the diverse communities of life enabling and involved in their procurement, plastic foods are also usually eaten alone and on their own. The opaque origins, transformations, and entities involved in their making and their movements, compounded with the antagonizing experiences associated with their purchase from corporations and kiosks and with their consumption in the village, radically undermine their flavor and texture, which many of my companions describe as dry (*kering*), bland (*tawar*), and unsatiating (*tidak memuaskan*). As Madelina put it, "Plastic foods are not nourishing because they do not taste of our forests and they do not taste of our lands."[32]

The contrasts identified between forest foods and plastic foods in turn shape women's divergent views on whether these foods can or should be eaten together. During the many debates over this question that I was privy to in my time in the field, some of my companions affirmed that combining forest foods and plastic foods within a single meal was better as it allowed the rich flavors of the former to disguise or offset the blandness of the latter, thus attenuating to some degree the hunger of those who ate the foods together. Other women, meanwhile, argued the exact opposite. These women claimed that mixing plastic and forest foods only heightened the tastelessness of the former and further undermined the nourishment derived from the latter, while also diminishing forest foods' beneficial effects on the skin and wetness of their preparers and consumers. Women in this camp often backed their argument regarding plastic foods' contaminating and contagious blandness by pairing it with these foods' uncanny ability to exacerbate, rather than satiate, the hunger of those who consume them. Patricia explained this to me not long after our first conversation, when we returned to the primary school yard on a Saturday to collect the discarded wrappers and dispose of them properly in the village bins. As we picked up the plastic packagings one by one with hand-fashioned metal forks under the scorching midday sun, my companion described how children who eat instant noodles often clamor for more food within just a few hours. Villagers who snack on processed biscuits rather than sago cakes, she continued, consume packet after packet throughout the day but always crave more. Many had now become "addicted" (*kecanduan*) to rice, which they would eat in copious amounts without ever feeling full. Plastic foods, according to Patricia, not only fail to satiate those who hunger after them but rather fuel and intensify their hunger.

For many women, then, the insatiability associated with plastic foods arises as much from their inadequate metabolic and nutritional properties as from their material-semiotic disconnection from the activities, knowledges, and interactions that together imbue foods with their nourishing attributes. As Patricia put it, "When you eat sago, you can go without food for an entire day. But when you eat plastic foods, you become even more hungry. The more you eat, the more you want to eat because there something is missing." My companion paused momentarily to wipe her sweaty brow and stretch her back that was sore from the repeated stooping and collecting. Then, she turned to me and added: "The stories are missing. The songs. The memories. The *ramai* and *damai*. The *semangat* and skin. This is a hunger that cannot be quelled. Like the oil palms and the companies, it keeps coming back and growing. It never goes away."

The hungers for sago and plastic described in this chapter position Marind as shared subjects in relation to contrasting objects of desire—forest foods versus modern foods. This unity in subjectivity, however, is troubled by the third in the trifecta of new and different hungers haunting the landscapes and life-forms of the Upper Bian. Described in synonymous terms by many women as the hunger for money (*lapar uang*) or the hunger for human flesh (*lapar daging manusia*), this form of hunger speaks in literal and figurative ways to the divisive effects of oil palm developments on Marind's gendered relationships to one another within the community and to the more-than-human ecology of the forest.

Some context on the social dynamics and impacts of agribusiness projects in the Upper Bian is warranted here. Since oil palm was first introduced to the area in 2010, a large number of primarily male villagers have become involved in grassroots land rights campaigning, advocacy, and lobbying to curb plantation expansion across their customary lands and territories. These struggles are often undertaken with the support of local and national NGOs and the humanitarian branches of the Catholic Church. In tandem, a small but growing number of equally primarily male Marind individuals have now ceded their lands to oil palm corporations in exchange for cash compensation or have sought employment in the plantations as fresh fruit harvesters, sprayers of pesticides, or mill workers. Hostilities and conflicts abound between community members standing for or against oil palm— some verbal, others physical. At the time of writing, disputes within clans over matters of land rights, surrenders, and payments had taken the lives of over a dozen individuals. Those working for the palm oil sector as laborers or middlemen were increasingly leaving their home villages to take up permanent residence within the plantation precincts, out of concerns for their own safety and that of their families (see figure 2.3).

Some women whom I spoke to, whose husbands and other male relatives had ceded their lands or now work within the agribusiness sector, affirmed they had done so under the pressure of corporate-hired military and police personnel, who are invariably present during land-related negotiations and consultations between communities and corporations. Other women, meanwhile, spoke of their husbands, uncles, and brothers being driven by their aspiration to participate more fully in the modern economy, to improve the material and social futures of their children and grandchildren, and to

Figure 2.3. An oil palm plantation, 2016. Marind laborers often take up permanent residence within plantation precincts. Photograph by Vembrianto Waluyas.

reap at least some degree of benefit or gain from the anyway-expanding plantation sector. Yet other women described their male relatives' decisions less as a matter of choice or desire than of survival and necessity. One such individual was Carlotta, a mother of three from the Kaize clan and a resident of Mirav village, who responded as follows to my query as to why her husband, Hugo, had decided to take up employment in the plantation industry: "Marind can fight all they want, but the truth is, oil palm is here to stay. The forest is disappearing. Finding jobs and making money is the only option if we are to continue feeding ourselves and our families. It is not that Hugo wants to live off oil palm or plastic foods. It is just that there is no other way—for him, for me, for our children."

For villagers who are opposed to oil palm development, in contrast, the actions of individuals like Hugo are revelatory of their pernicious hunger for money and human flesh. This view was especially prevalent among those women who voiced deep grievances to me regarding their structural and everyday exclusion from land-related decision-making processes, in a society where customary tenure is predominantly in the hands of men and intergenerationally transmitted through the patrilineage.[33] Mirabela, the leader of the failed food foraging expedition described in the opening of this chapter, explained the hunger for money and human flesh to me on our way back to her home that evening in Khalaoyam. Men who hunger for money, she said, agree to the surrender of communally held lands without consulting their broader clan constituents, in corporate meetings that take place in Merauke City or distant plantation headquarters, rather than in the villages. They rarely distribute compensation received with fellow clan or community members. Their desire for material wealth, Mirabela added, blinds them to the long-term impacts of their decisions on the well-being of the forest and of Marind men, women, and children present and to come. Instead, men who hunger for money collude or cooperate with oil palm corporations to further their individual and material interests—even as they remain oblivious to the derisory sums of compensation they receive in exchange for intergenerationally inherited and managed swaths of customary land, and which fall well below market value.

The hunger for money is also said to drive individuals to spend their cash on items or activities that are deemed wasteful, selfish, or irresponsible by others within the community.[34] For instance, Marind men who had surrendered their lands to corporations or taken up employment in plantations were often criticized by their spouses and sisters for investing their money in expensive refrigerators, state-of-the-art mobile phones, and digital flat-screen televisions—even though food supplies are in dire deficit in the villages, and even though there is no regular signal or electricity in these villages to operate refrigerators, phones, and televisions in the first place. Others were said to fritter away their cash on hard liquor (*miras*) sold illegally in village kiosks that they would then consume under the cover of night in hidden patches of forest or at the outskirts of settlements, either alone or with groups of other men. These individuals would then return to their homes in a state of total inebriation and become violent toward their families and friends. Alcohol intoxication, women explained, not only poisoned men's own skin and wetness but also made their minds and hearts sick, and consequently rendered them even more incapable of recognizing and remedying the hungers afflicting their wives and children. Yet other men, meanwhile, were blamed for spending their money not on alcohol or material commodities but on sex workers in the brothels of Merauke City, thereby putting themselves, their spouses, and their offspring at risk of potentially deadly, sexually transmitted diseases such as HIV/AIDS that, like donovanosis, influenza, and many other illnesses, are said to "eat" the bodies of their hosts and victims. Rather than sharing money and the opportunities it affords among the broader communities who entertain ancestral kinships with communally held lands and who collectively benefit from the nourishing, multispecies futures these lands sustain, men waste or "throw away" (*buang*) their money either on pointless purchases or on perilous promiscuities. As Mirabela evocatively put it, "These men, their hands stink of dollar bills. Their fingers are stained forever red—like the 100,000-rupiah bills, the blood of the dying forest, the blood of Marind fighting to protect the forest, and the blood of Marind at war with each other because of oil palm. These men—all their money disappears on mobile phones and liquor. Their children and wives go hungry. Their hunger eats them up."

Mirabela's criticism points to the deleterious effects of the hunger for money on both the individual concerned and their social circles. Men who hunger for money forget how to walk the landscape in search of food with their kin and instead spend most of their time in the city or plantation, accumulating all manner of goods, frequenting sex workers, and losing their minds and bodies to alcohol, to the detriment of their families and communities back in the village.[35] They no longer live or eat in the forest with their human, plant, and animal siblings or exchange life-sustaining skin and wetness with the sentient environment. Instead, they dwell in concrete barracks, surrounded by industrial oil palm plantations and non-Papuan workers, feeding off plastic foods prepared and served in the confines of anonymous concession canteens. Over time, these individuals become disconnected from the sounds, songs, and stories of the grove, the pasts and relations embedded in forest foods, and the serenity and liveliness of the living landscape. Their knowledge (*ilmu*) of the forest diminishes and is no longer passed on to their children and grandchildren.[36] Echoing the insatiability provoked by plastic foods described earlier, men who hunger for money are also often alleged by women to never be content with how much they earn or with what they purchase.

At the same time, blame and pity, as well as hesitation and uncertainty, often sat awkwardly alongside each other in women's moral valuations of men's hunger for money. This was especially the case among those women whose husbands had taken up labor in monocrops and who often expressed sadness for their spouses now having to abide by stringent work routines, respect the strict orders and disciplinary authority of their bosses, comply with the rigid hierarchical structure of the corporate body, and endure the dreary monotony of plantation labor in order to receive the money they desperately and constantly hunger after. Even then, men working in the monocrops often eke out a livelihood at the brink of precarity. As Carlotta noted, laborers like her husband, Hugo, tend to be hired as seasonal, rather than permanent, employees. They are vastly underpaid compared with their non-Papuan fellow workers. In stark contrast to the freedom (*kebebasan*) associated with forest food procurement activities, men like Hugo who are subject to the exploitative system of debt bondage receive no salary at all, often for indefinite periods. Their skin becomes dull and their wetness depleted as they labor in the plantations, exposed to toxic pesticides and to the polluting fumes of bulldozers, trucks, and processing mills.

Echoing the cultural significance of "famine" (*gomara*) among Wamirans in Papua New Guinea, hunger for money in Marind parlance thus constitutes a deeply gendered and morally inflected evaluation that communicates an inherent tension between the pursuit of individual desires attributed to men, on the one hand, and the imperative of meeting collective needs expressed by women, on the other.[37] The gastropolitical valences of the hunger for money take on particularly sinister and visceral undertones in its synonymous expression, "hunger for human flesh" (*lapar daging manusia*). According to Mirabela, the hunger for human flesh refers to the detrimental effects of individualistic behaviors on the bodies, nourishment, and futures of others. As the benefits and wealth promised by oil palm corporations increasingly divide Marind couples, families, and clans once bound through kinship and custom, co-optation and conflict have intensified across the villages of the Upper Bian. Hungers formerly experienced by Marind collectively in the context of seasonal changes and associated food availability, together with hungers serving as moral sanctions to preserve respectful protocols of food procurement, lose their unitary and uniting force. Social harmony afforded by acts of commensality in and from the forest gives way to tensions and frictions, as villagers are increasingly pitted against each other in disputes over territorial rights and monetary compensation.

Seen from this perspective, individuals who participate in the oil palm sector through their land surrenders and labor endorse and enable the destruction of the forest that once sustained them. In doing so, they undermine the fleshly skin and wetness of their human and other-than-human kin, at the same time as they are themselves consumed by an incessant desire for cash and commodities. The repercussions of this concomitantly self- and other-destroying cycle, expressed through the carnal metaphor of eating human flesh, extends across species and generations. Unlike the reciprocal and morally valued forms of nourishment animating forest foodways, the hunger for flesh and money entails a destructive and unidirectional form of consumption—one where people symbolically feed off each other, to the detriment of both parties, and that of the forest ecologies increasingly being obliterated to make way for industrial plantations. As Mirabela's sister Costanza put it, "In the past, Marind all ate together from the forest. But now, Marind turn against their own kin. Men sell off the land to the corporations without our consent. The oil palm eats our forests. Meanwhile, the clans eat each other up [*suku makan suku*]."

3

OF ROADS AND OTHER
HUNGRY BEINGS

Adriana, a middle-aged mother of three from Bayau village, had been sitting by the road since the first light of day (see figure 3.1). I encountered her around six in the morning, while making my way by foot to the local church to meet with the head priest and discuss a meeting on land rights due to take place that afternoon. I recognized Adriana at a distance from her thick, long, and tousled hair, which she tasked me with untangling, combing, and oiling on the many evenings we spent together in her home in Bayau. It was only when I drew closer that I saw the cadaver of a juvenile pig lying beside my friend, shrouded in a swarm of frenzied flies.

Adriana told me the animal had been crushed by an oil palm fruit truck earlier that morning, slightly farther down the dusty track. The driver, an Indonesian man in his early twenties, had stopped to examine the animal following the collision. He must have decided its tusks were too small to sell, as he had departed almost immediately, leaving the carcass where it was. After the vehicle left the scene, Adriana had kneeled beside the corpse and uttered a song that celebrated their shared belonging to the Basik-Basik (pig)

Figure 3.1. Adriana, a Marind woman, and one of her grandchildren, 2017. Photograph by the author.

clan and that also mourned the death of her brother, Felipus, who, like the animal before us, had been "eaten by the road" (*dorang dimakan jalan*) in a fatal vehicle crash two years prior. Then, Adriana had moved the corpse to the side of the road and covered it with a bunch of leaves and fronds gathered from nearby bushes. She told me she had performed these actions out of respect and mourning for her deceased kin. It had suffered a violent, sudden death. It deserved a companion, a song, and a dignified place of rest.

Adriana had originally come to the road that morning to await her daughter, Mia, who had gone to sell vegetables at the market in Merauke City. Mia's absence had lasted over three weeks—far longer than planned. Adriana had been waiting here for two days. She was anxious, distracted, and hungry. Mia was the second of Adriana's children to leave the village for the city. Her mother worried she would not return. Her eldest son, Serafinus, never had. Over the preceding week, Mia and Serafinus had appeared to Adriana every night in her dreams, surrounded by highways, cities, plantations, and buildings that Adriana herself had never before seen or visited but that appeared real enough in her nightly visions. My friend told me her children were being eaten by the road—one after the other. She told me the road was eating many other kinds of beings. The forest. The river. The groves. Adriana's sibling, the pig, lying eviscerated beside us.

Soon afterward, Adriana's husband, Gilbertus, hobbled over from the village. Even from afar, I knew it was him from the limp of his lame right leg. Catching Adriana's last words as he reached us, Gilbertus told me that he, unlike his wife, had been to many places—Merauke City, Jayapura, even Jakarta. But a dream had summoned him back to the village. When he arrived there, he discovered that his land had been eaten by bulldozers. All that remained were dust, vehicle tracks, and felled trees. Gilbertus hoped his daughter had not been eaten and would return. But the road and cities, he added, are powerful and dangerous. Like the corporations and government, they are always hungry. Gilbertus spoke from firsthand experience. His own right leg had been crushed—or, in Gilbertus's words, "eaten"—by an oil palm company's four-wheel-drive, crashing frenetically down the same road where we were now sitting and speaking.

Our conversation was interrupted by a deep rumble arising in the distance. Adriana raised her head with anticipation. A rickety jeep appeared in the horizon, loaded with jute bags and cardboard boxes. The jeep ground to an awkward halt at the entrance of Bayau. Once the diesel fumes subsided, a dozen or so Indonesian plantation workers crawled out of the vehicle, carrying crates of live chickens and cartons of instant noodles. The dust had barely settled when the jeep engine revved to a start. It had many more villages to visit before returning to the city. Adriana and Gilbertus bowed their heads and sighed, looking downcast. They told me they were tired and hungry, but they would return tomorrow and wait again. Together, they would wait once again for their daughter, by the side of the hungry road.

This chapter explores the transformation of Marind and their environments into *objects* of hungers arising from an array of invasive and rapacious forces. This typology of hunger distinguishes itself from the hungers explored in the previous chapter, wherein Marind are positioned as *subjects* of hunger for sago, plastic foods, money, and the flesh of fellow kinsmen. It also contrasts starkly with the mutual and intergenerational dynamics of eaten and being eaten that characterize forest foodways, in that the consumption of Marind bodies and ecologies by roads, cities, and government and corporate bodies is unilateral and nonreciprocal. Like the hungers of Marind for sago, plastic foods, money, and the flesh of fellow kinsmen, the hungers of foreign entities manifest primarily in the physical depletion of the bodily skin and wetness of those subject to their effects. But these hungers also take more ambivalent and covert forms. They include the haunting remains of kindred animals trampled by vehicles on the road, the racialized stigma and deception associated with the city, and the mind-altering effects of foreign forms of sorcery wielded by government and corporate actors. Together, these effects conjure hunger as an attribute of diverse infrastructural and institutional assemblages, whose destructive dispositions are idiomatized by local women as a form of masculinized and pathological hyperphagia.

The chapter begins by examining how villagers subjected to the hunger of roads lose their connections to the forest ecology and forest foodways as they are lured away, at times indefinitely, from their settlements and communities, and how animals eaten by roads become objects of ritualized singing and mourning by those who encounter them. I then consider how the alien environments of cities in Merauke and beyond consume the bodies and behaviors of Marind individuals who visit them by stripping them of their sense of agency and dignity, subjecting them to racializing violence, and rendering women especially vulnerable to the often unspoken harms of sexual violence and sexually transmitted diseases. The final section of the chapter explores the insatiable hunger for land and profit that many women associate with corporations and the government, the pernicious acts of sorcery through which these mutually enforcing entities come to exert control over Marind landscapes and life-forms, and the ambiguous forms of responsibility and moral injury experienced by Marind men whose minds become targets of state-corporate manipulation.

Roads

Roads (*jalan*) are one of many hungry beings that, together with Marind and their forest kin, are said to haunt (*menghantui*) the famished landscape of the Upper Bian. The development of these roads has accelerated in conjunction with monocrop expansion since 2008 across the region, alongside the construction of processing mills, palm oil refineries, and private airports for use by plantation managerial staff. Some roads connect Marind villages to one another and to the local township of Timase. These roads, however, are rarely used by local community members, who prefer to walk to neighboring settlements in groups, or travel by canoe up and down the Bian River, because doing so allows them to share skin and wetness with their surrounds and is deemed a more sociable and convivial way of traveling across and with the landscape. Other roads link Marind villages to Merauke City, which lies approximately 250 kilometers from the nearest settlement of Bayau and constitutes the largest urban center and capital of Merauke Regency. Frequented mainly by village men, these roads connect Merauke to other regions of West Papua via the Trans-Papua Highway (Jalan Raya Trans-Papua), a megadevelopment project officially initiated by the Indonesian government in 2013 and intended to enhance transportation and mobility across West Papua's southern, eastern, western, and northernmost areas. Other roads in the Upper Bian include privatized dirt roads built by agribusiness and timber corporations within and across their plantations. Restricted in principle to company workers and staff but often clandestinely used by local community members, these roads link different plantations to one another and to newly built private airports and facilitate the transport of fresh fruit bunches, crude palm oil, and refined palm oil to and from concessions, mills, refineries, cities, and ports.

As infrastructures of connectivity, roads have long played a central and contested role within colonial imaginaries of modernization, technology, and nation-building in Indonesia and elsewhere.[1] This is no less the case in West Papua, where road construction projects are actively promoted by the Indonesian government and by corporations as a means of enhancing the movement of people and resources and boosting economic development throughout the region. Roads, however, are objects of great controversy among Upper Bian villagers, particularly among women.[2] For starters, most Marind are unable to afford a vehicle of their own, such that their travel along public roads requires renting a jeep or minivan from non-Papuan, male settlers or paying for a seat when vehicles stop by the villages to drop off passengers. The growing reliance on motor vehicles, together with the dependence on cash and on the labor of non-Papuan men that road travel entails, undermines Marind's autonomy of movement at the same time as it contravenes the valued practice of walking in the company of one's kin, which in turn limits people's capacity to engage sensorially and kinesthetically with the landscape and its diverse ecology of dwellers, or what Tyson Yunkaporta, an Apalech clan member and Indigenous Knowledges scholar, describes as a "haptic relationship with Country."[3] As Adriana explained while we sat together awaiting her daughter that morning, "When we travel by car on the road, we do not share skin and wetness with the soil or rivers. Everything moves so fast, and we cannot pay attention to what is going on around us. We are trapped in a metal box, in a foreign place, with foreign men."

While Marind are very much aware of the human and institutional forces driving infrastructural expansion in Merauke and beyond, they often attribute the destructive effects of these developments to the hunger of roads themselves. Much like the Baining of New Ireland, Papua New Guinea, who associate the road with the severance of one's social ties and the threat of starvation, many of my companions characterize the road as a place of hunger, solitude, and dryness because there is no food, shade, or kin to be found along or upon it.[4] Alongside failing to offer nourishment to those who encounter them, roads are also said to prey on the bodies of those who travel them. Roads "eat" (*makan*) Marind by physically taking them away from their home villages and lands. In doing so, they subvert and rupture the socialities, relations, and intimacies that bind nuclear and extended families and clans to one another.

For local women, who rarely have the opportunity to travel beyond their villages in motor vehicles, the road is seen as a distinctly masculine realm, used primarily by male villagers, corporate representatives, NGO workers, and government officials, and built also by male non-Papuan construction workers. Marind men who frequent the road, these women explained, expose themselves to the influence of other, foreign men. Among them are military forces transiting between garrisons, settler traders transporting supplies from the city to the villages, and corporate representatives escorting investors and developers to and from their plantations. When prolonged or frequent, such encounters are said to deplete the skin and wetness of Marind men, who gradually forget their Papuan roots and culture; their relationships and responsibilities toward their wives, children, and wider kinship networks; and their ancestral ties to the forest and its myriad life-forms.

In its most tangible form, the hunger of roads causes Marind persons who travel along them to disappear completely. Like Adriana's daughter Mia and son Serafinus, Marind eaten by the road often initially leave the village for short periods, and with a particular objective in mind—to sell vegetables at the market, seek medical aid at the hospital, or discuss a land negotiation deal with a corporate representative. And yet many of these individuals end up not returning to their native homes—either for protracted periods or at all. Heated speculations and discussions in the villages would often intensify following such events, as people questioned whether and why their kin had been waylaid along the way, who they had encountered along the road, if they had suffered an accident or become lost, or for what reason they no longer wanted to return home. All these conjectures conjure the powerful and predatory lure of the roads themselves over the movements, desires, and actions of those who encounter and use them.

At the same time as they take kith and kin away from home, roads also provide an easy conduit for threatening, foreign entities to enter the Marind lifeworld. These entities include non-Papuans who have migrated to Merauke through either state-sponsored or spontaneous resettlement, who occupy customary territories, and who are structurally privileged over Papuans in terms of employment and social mobility. They also include soldiers of the Indonesian national army, garrisoned at barracks across Merauke, whose omnipresence and surveillance create fear among local villagers and remind them of their ongoingly militarized occupation under settler-colonial rule. The road further enables government officials and corporate representatives to access rural settlements and organize meetings that are invariably attended by police and military forces, and during which villagers are coaxed (or, more often, coerced) into surrendering their lands to oil palm projects.

Roads are additionally threatening because they destroy the living forest, rupturing the patterns of migration and subsistence of forest organisms and causing them to flee their native habitats.[5] As Rubina, a widowed mother of two and a member of the Balagaize (crocodile) clan living in Khalaoyam village, explained to me while we walked along the dirt road to visit her relatives in neighboring Bayau, "Roads are made for humans. But they also eat the forest and frighten away our amai. The more roads are built, the harder it becomes to hunt and forage. The animals go hungry, and Marind go hungry. Everyone is eaten by the road." Like Rubina, many of my female companions described roads as tearing across the landscape in ever-more-numerous capillaries of dust, fumes, and asphalt. People spoke of these proliferating infrastructures devouring the trees and vegetation that lie in their way, reducing them to piles of unrecognizable rubble and charred remains. They claimed that roads not only eat away at the futures of animals by destroying the ecologies and resources they need to survive but also render animals vulnerable to the dangers of passing trucks, vans, and bulldozers that regularly run over the cassowaries, tree kangaroos, possums, and other organisms attempting to cross them. The rotting pig that Adriana and I encountered, for instance, was one of many animals that had been forced to reckon with the presence of roads as invasive and unfamiliar infrastructures yet are not equipped with the knowledge or instinct to survive them. As a result, many Marind today encounter their forest kin not as living organisms and sources of food in their native environments but as the trampled remains of beings that themselves have been eaten by the road—roadkill.

I use the term *roadkill* here as a shorthand. Even though, on one level, the word speaks to the agency of roads as threatening presences, Marind women to whom I translated and explained the English term challenged its aseptic and neutralizing connotations, purged of agency and affect, because it does not come anywhere close to capturing or conveying how they themselves experience or encounter nonhuman deaths on the road. Instead, women spoke of traveling the road in the silent company of "mangled bodies" (*badan yang hancur*), "leaking entrails" (*isi perut yang bocor*), "broken limbs" (*tubuh yang rusak*), and "blood-stained feathers" (*bulut yang penuh darah*)—the almost unrecognizable yet all-too-familiar remains of their cherished kin turned disfigured carcass. Many described feeling "haunted" (*dihantui*) by these remains—some personally witnessed, many more anticipated—when they prepared themselves to travel by foot from their settlements to the forest to forage, hunt, and fish; to journey to neighboring villages to visit family and kin; or to commute by public jeep or motorbike to the city. At worst, Marind witness "roadkill" when the killing is not over. This was explained to me by Cosmina, a twenty-two-year-old woman of the Sami (snake) clan and a fellow instructor at the primary school where I volunteered as an English teacher, with whom I frequently journeyed to the district capital to purchase provisions for the village. Animals and birds fatally injured, as Cosmina described during one such journey, are often found caught in the last throes of dying, their bodies jerking, their gazes panicked, their growls and shrieks piercing. Such encounters provoke immense grief, anger, and pain among travelers. Nothing can be done in the face of these deaths at once slow and violent. But, as Cosmina stressed, "One must nonetheless stop. One must turn off the engine—get off one's motorbike. One must stand by one's agonizing kin. One must look, and not turn away. And then, one must sing."

Sami, Sami, kau lincir, kau luncur
Sami, Sami, you slip, you slide
Adiknya hutan, adiknya dusun
Sibling of the forest, sibling of the grove
Sami, Sami, kau tenun, kau goyang
Sami, Sami, you weave, you sway
Adiknya sungai, adiknya rawa
Sister of the river, sister of the swamp

Sami, Sami, kau lahir dari tanah liat dan pasang surut
Sami, Sami, you are born of clay and tide
Kulit kau licin dan berkilau, terpola oleh tanah
Your skin is sleek and shiny, patterned by the land
Diam-diam, kau melintasi tanah
Silent and shy, you slither across the land
Memindahkan tanah, memindahkan daun, kau membentukkan tanah
Moving soil and leaf, patterning the land

Di sini ketemu kau, adik ular Sami
Here I find you, Sami, snake sister
Badanmu hancur, <u>*dubadub*</u> *hilang*
Your body crushed, your wetness gone
Melihat kau susah, tinggalkan kau susah
I cannot bear to look at you, I cannot bear to leave
Truk dan mobil dan buldoser su ambil nyawamu
The trucks and cars and bulldozers, they took away your life
Tinggal kau di sini, tunggu mati
They left you here, waiting to die
Dorang hancur kau pu <u>*dubadub*</u>*, hancur kau pu harga diri*
Robbed you of your wetness, robbed you of your pride

Di sini ketemu kau, adik ular Sami
Here I find you, Sami, snake sister
Darahmu begitu gelap, matamu pegitu pucat
Your blood so dark, your eyes so pale
Sami, Sami, sa terada untuk kamu, sa tak bisa menyelamatkan kau
Sami, Sami, I was not here to save you, I could not spare you death

Sami, Sami, berapa lama kau di sini, tunggu mati sendiri?
Sami, Sami, how long have you been dying here alone?
Berapa truk su menginjak-injak kau pu <u>igid</u>?
How many trucks upon your skin have gone?

Sami, Sami, sa tidak akan pigi, sa tidak akan jalan
Sami, Sami, I will not turn away, I will not leave you
Dengan daun-daun sa akan bungkus kamu
In leaves and fronds, I'll wrap you
Dengan tangan dan kaki sa akan angkat kamu
With my arms and my legs, I'll lift you
Ke tempat diam dan hijau sa akan bawa kamu
To a quiet, green place, I'll carry you
Ke tempat nenek moyang kamu lahir
To that place where your fathers and forefathers were born

Di sana, kau akan cari damai
And there, you will find peace
Di bawah naungan hutan yang sejuk, kau akan tidur
In the cool shade of the forest, you can sleep
Di sana, kau tidak akan menderita sakit dan debu
There, no pain or dust will haunt you
Hujan dan tanah, de akan menjaga kamu
The rain and soil will protect you
Mimbu buruk, de akan lepaskan kamu
This nightmare will release you

Adiknya hutan, adiknya dusun
Sister of the forest, sister of the grove
Sami, Sami, lahir dari tanah liat dan pasang surut
Sami, Sami, born of clay and tide
Kitorang satu keluarga, kitorang satu kulit
You and I are kin and skin
Terimalah lagu saya ini
I beseech you, accept from me this song
Melalui lagu ini akan kau hidup terus
Through it you will live on

These lyrics were composed by Cosmina and her elder sister Oktavia, upon discovering the pulverized remains of her clan's sibling, the snake

Figure 3.2. The remains of a snake, 2018. Many Marind mourn the death of beings eaten by the road by way of songs. Photograph by Vembrianto Waluyas.

(sami), along a recently constructed stretch of the Trans-Irian Highway near Khalaoyam village (see figure 3.2). Like many other community members, Cosmina has begun to mourn the death of forest beings eaten by the road through the medium of improvised songs. Echoing the lyrics composed by Ana that open this book, songs about roadkill, Cosmina explained, commemorate and celebrate the origins and lifeways of Marind's forest kin. They speak to the ancestral and personal connections between these organisms and the individuals who discover them. Songs about animals eaten by the road also enable Marind to express their shame and remorse for not being present, or able, to spare these organisms a violent and torturous death. These are songs of abandonment and guilt that condemn and decry the theft of dignity and pride that death by road entails.

For, as Cosmina's lyrics intimate, the *form* of dying here matters as much as the *fact* of death itself. Unlike the hunting and consumption of organisms in the forest that are accompanied by ritualized acts of respect and reverence and are undergirded by the logic of reciprocal nourishment, organisms eaten by the road are flattened into mutilated and eviscerated remnants of their former living selves. They are left to rot, suffering, alone, humiliated, and gasping for that vital, last breath of air that will not save them. Severed from their homes and kin in the forest, these organisms undergo what the

Australian anthropologist Deborah Bird Rose calls "double death," or deaths that can no longer sustain regenerative, ecosystemic flourishing, nor nourish the humans who witness them.[6] In this context, songs about vulnerabilized nonhuman beings come to embody a last rites of sorts—a reckoning with the enormity of untimely, more-than-human deaths and bodily lacerations that repeat over and over and over again under the indifferent weight of passing trucks and bulldozers.

The mourning of animals eaten by the road is often undertaken collectively by Marind women. When an individual encounters a dead or dying animal or plant with which their clan shares a particular kinship bond, they utter a distinctive wail, drawing the attention of those nearby, who will drop their activities and rush to their side. On one such an occasion, I was asked to join a group of villagers in standing—or, more often, kneeling—in a circle around the body of a crushed tree kangaroo (<u>walef</u>) that had been found by Oktavia, a member of its clan, on the outskirts of Bayau village. My companions stroked the deceased macropod's body repeatedly and reverently, holding onto and reenacting even at the moment of death the modes of haptic sociality that animate everyday, lived relations with nonhuman beings in the forest. If the animal or bird is already deceased, as was the case here, the group would proceed to imitate its voice, grunt, or song to attract the attention of its own kin. "That way," Oktavia explained, "the sibling's family will know that one of their own has been eaten by the road. That way, they, too, may mourn its death. They, too, may heal their pain."

Soon afterward, Oktavia began to sing in a slow, deep, guttural voice—searching for words, improvising lyrics, swallowing back tears, composing grief. When she stumbled and eventually stopped, her adolescent daughter Aurelina took over, fleshing out the song with her own meanings and memories. Human words were interspersed with mellifluous whistles, deep caws, husky hoots, and gravelly grunts, as those among us who did not sing continued to give voice to the voices of those we mourned. At one point, a bird in the forest responded with a distant, muted call. The call rippled through the air, leaving in its trail an even greater silence. "Now," Oktavia said, "we know that the forest is listening. We know that the forest, too, is grieving."

Songs about roadkill composed and collectively uttered by women like Oktavia and Aurelina constitute expressions of posthumous respect and reverence for beings murdered without ritual, restraint, or purpose. They are rituals of remembrance for deaths that count for absolutely nothing and that go completely unaccounted for under the exterministic and extractive logic of technocapitalist regimes—deaths, as Aurelina decried, that are not even sacrificial in that they achieve or benefit nothing and no one. These deaths produce errant, famished souls that haunt the landscape and are haunted by their own torturous deaths. Sometimes, these deaths are so sudden, so unexpected, that victims remain unaware of their own passing. In such instances, songs, according to Cosmina, "help the lost souls of the dead understand and accept that they are no longer of this world. Songs remind them of everything they were, and everything they can no longer be. Songs help them let go."

As the lyrics of Cosmina's song intimate, songs about animals eaten by the road, as expressions of grieving and conduits for healing, are accompanied by other acts of commemoration that together seek to offer forest creatures subjected to a harrowing and lonely death something akin to a peaceful afterlife. At the end of the singing for the crushed tree kangaroo, for instance, the animal's remains were wrapped by my companions in fronds, carried to the forest, buried in the soil, and covered with offerings of leaves, sago flour, nuts, and shoots. In the weeks that followed, women from Bayau village regularly formed groups and went to visit and pay their respects to the tree kangaroo at its resting place, in a landscape increasingly dotted with these makeshift nonhuman burial grounds. Here, they sang songs that were either newly improvised in situ or that repeated lyrics previously created by others and that had since become memorized in the community. Often, they invited me to join them in bringing and offering small food gifts to the dead, and more often again the silent companionship of yet another victim salvaged from the dusty road. Among those we brought to the tree kangaroo's burial site in the months that followed its passing were a crushed black-crested bulbul, yellow-feathered and lighter than a betel nut; the mangled casque of a cassowary, its feathers and claws stripped and sold by plantation workers; the clumps of hair of a mature wild boar, thick and matted with clots of blood and froth; and a humble crow, its plumes coal black and blue, gaze dull.

Each of these beings, too, was mourned and celebrated through songs that echoed the interconnected yet distinctive lifeways of organisms whose textured pasts and thwarted futures Marind "re-member" with their voices and words.[7] In grieving animals eaten by the road, women like Adriana, Oktavia, and Cosmina thus enact what Hi'ilei Julia Kawehipuaakahaopulani Hobart, a Kānaka Maoli food studies scholar, and Tamara Kneese, a US-based media studies scholar, call "radical care."[8] They refuse *not* to mourn lives deemed ungrievable under the exterministic logic of plantations and their infrastructural assemblages.[9] Instead, these women insist on carving fleshly spaces and solemn moments for multispecies grief and grieving. In doing so, they embrace mourning as a form of resistance to another, potentially more lethal, kind of death—the death of mourning itself as a necessary stance of respectful recognition and reverence for the profound moral and ecological ramifications of both nonhuman life and nonhuman death.

Cities

Alongside roads, cities (*kota*) constitute another major infrastructural actor within the emergent ecologies of hunger consuming landscapes and lifeforms in the Upper Bian. Three cities in particular bear a prominent place within women's discourses around the rapacious appetites of urban geographies. The first is Merauke City (*kota* Merauke), the capital of Merauke regency, the closest urban center to the villages where I conducted fieldwork, and the home of the regency's major governmental and corporate headquarters, and medical and educational facilities. The second is Jayapura, the capital of Papua Province, which is located approximately 660 kilometers north of Merauke City as the crow flies. The third is Jakarta, the capital of Indonesia, which lies a six- to nine-hour flight away from Merauke City. While almost all my female friends had previously traveled to Merauke City, only a handful had visited Jayapura, and even fewer had set foot in Jakarta.

Much like the characterization of cities as figures of death, domination, and rupture among the Korowai of lowland West Papua, the hunger attributed to cities by my companions is intrinsically linked to their association with danger (*bahaya*) and foreignness (*asing*).[10] For instance, many women with whom I traveled to Merauke City to obtain supplies for the village and primary school spoke of feeling afraid and vulnerable when visiting urban zones because they were unfamiliar with the ways in which cities work and how city people behave. When in town, they often expressed profound discomfort and embarrassment when trying to cross roads because they did not understand the traffic light system. Others experienced uneasiness when trying to order foods they had never heard of from printed restaurant menus. Yet others reported feeling frustrated and stupid when having to ask passersby for directions because they were ignorant of street names.

In the city, my friends reported, their knowledge (*ilmu*) of the forest is useless because the built environment offers them no intelligible spatial or temporal reference points against which to situate themselves or their movements. Here, there are no birds or wind or natural relief to offer direction or guidance (see figure 3.3). Indeed, the very possibility of walking in

Figure 3.3. Merauke City, 2013. Cities are widely associated by Marind with danger and foreignness. Photograph by Paula Mahuze.

urban spaces—a central dimension of knowing and being in the forest—is preempted by the fact that pavements are often nonexistent and motor vehicles the default mode of transport. Contact with the skin and wetness of the earth is also negated by the insulating asphalt, concrete, or tiled surfaces of cities and their buildings, and by the imperative to wear shoes when visiting urban places. In the image of these unnatural materialities, cities are places where food, transport, and other services can only be obtained with cash, and where the only foods available are of the "plastic" variety. The dependence on money to survive in cities is a major concern for many Marind women, whose financial resources are limited and usually managed by their husbands or other male relatives, and who often find it difficult to gauge whether what they are asked to pay is relative to the value of what they purchase.

Women in the villages of the Upper Bian who had traveled to Merauke City also often described urban areas as unpleasantly "loud" (*keras*). These places, as Susana, a middle-aged woman from the Samkakai (wallaby) clan and a resident of Mirav village, recalled from a recent visit, are saturated with the sound of speeding vehicles, hollering street hawkers, megaphone advertisements, beeping horns, and foreign languages—Javanese, Batak, Madurese, and others. Unlike the collective sense of liveliness (*ramai*) that Marind associate with the forest, the liveliness of the city takes the form of a sensory overload that is disorienting, anxiety-provoking, and exhausting. Finding peace (*damai*) is virtually impossible in this continuously moving environment that is animated not by forest animals or plants but rather by man-made machines and buildings. Similarly, Susana continued, the layout of cities is determined by artificial man-made road signs, whose toponymies refer to political events or male political figures in Indonesian history that Marind are either unfamiliar with or, more often, that conjure to them their violent history of militarized settler occupation under Indonesian rule.

Susana pointed out these traumatic inscriptions of colonial pasts as we walked through Merauke City following a visit to her husband's relatives in the southern suburbs. They included a road named Trikora after the militarized annexation of Papua in 1961, a square named Pepera after the co-opted West Papua referendum of 1969, and an administrative government complex named Wiranto after the military general responsible for the torture, mutilation, and massacre of over 150 West Papuans in Biak in the summer of 1998. At each of these sites and their respective signposts, Susana would stop and explain the horrifying acts that had taken place during these events, pausing to swallow her tears of grief and rage, and referring to these monuments and markers as "scars" (*bekas luka*) that remain indelibly inscribed on the skins of Papuan lands and Papuan people.

At the end of a harrowing, three-hour pilgrimage through the city, we finally reached our motel. Before we entered the building, Susana pointed to the dusty LED hotel sign flickering above us and read out the establishment's name: "Indonesia Jaya." Victorious Indonesia.[11] She laughed dejectedly and said, "Indonesia Jaya. Irian Jaya.[12] Victory, they say. For me, walking through the city is like walking through the past of *tanah Papua* [the Papuan land]. This is not a past that lives in the forest or the grove, or the past that we share with our plant and animal <u>amai</u>. This is a past of violence, colonization, and invasion. It is a past of Indonesian victory—not Papuan victory. It is this past that haunts us when we walk the city. It is this past that haunts Marind and Marind's famished land."

Cities are viewed with fear and suspicion by Susana and other villagers for many other reasons. As noted earlier, these places are said to eat Marind who visit them by draining them of their preciously earned cash, which is expended on items and activities sold or provided by non-Papuan settlers, who often trick villagers into paying more than what foods and other commodities or services are worth—public transport, restaurant meals, or hotel rooms, for instance. The all-consuming force of cities also takes on symbolic and political valences as sites where decisions about the short- and long-term future of Marind peoples and places are made by non-Papuan government representatives. These decisions, which include the demarcation of new administrative districts, the allocation of land to agribusiness corporations, the development of new villages for non-Papuan settlers, and the construction of new roads, are said by Marind to eat away at the landscape and its native inhabitants, both human and other-than-human. They are decisions made primarily by non-Papuan men rather than women, behind closed doors in government buildings, far away from Marind villages, without local communities' consent or consultation. They result in the intensified appropriation and exploitation of Marind territories and resources. They are instituted by state representatives of Indonesian origin, whose monopoly over governance and administration sits within a broader trend of Papuan minoritization in the cities of Merauke and Jayapura, where settlers now represent over 62 and 65 percent of the population, respectively.[13]

The consumption of Marind in and by urban infrastructures also manifests in their changing bodies and behaviors. Men from the villages in particular, who spend more frequent and extended periods in urban centers compared with women, are said to develop unhealthy, wasteful, and depraved habits during their time in the city. Many women, for instance, spoke of their male relatives gradually become accustomed to, and reliant on, purchasing alcohol, visiting karaoke bars, and frequenting sex workers. They would often get drunk, lose or be robbed of their meager possessions, and end up in violent brawls with strangers. They would begin to develop a taste for plastic foods and money and to forget the flavors of sago and game. Their skin would lose its dark gloss and wetness as they spent most of their time indoors in hotels, restaurants, and brothels. The absence of collective, strenuous physical labor in urban environments was also said to breed laziness and apathy among city dwellers, who became increasingly reluctant to travel anywhere by foot, including to visit their kin and friends, or to return to the village promptly, if at all.

At the same time as they eat away at the bodies and dispositions of their inhabitants, cities are also said to eat Marind by rendering them vulnerable to demeaning treatment and racialized discrimination on the part of non-Papuan settlers. This perspective was shared with me on numerous occasions by Klara, a widowed mother of three from the Samkakai clan and a resident of Mirav village, who supported her family by selling fruit and vegetables once a month at a local market in Merauke City. "The city," Klara told me, "is a foreign land, populated by foreign people who do not share our dark skin and curly hair. It is a place that eats our pride and identity as Papuans [*makan kitorang pu bangga, pu jati diri*]. It is a place that makes us feel small, and dirty, and unwanted."

The racialized alienation and marginalization that Klara and many others have experienced in the city resonate with their diminishing treatment at biomedical institutions like hospitals and clinics, as described previously, and similarly take on multiple different forms. For instance, some villagers with whom I traveled to purchase supplies in the city were denied entry to hotels and guesthouses I had booked for us, or reported having previously been refused lease contracts for rental properties owned by non-Papuan settlers because they were deemed financially insecure, lacking in basic hygiene, and therefore likely to make the establishment "dirty" (*kotor*) and "smelly" (*bau*). Other villagers spoke of having been denied service at restaurants because their shirts were torn and stained, or because their children were barefoot. When attempting to hire vehicles or use public transport, my companions were often directed to sit at the farthest end of the public jeeps because their dark skin might otherwise "frighten" (*menakutkan*) children passengers. They were also invariably asked to pay up front before entering the vehicle, unlike non-Papuan customers like myself, from whom payment was only expected on arrival at the destination.

Resonating with the West Papuan independence activist Filep Karma's characterization of his people as being perceived "like half-animals" (*seakan kitorang setengah binatang*) in the gaze of Indonesians, Marind whom I accompanied to the city were frequently confronted with racial insults, slurs, and jeers when they walked the streets—"monkey," "pig," and "dog," among others.[14] They were also often derided by kiosk, restaurant, and hotel owners or employees for their lack of knowledge of city ways—how to read a receipt, turn light switches on and off, or read directions off a map. "In the city," reported Mariska, an elderly Marind woman of the Uabarek (coconut) clan and a resident of Mirav village, "Indonesians make us feel stupid—like we know and understand nothing. They belittle us. They make us feel like animals. They eat up our self-esteem [*dorang makan habis kitorang pu harga diri*]."

Last but not least, the erosion of Marind's sense of pride and dignity in the city environment is compounded by their bodily exposure to sexually transmitted diseases, which are increasingly prevalent in Merauke and Jayapura cities, and the effects of which my companions also describe through idioms of consumption. Women often characterized cities are dangerous places because they make people sick with the deadly "four-letter disease" (*sakit empat huruf*), or HIV/AIDS. This disease, as Mariska explained, eats the flesh of those who contract it, leading to the gradual wasting away of their skin, muscles, and bones. It begins by contaminating the bodies of Marind men who frequent sex workers in the city and then infects those of their wives and children when men return to their villages. No remedy exists for this lethal sickness, which few community members seek treatment for due both to the financial costs involved and to the prevalent shame and stigma associated with the disease.

Women are said to be particularly vulnerable to sexually transmitted diseases in light of the frequent instances of sexual harassment and abuse they experience in cities—a space that, like roads and also plantations, many of my female companions also associate with men and masculinity. Such instances are common during nighttime, when women become easy prey for inebriated groups of Papuan and non-Papuan men who roam the dimly lit streets or lurk in the empty corridors of cheap motels. Several young Marind girls shared stories with me of being taunted and catcalled when walking outdoors, either on their own or in groups. Others had been poked, prodded, and fondled on public transport. Yet others had had their hotel rooms broken into by groups of drunken men. Fear, shame, and the unsaid shrouded these harrowing accounts, as women expressed through their words as much as their silences the unrestrained sexual appetites that the city seems to unleash among its dwellers.[15] As Mariska's eighteen-year-old granddaughter, Pia, described, "In the city, hungry men want to eat our bodies. After men eat our bodies, then shame eats our bodies. This is what the city means for Marind women—hunger, danger, and shame."

Corporations and Government

Just as hungry as the cities and the roads that connect them are the government (*pemerintah*) and oil palm corporations (*perusahaan sawit*). A number of similarities between these two masculinized entities explain their frequent conflation within the discourse of many local women. Government and corporate bodies, my companions noted, work in conjunction with one another in the planning, design, and implementation of agribusiness, infrastructure, and other large-scale, land-based projects. Their composition is overwhelmingly dominated by non-Papuan men. Their collusion also manifests in the frequent (if informal) engagement of military and police forces by agribusiness conglomerates as security personnel, plantation patrols, and even company shareholders. Nepotistic relations between government bodies and corporate organs, alongside endemic state-corporate patronage and clientelism, blur the boundaries between the private and public spheres, with both entities sharing a seemingly insatiable hunger for land, resources, and control.

The hungers that Marind attribute to the state and to corporations invoke comparable characterizations in Melanesia and beyond of people being "consumed" or "eaten" by rapacious institutional forces and actors, including corrupt politicians, plantations, factories, mines, and white people.[16] Among Marind, these hungers are frequently expressed through the idiom of *suanggi*, a Malukan-Malay word used throughout North Sulawesi, the Bird's Head of Papua, and in some eastern Indonesian communities to refer to witches, sorcerers, or other figures of evil.[17] *Suanggi*, as Selena, a middle-aged mother of two from Mirav village, explained to me, is used to describe perpetrators of malevolent and supernatural actions who are of non-Papuan origin and usually male. These include forms of sorcery introduced in precolonial times by Indonesian plume traders and bird hunters, as well as those practiced today by settler populations who control, occupy, or otherwise exploit Merauke's natural resources. The foreign origins and wielders of *suanggi* are what differentiate it from kambara, an endemic form of sorcery practiced exclusively by Marind men and within Marind communities, and one that declined dramatically following Dutch colonization and the conversion of local communities to Catholicism and, to a lesser extent, Protestantism. Like perpetrators of kambara in the precolonial past, the powers of *suanggi* wielded by the government and corporations constitute a source of deep and widespread fear among Upper Bian villagers, and especially among women, who are subject to the adverse effects of both regimes of sorcery but unable to wield either regimes themselves. Their differences in origins and agencies notwithstanding, kambara and *suanggi* alike are characterized by their male perpetrators as well as their insatiable greed and sociopathic self-interest.

For instance, Marcelina, a young mother of two and a member of the Mahuze (dog) clan based in Mirav village, described how corporate wielders of *suanggi* are always hungry for more land, just like kambara practitioners are perpetually seeking out the flesh and blood of their victims. Both groups are said to inflict illness, injury, suffering, and eventually death on their targets by eating their bodies from the inside out. Marcelina further compared wielders of kambara to oil palm corporations that sap the life-sustaining flesh and fluids of Marind and their plant and animal kin by converting the sentient forest into arid plantations and diverting streams and rivers for irrigation purposes. Corporations, Marcelina continued, are also like kambara practitioners in that they can replicate themselves and be in several places at once. Their concessions, for instance, multiply across the landscape under myriad different names and logos. Their sorcery powers are spread out across the many divisions and individuals who together compose the distributed body of the corporation—from high-level decision-makers to menial plantation laborers. Just as <u>kambara</u> operate elusively and cannot easily be identified physically, Marcelina added, corporations control their concessions at a distance, from locations that she herself had never visited but had come to learn about during government consultations and from maps secured for communities by local NGOs—Jayapura, Jakarta, Singapore, and Kuala Lumpur. The authority of these corporate bodies, my companion noted, is everywhere (*ada dimana-mana*)—even as their agents often remain invisible (*tra terlihat*).

The destructive and pernicious forms of *suanggi* wielded by foreign government and corporate actors is further enhanced by their perceived superiority in scope and effect when compared with Marind's own now largely abandoned practice of <u>kambara</u>.[18] According to Marcelina, <u>kambara</u> is an endogenous and localized form of sorcery that can only be inflicted by Marind men against other Marind men and women. Women may not be able to harness the powers of <u>kambara</u> themselves, but its roots, effects, and antidotes are by and large familiar to most community members, irrespective of gender differences. For instance, <u>kambara</u> practitioners are known to acquire their powers from the ancestral spirit Ugu, who bears a mythical grudge against humans. They attack their victims by contaminating their food or casting spells on them in the forest, often with the aid of co-opted plants and animals. These lethal effects can be countered by medicine men (<u>messav anim</u>) who invoke Ugu's nemesis, the ancestral spirit Sosom, to their aid.

Suanggi, in contrast, operates exogenously. In other words, Marind are vulnerable to *suanggi*, but neither Marind men nor women can inflict *suanggi* on others because its origins, techniques, instruments, spells, and remedies are unknown to them. As Serafina, a mother of four and a member of the Kaize (cassowary) clan based in Khalaoyam village, explained, "The problem with *suanggi* is that we do not know where it comes from, what it wants, or how to prevent it from eating us." Conversely, *suanggi* are immune to the effects of <u>kambara</u> because <u>kambara</u> can only be inflicted by Marind on other Marind. The result is a deeply uneven field of forces in which Marind are doubly vulnerable to both internal and external forms of supernatural violence.

The supernatural powers of government and corporate perpetrators of *suanggi* are heightened by their intrinsic association with one another. For instance, corporations routinely work in collusion with military personnel, whose deadly and elusive operations Marind widely describe through the idiom of *suanggi*. The expansion of industrial oil palm monocrops, owned and operated by multinational conglomerates, and the proliferation of roads and cities are supported by government policies and prerogatives of achieving national food sovereignty, local economic development, rural urbanization, and transregional connectivity. Roads, cities, and plantations have also enabled a growing influx of non-Papuan settlers who are seeking employment in the agribusiness sector, occupying customary lands, and introducing new forms of sorcery into West Papua from across the Indonesian archipelago. Many of these settlers hail from Java, a region that many Marind associate with the dark arts of the *dukun*, who wield their supernatural powers to inflict revenge through hexes and incantations. While instances of <u>kambara</u> decreased following Dutch colonization and missionization, the arrival of foreign corporations and non-Papuan settlers means that *suanggi* is now on the rise.

Finally, whereas <u>kambara</u> entails a physical assault on an individual and their instant demise, *suanggi* is said by villagers to operate through the subtle powers of mental manipulation, or what many of my companions called an "eating" of one's thoughts, feelings, or awareness (*makan kitorang pu pikiran, pu perasaan, pu kesadaran*). Usually occurring during face-to-face encounters, these manipulations involve a takeover of control over the minds, words, and actions of community members by company and government actors in ways that further corporate and state interests.

I collected several such accounts of possession from Upper Bian villagers during my time in the field. One was shared with me by Pius, an elder from Khalaoyam, who described his experience of being eaten during a consultation with an oil palm corporation in Merauke City in late January 2015. Pius, who had been invited to the meeting as a spokesperson for his community, stood firmly opposed to the company's development project. Yet, as Pius reported, from the moment he entered the meeting room at the corporate headquarters, his mind became instantly "empty" (*kosong*). He could not remember what he said or heard, or even whom he met and spoke to. Three weeks after Pius's return to Khalaoyam, bulldozers appeared in throngs near the village and started systematically felling the fruit trees across his community's land. When Pius intervened, he was handed a contract signed by his own hand, surrendering three thousand hectares to the company at less than 10,000 rupiah (US$1) per hectare, and for a minimum term of twenty-five years.

In another case that I documented, Alex, a young man from Mirav village, was nominated by his clan to seek compensation from a corporation that had destroyed over a third of their sacred sago groves to make way for an oil palm nursery, without the community's consent. Over the preceding six weeks, Alex prepared meticulously for the negotiation, consulting all manner of documents, laws, and regulations and also seeking my guidance as former policy adviser to buttress his case. And yet he, too, reported having no recollection whatsoever of the nature or proceedings of the meeting after it happened. For hours later, in his hotel room, he tried in vain to recall what had been discussed and decided, but to no avail. The next morning, Alex found a crumpled, signed contract at the bottom of his satchel while searching for his motorbike key as he prepared to head back to Mirav. According to the document, the young man had agreed to a surrender of two thousand hectares of land to the aforementioned corporation. No mention was made of the compensation he had been charged by his community to seek out. According to his wife, Florensia, it took Alex over three months to overcome his shock, fear, and shame and to eventually find the courage to return to the village and disclose the fateful outcome to his community.

While women widely characterize oil palm companies and government representatives as wielders of pernicious *suanggi* powers, many are also split over whether the behaviors of men, including Pius and Alex, can always or necessarily be attributed to corporate sorcery attacks. Some, for instance, were adamant that men were using *suanggi* as a convenient pretext to maintain a semblance of innocence for decisions they had in fact made consciously and deliberately. This view was vehemently countered by women who claimed to have succeeded in persuading their husbands and brothers not to surrender lands in the course of numerous private conversations at home, and who affirmed that *suanggi* was the only possible explanation for why their male relatives had suddenly reverted to entirely opposite decisions during consultations that took place just days later. For all their convictions, however, these women could not explain exactly *how* corporations controlled the actions of their male relatives. Hesitations of all kinds abounded in their theorizations of men's agency in relation to that of predatory state and corporate actors.

For some, the events described here are understood as enabled by the ambiguous nature of the physical locations in which they occur—the cities, plantations, and corporate and government headquarters as infrastructures are themselves shrouded in "uncertainty" (*abu-abu*) and are far removed from the familiar and known spaces of the forest and village. In these alien places, corporations were said by others to manipulate their victims' minds through the medium of food, and particularly plastic, processed commodities such as instant noodles and biscuits, that are habitually offered to participants during multistakeholder consultations and that women often

Figure 3.4. Irrigation system on an oil palm plantation, 2019. Polluted waterways cause people to "lose themselves" to the influence of toxins. Photograph by the author.

implore their male relatives not to touch or consume prior to their travels to the city, lest the food affect their decisions and actions. Yet other women believe that corporations gain control over men's thoughts and bodies not only in faraway locations but also closer to home—namely, through the intentional contamination of local water sources with pesticides, mill effluents, and fertilizers (see figure 3.4). Individuals who frequently bathe in or drink from polluted rivers, they noted, "lose themselves" (*hilang diri*) under the influence of these toxic substances. They develop an addictive hunger for money and plastic food, which they seek to quell by leaving the village and working on the plantations, where their skin and wetness are only further exposed to the corrosive and contaminating effects of plantation chemicals. Laboring for minimal pay, working under precarious conditions, and increasingly captive to the hold of *suanggi*, the bodies and labors of these zombified beings are said to be eaten by the rapacious and powerful strangers who employ and exploit them.

Marind women's discourses surrounding the destructive consumption of Indigenous bodies amid natures themselves put to work within the state-corporate agribusiness nexus resonate powerfully with the writings of the Martinican authors Aimé Césaire and Patrick Chamoiseau, who describe the shared subjection of Black bodies and physical landscapes to the cannibalistic violence of the rapacious plantation machine.[19] These discourses find further resonance in the memories of rural Brazilians who describe their bodies, gardens, forests, lands, and livelihoods as having been "eaten up" by sugarcane plantations, and also in the memories of Indigenous Toba of the Pilcomayo River in Argentina who characterize sugarcane plantations owners as anthropographic "Big Eaters" profiteering from the laboring flesh of indentured workers.[20]

Each form of *suanggi*-induced behavior furthers the interests of its foreign perpetrators—from the forceful appropriation of land by corporations to the acquisition of a cheap and exploitable labor force, and the proliferation of an introduced and lucrative cash crop. Each behavior in turn adversely impacts the victim of *suanggi*, together with their broader social networks. Mia and Serafinus's mother, Adriana, with whose deceased kindred pig sibling I had once sat beside the road, described this vicious and distributed spiral of harm as follows one evening, as we sat in the village square chewing betel nut and chatting: "Marind eaten by the road do not return to the village to feed their kin. Marind eaten by the city abandon their roots and skin in the forest. Marind men whose minds are eaten by the government and companies sell off our land and become hungry ghosts in the plantations. Meanwhile, the forest disappears to make way for oil palm, and everyone else, too, goes hungry—Marind and amai today, tomorrow, and many more generations to come. And so, I wonder—what kinds of ancestors will Marind men and women become?"

The culpability and complicity of Marind men in this vicious cycle as those whose minds, in Adriana's words, "are eaten by the government and companies" and who "sell off our land and become hungry ghosts in the plantations," uncover how the violence of ecological harms and social breakdown on the Papuan plantation frontier operates alongside the concomitant violence of moral injury that is inflicted on male villagers whose enlistment and participation in plantation labor are deemed necessary for survival but that also fundamentally transgress collective moral beliefs, values, and ethics.[21] The intergenerational dimensions of this moral injury surface particularly in Adriana's question over the "kind of ancestors" both Marind men and women will become—what they owe to their existing predecessors and successors, and to themselves *as* future predecessors in the eyes and for the skin of those to come.[22] As my companion intimates, the temporal effects of being eaten by roads, cities, and government and corporate actors are not only immediate, individual, or bounded in space and time but also latent, dispersed, cumulative, and irreversible. They materialize gradually over multiple geographic, social, metabolic, and temporal scales, undermining relationships among Marind men, women, clans, and villages and jeopardizing in turn the futures of their diverse forest kin. Eventually, the hungers of predatory foreign others transform the eaten themselves into agents of a generalized destruction that ripples across space, species, and generations.

4

MAKING SENSE
OF HUNGER

I first met Veronika and Matthias in the summer of 2015, when based in the village of Mirav for an initial fieldwork period of three consecutive months. Members of the Kaize (cassowary) and Gebze (banana) clans, respectively, both in their mid-thirties, and married since the age of sixteen, the pair had tried to conceive for many years. Veronika had suffered three miscarriages in the prior eighteen months—a fact she confided in me following a visit to the local clinic together to obtain medication for her chronic anemia. She believed she was unable to bring a child into the world because the absence of forest foods had dried out her womb. Veronika's husband, Matthias, meanwhile, attributed the couple's difficulty in bearing offspring to the burdens (*beban*) both of them suffered as active members of the local land rights movement: the stress of losing their lands to oil palm; the frustration of not being heard and heeded by corporations; and the sadness of seeing their forests dying, one after the other, like their babies. Two months into my stay in Mirav, good fortune struck when Veronika became pregnant and managed to bear a baby boy to term. The couple named them Oskar, after Matthias's grandfather.[1]

Until the age of four, Oskar suffered intermittently from bouts of diarrhea and a weakness of the limbs that manifested in a limp body and a tendency to sleep for worryingly long hours. During subsequent visits to the field, I noticed in the child's outward-bending legs the symptoms of the early onset of rickets, a softening and weakening of bones caused by prolonged vitamin D deficiency and a consequent inability to absorb calcium and phosphorus. Over the spring of 2019, when I was once again based in Mirav for a six-month stint, Oskar's condition deteriorated severely. They lost weight rapidly, and their skin became gray and loose. They no longer cried or whimpered but rather lay in bed in a state of glazed, semitorpor. The child had almost entirely lost their appetite. Veronika attempted to breastfeed Oskar, but it had been months since she had any milk to give. The baby in her arms, she told me, weighed less than a cassowary feather.

Eventually, Veronika and Matthias borrowed money from relatives, supplemented with some funds I offered up, to travel with their child to Timase township and seek medical aid. At the clinic we visited together, Oskar was seen by a young nurse who weighed them, took their pulse, and measured their wrists, torso, ankles, and head. At just over ten kilograms, Oskar was severely underweight for their age. The nurse put Oskar on a glucose drip and filled out a prescription for biofortified milk powder that would last about a month. "More vegetables, more fish," she said. "More red meat, too. Less sago. Sago is low in vitamins and proteins. It's an empty food [*makanan kosong*]."

We returned to Mirav that same afternoon. Later in the evening, I sat with Veronika and Matthias on the front porch of their hut and helped mix the milk powder with boiled water while Veronika massaged Oskar's belly, reciting Marind spells to heal their weak body (see figure 4.1). My companion began to cry silently. She said it was her family's fault, and not her own or Matthias's, that Oskar was sick. Her father had recently sold half their clan's land to an oil palm company, and all the forest on it had been cleared. The ancestral spirits (dema) were angered by this and had punished the clan by inflicting hunger and sickness on her child.

Matthias, who had been adding up the amounts of the various medical bill receipts beside us, hushed his wife and said things weren't that simple—that she did not understand. Veronika remained silent until Matthias left the room to gather firewood for the dying hearth. Then, she leaned toward me and said: "He thinks I don't understand—of course I understand. I understand that there are all kinds of explanations for why hunger is spreading across our lands. There is the anger of our dema. There is the greed of a world that wants to stay blind to our suffering. There is colonization

Figure 4.1. Veronika, a Marind woman, 2019. Photograph by the author.

and genocide. There are people who think hunger is progress, and there are people who think hunger is sacrifice. Everyone knows what hunger feels and looks like—but no one agrees on why it exists and why it won't go away."

This chapter examines how Marind women understand and critique hunger's origins and causes. In attending to hunger's contested etiologies, the chapter complements and contextualizes Marind's understandings of hunger as a condition that transforms according to its relative subjects and objects, within a more-than-human world wherein "every eaten is also an eater."[2] What emerges from this chapter is that the "what" of hunger is just as important to my female companions as its "why." This "why," as I demonstrate in what follows, is not only dispersed across different actors and forces but also intensely debated among Marind women themselves.

Over the course of my fieldwork in the Upper Bian, deliberations surrounding the causes of hunger's intensification and multiplication arose across a range of settings and interactions—during women's foraging expeditions with kin in the forest, over shared meals with extended female relatives in the settlements, or as part of organized women's discussion groups at village-wide or intervillage levels. Other debates were initiated by women while we queued to receive welfare food packages from local oil palm corporations, waited for consultations at the township hospital, or purchased plastic foods from the local village kiosk. Not surprisingly, deliberations surrounding hunger's etiology intensified markedly when illness and death afflicted the communities—for instance, when malnourished infants met an untimely end, when young women collapsed from exhaustion during sago-processing activities, or when parents like Veronika and Matthias were forced to seek medical help for their ailing children.

Disagreements among women in the field around hunger's causes were also compounded with, and often prompted by, arguments surrounding individuals' food choices, decisions, and preferences—for sago, plastic food, or money—as these arose in the course of everyday life. As they engaged collectively in the epistemic labor of making sense of hunger, my friends often shifted from one explanatory mode to another and back—at times perceiving them as mutually exclusive, at others complementary, their own everyday food decisions not always aligned with the etiologies they alternately eschewed or endorsed.

What became apparent through these many moments and musings was that hunger's etiologies were neither static, singular, nor subject to individual or collective consensus. Much like the meanings of hunger vary depending on who is perceived as being fed, feeding, or famished, so too hunger's drivers encompass an array of subjects, whose effects multiply across equally different if interconnected sites and scales. The morally inflected and gendered gastropolitical frictions I draw on in this chapter thus speak to the creative and critical ways in which Marind women theorize the plural condition and causality of hunger within diverse and overlapping "geographies of blame."[3] At the same time, these frictions also highlight a lack of concurrence and an excess of hesitation among women over hunger's moral and metaphoric meanings, distribution, and protagonists—one that in some ways exacerbates, rather than alleviates, the ecocosmological ruptures and biosocial breakdowns associated with the experience of hunger itself. These contested etiologies of hunger render manifest the various and vying epistemological frameworks through which women attempt to explain hunger's haunting and non-innocent presence, all within a broader crisis of signification in which the question of whom hunger harms is indissociable from the question of whom hunger benefits.

The chapter begins by considering the attribution of hunger by some women to the retributive actions of ancestral spirits (dema) who created the Marind lifeworld at the beginning of time, and whose punitive measures are prompted by local men's failure to protect and preserve forests and forest foodways from the deleterious impacts of agribusiness expansion on present and future generations. I then examine how hunger is understood by women as a consequence of top-down Indonesian national food security policies and projects, discriminatory or tokenistic national and regional laws, the apathy and indifference of foreign nation-states and transnational organizations to Papuans' suffering under Indonesian occupation, and the global consumer communities that become indirectly and unwittingly complicit in plantation violence through their everyday food choices and purchases. Finally, I consider how the idiomatization of hunger as a form of willing martyrdom, tied to the promise of future salvation within the religiously inflected discourses of some women, sits awkwardly alongside its interpretation by other women as an expression of progress and modernity, as an invitation to cultivate other kinds of appetites in a changing world, and as a precondition for the operations of capitalism itself as a system premised on the predatory consumption of certain places and peoples to the advantage of others.

Moral Failure and Ancestral Punishment

Veronika was one among many of my female companions to interpret hunger as a punishment meted out on Marind by ancestral dema. As she explained to me over a meal of stewed sago while we camped in a bamboo grove near her clan's ancestral birthing ground, dema are the creators of Marind clans and their respective plant, animal, and elemental kin (amai). Their undertakings are described in a vast and esoteric body of intergenerationally transmitted stories and lore that Marind consider to be sacred (sakral) and whose intricate details are generally known only to Marind men. Dema, Veronika continued, are venerated by Marind for their life-sustaining potencies at the same time as they are feared for their destructive dispositions and punitive capacities. These spirits can reward Marind for their good deeds in the form of good fortune, longevity, and fertility.

But they can also punish community members if they fail to demonstrate due respect and reverence toward dema or toward the life-forms and land-scapes that dema brought forth. Such measures can take the form of dramatic climactic events such as extreme droughts, rains, or floods, as well as protracted hunger, illness, injury, and even death.

In the precolonial period, medicine men and medicine women (mes-sav anim) were able to temper or appease wrathful dema through the performance of elaborate pacification rituals, spells, and incantations. Harmonious relations with dema were also maintained through a range of other collective practices, including inter- and intraclan rainmaking rites, mythical reenactments of dema feats, and, in particular, great feasts (angai).[4] As the Dutch anthropologist Jan van Baal documents, and my conversations with Marind corroborated, angai involved different groups of individuals, including nuclear families, clans, and moieties, and served to bind social groups together through the cooperation of labor, the pooling of material resources, and the satiation of collective hungers via the consumption of valued forest foods that were communally procured, prepared, and shared.[5]

While Dutch rule and missionization in the early twentieth century led to the abolishment of angai, together with related ritualized practices such as headhunting raids, fertility cults, and ancestor worship, dema continued to live on in the realm of the forest and exert their influence on Marind and their plant and animal kin. Over the last decade, however, the moral and material relations between dema and Marind have been radically reconfig-ured by the arrival of oil palm—a cash crop that was introduced by a foreign government and foreign corporations; that does not partake in the kinships binding Marind to ancestral spirits and kindred organisms; and that is often described by Marind as a hungry and rapacious being consuming native forests, lands, and waters through its relentless proliferation.[6]

As described earlier, villagers are increasingly split between those who continue to staunchly oppose oil palm projects and protect the forest through grassroots campaigns and advocacy, and those now collaborating with the agro-industry in the hope of achieving material gain, education, and employment. Ancestrally ordained solidarities between clans and phratries are giving way to factions and frictions, weakening Marind's collective ca-pacity to curb the proliferation of industrial monocrops. Relations of food, flesh, and fluid that once sustained inter- and intraclan bonds and their relations to the land and its life-forms are disrupted by conflict between those standing for or against agribusiness, and the many more individuals positioned somewhere in between. Echoing the cultural dynamics of food insecurity described by the Euro-Canadian anthropologist Michelle Mac-Carthy in the Trobriand Islands, plantation-driven changes in the Upper Bian thus threaten local food security at the same time as they rupture the very fabric of Marind social orders, gendered identities, and ecological relations, in a cumulative process that many of my companions idiomatize through the language of hunger.[7] Recall here the words of Costanza: "The clans eat each other up."

The unending and intensifying forms of hunger afflicting Marind are understood by some women as the purposeful intervention of <u>dema</u> who punish Marind communities for their own failure to protect and preserve the forest from destruction.[8] This failure is attributed in particular to Marind men as the primary decision-makers when it comes to land management, use, and sale. As intimated by Mirabela and Costanza, whom I quoted earlier, men who endorse the oil palm sector by surrendering their lands to agribusiness companies violate the material, affective, and cosmic "mutuality of being" that binds humans, plants, animals, and spirits within the sentient ecology of the forest.[9] They spend extended periods in Merauke City, working office jobs and hungering after plastic foods. They forget the sounds of the forest, the voices of its birds, and the stories of its ancestral creators. Lured by the promise of material wealth, these individuals neglect the consequences of their decisions and choices for the fate and future of the forest and its diverse inhabitants. Marind men who side with capitalism thus subject themselves and others to the violence of ancestral retribution in the form of hunger. In doing so, they exacerbate the profound ecosocietal breakdown of land, species, people, and spirits wrought by agro-industrial developments.[10]

And yet Marind women's interpretation of hunger as an ancestral punishment for wrongs attributable to male villagers was complicated by what many of my companions identified as a troubling conundrum faced by men themselves. Part of this conundrum already surfaced in the previous chapter, which examined how men's agency and responsibility for land surrenders are muddied by the pernicious forms of mind control exerted over them by corporate and government representatives as foreign sorcerers, in the alien environment of faraway cities. Another dimension of this conundrum was expressed by Perpetua, an elderly widow from Bayau village, by way of a song composed together with her sisters and daughters of the Kavzum (eel) clan during a fishing expedition on the banks of the Bian River (see figure 4.2). Having fastened the hooks to the lines and preparing herself to cast them into the waters, Perpetua pointed out to me the greasy sheen of the river's mottled surface, which she attributed to the toxic waste and discharges released daily from

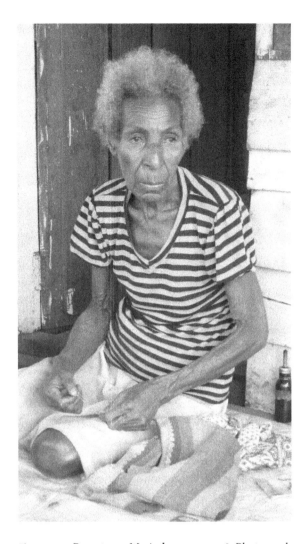

Figure 4.2. Perpetua, a Marind woman, 2018. Photograph by the author.

a nearby palm oil–processing plant. Rocking the boat gently with her arms to attract the fish below, my companion began to sing the following refrain:

> *Ceritanya ikan berada dalam darah kita*
> In our blood, we carry the story of a fish
> *Yaitu ceritanya <u>kavzum</u>*
> The story of the riverine eel

Belut de makan dari lumpur dan berlahir dalam rawa
That feeds in the mud and is birthed by the swamp
Dulu, kitorang Marind semua hidup macam ikan
In the past, all Marind lived like fish

Perpetua cast the nets into the water, and her daughter Virginia picked up the song where her mother had stopped:

Berenang bersama di sungai Bian
Swimming together down the waters of the Bian
Jauh, jauh, jauh dalam sungai sungai Bian
Deep, deep, deep down the waters of the Bian

Tapi sekarang, kitorang Marind macam ikan dalam sungai
But now, Marind are like fish caught in a river
Sungai yang mengalir ke hulu ke hilir bersama-sama
A river that flows upstream and downstream at the same time

<u>Dema</u> *menghukum kitorang ketika hutan dihancurkan*
The ancestral spirits punish us when the forest is destroyed
Pace-pace, de bersalah, de kasih dorang tanah
Because the men have committed wrongs, the men have given
    away the land
Sementara itu, perusahaan de pake suanggi makan pace-pace pu
    pikiran
Meanwhile, corporations eat our men's minds with *suanggi*
Bikin pace menyerah kitorang pu tanah
They make men relinquish our lands
Menyerah pada dorang yang makan kitorang pu hutan, kitorang
    pu masa depan
To those who eat up our forests and futures

Enters here the voice of Perpetua's sister, Alexandrina, who had been sitting beside us and fashioning sago fiber sacks to collect the harvested fish:

Apapun yang pace-pace coba, de tidak bisa bergerak, tidak bisa
    pilih yang benar
No matter how hard they try, the men cannot move, or do the
    right thing
De tidak bisa maju, dan tidak bisa mundur

They cannot go forward or backward
De didorong ke satu arah, terus didorong ke arah lain
They are pushed one way and then the other

Finally, again, Perpetua, singing and swaying, casting lines and repeating:

Lagi dan lagi dan sekali lagi lagi, pace-pace de bersalah
Over and over and over again, the men are in the wrong
Lagi dan lagi dan sekali lagi lagi, pace-pace de juga terjebak
Over and over and over again, the men are also stuck

In comparing her male counterparts to aquatic creatures jolted to and fro by opposed river currents, Perpetua and her female relatives' song conjured the paralyzing double bind that Marind men face in the context of ancestral spirits who demand that Marind protect the forest, on the one hand, and agribusiness operators who impose monocrop projects without local consultation or consent, on the other. These projects are often presented to communities as a fait accompli and a necessary measure in achieving national food security, regional economic development, and poverty alleviation. Local communities have little capacity to determine where and whether these projects are implemented, how, and to what effect. Importantly, their capacity to resist agribusiness expansion is undermined by the supernatural powers wielded by corporations themselves as perpetrators of *suanggi*—powers that, as noted in the previous chapter, vastly transcend those of Marind's own former native sorcerers and also operate in unfathomable ways.

Exemplifying what the British anthropologist Gregory Bateson terms a "schizophrenogenic" environment, Marind men are thus caught between the mutually opposed injunctions of ancestral spirits, on the one hand, and corporate sorcerers, on the other.[11] Men cannot satisfy one party without facing the threat of violence from the other. Instead, they are confronted with the irreconcilable demands of two conflicting "regimes of violence"—both of which, ultimately, result in intensifying and proliferating hunger for both them and their kin.[12] This state of affairs brings many women like Perpetua and her female kin to hesitate in placing the primary blame for hunger on the actions and intentions of their male counterparts alone.

The double bind faced by Marind men has further implications for the agency of Marind women themselves. Specifically, it conjures women's own sense of being "stuck" (*terjebak*), in Perpetua's terms, between the demands of custom that require women to abide by the decisions of male relatives, and the urgency of challenging these patriarchal norms in the face of radical and rapidly unfolding socioenvironmental changes.[13] Other companions in the field, meanwhile, identified another, far more disconcerting, asymmetry in power at play—that operating between ancestral spirits and corporate entities as wielders of different forms of supernatural authority. As Perpetua's sister, Alexandrina, reflected following the utterance of her song:

> Since time immemorial, <u>dema</u> controlled the world and the beings within it. They punished our wrongs by inflicting us with hunger. If <u>dema</u> were angry, the <u>messav anim</u> [medicine men] would perform rituals to pacify them. But now, there are no more <u>messav anim</u> in our communities. Instead, corporations control the world and inflict us with hunger. <u>Dema</u> might be powerful—but even they cannot do anything to stop oil palm. What does this mean? Have <u>dema</u> lost their power? Are <u>dema</u> working with the corporations? Are corporations the new <u>dema</u>? No one knows for sure.

On the one hand, then, ancestral spirits affirm their power by imposing punitive hungers on Marind who contravene tradition and custom. But for all their omnipotence, these same ancestral spirits appear incapable of preventing industrial oil palm plantations from proliferating and foreign corporations from profiteering. This scenario in turn suggests a disempowerment—or worse, co-optation—of <u>dema</u> *themselves* by corporate actors within an emerging social order in which, as Alexandrina put it, foreign entities now govern in powerful yet inscrutable ways the ecological, social, and supernatural terrains of the Marind lifeworld.

In the face of these transformations, Marind men's degree of agency and complicity in the production of hungers, too, comes into question. As Perpetua reflected:

> The men are the ones making all the decisions about the land. That's why we accuse them of causing our hunger. But maybe the men's hands are tied too. Maybe their power is nothing compared to that of corporations and of <u>dema</u>. The men are responsible. But they are also vulnerable. We Marind women blame the men. But if we were the men and if we had the power to make decisions, then would we decide differently? Would we act any different? This, we cannot know because we do not hold that power. This is why the cause of hunger remains *abu-abu* [uncertain].

While some women interpret hunger as an ancestral punishment meted out by <u>dema</u> and prompted by local men's moral failures, others identify the etiology of hunger in the demands and dynamics of entities that lie well beyond, yet directly impinge on, the Marind lifeworld. Rather than blaming ancestors, corporate sorcerers, or male relatives, these women, who tend to be of a younger generation and have completed secondary education, located the root cause of hunger in the extractive violence of the nation (*bangsa*) and the world (*dunia*). Here again, the indomitable power of these forces is often seen to transcend the agency of Marind men and therefore absolve these men to some extent of their responsibility in the production and proliferation of hunger. One individual to maintain such a view was Cistina, a twenty-five-year-old mother of two, a member of the Samkakai (wallaby) clan, and a nurse in training from Bayau village, who explained, "Sure, our men make the decisions to surrender the land. But even our men are powerless in the face of the nation and the world—just like we are powerless as women in the face of the nation and the world. In this respect, Marind women and men are just the same."

In invoking the nation, individuals like Cistina speak to a prevalent figure within official Indonesian food sovereignty discourses, wherein the nation is imagined and anthropomorphized as a "hungry" being in need of feeding by the state.[14] In line with its historical and archipelago-wide usage, the figure of the nation has been central to the rhetoric surrounding contemporary oil palm developments in Merauke, which are promoted by the government as central to "feeding Indonesia and then the world."[15] This construct of the nation, however, is one that many Marind conceptualize as distinctly Indonesian rather than Papuan. It is one that they do not identify themselves as belonging to, or willingly participating in, and that they instead perceive themselves as being coerced and consumed by. The nation and its hungers in turn sit within a broader constellation of settler-colonial violence, buttressed by top-down legal, economic, ideological, and (geo)political infrastructures that position Papuan lands, environments, and bodies as victims (*korban*) of ongoing exploitation, vulnerability, and abuse. The hunger of the government takes on distinctive political hues in light of West Papua's forceful incorporation into the Indonesian nation in 1969—a form of control through symbolic ingestion that my companions often invoke in describing their country as "being eaten by the state." In the words of Cesarina, a young mother of three and a midwife from Khalaoyam village, "When Indonesia took over Papua, they forced us into a nation that is not ours. They ate up our futures, our autonomy, and our freedom."

For women, including Cistina and Cesarina, the notion of the nation as a rapaciously hungry entity is also indissociable from the predatory logic of the laws (*hukum*) governing land and natural resources in West Papua, and which have been instrumental to the naturalization of Indigenous Papuans' territorial dispossession, economic marginalization, and political disempowerment under settler-colonial rule. These laws undermine Papuans' access and rights to land, which in turn bears direct implications for their ability to sustain forest foodways and themselves become good food for their other-than-human kin.

Among the many regulations that my companions described as "eating up" Papuans' freedoms is Otsus (*otonomi khusus*), a special autonomy law passed by the Indonesian government in 2001 to enhance the decision-making capacities, development opportunities, and economic benefits accrued by Papuan people. The implementation of this regional law, however, was radically weakened under the rule of Megawati Sukarnoputri, when political and economic power reverted into the hands of the central government in Jakarta. Since its promulgation, Otsus has continuously failed to deliver its anticipated outcomes for local communities or enhance their voices on the political stage, whether in the context of grassroots food sovereignty movements or the context of achieving inclusive decision-making processes in relation to land use, management, and ownership. The disappointment and deception associated with the once-promissory law of Otsus was captured by Cesarina's younger sister Paolina, a women's community organizer with whom I had previously collaborated closely in land rights advocacy cases, who affirmed that "Otsus was created to make Papuans feel special [*khusus*]. But, in reality, Otsus is just a toy in the hands of the politicians. It masks hunger and poverty with the language of rights and autonomy. It conceals the fact that Papuans are victims [*korban*] of the violence of the law. This is why we don't want Otsus."[16]

Other women, meanwhile, identified the structural causes of hunger at the level of national laws, which invariably take precedence over local and provincial decision-making processes, legitimate agribusiness, and other land-based developments in the name of national interest, and thereby undermine the capacity of local communities to assert their rights to land, food, and livelihoods. Legal instruments cited by these women included Regulation No. 40 of 1996 on Business Use Permits, which extinguishes customary land rights and gives the state the authority to determine the legal status and ownership of territories following their cessation to corporations. They also included Regulation of the Ministry of Agriculture No. 26 on Guidance on Plantation Business Permits, which controversially raises the maximum landholding per company in West Papua to two hundred thousand hectares (or twice the maximum concession size in all other parts of Indonesia) in light of the perceived availability of "idle lands" (*tanah terlantar*) awaiting economic exploitation across the region.

Many among my companions were also critical of the Indonesian Constitution, which recognizes and respects the traditional rights of Indigenous Peoples (*masyarakat hukum adat*, or customary law communities in Indonesian) but only so long as these rights and traditions are continually practiced and align with the social development prerogatives and principles of the Republic of Indonesia. A similar logic undergirds Indonesia's Basic Agrarian Law of 1960, which recognizes customary law pertinent to land, water, and air space only so long as it is not contrary to national interest and state law. Both instruments exemplify what the American anthropologist Elizabeth Povinelli describes in the Aboriginal Australian context as "the cunning of recognition," or state-sanctioned institutional processes that purport to encourage multiculturalism and diversity but that ultimately perpetuate unequal systems of power by demanding that Indigenous Peoples identify with an impossible standard of "authentic" traditional culture.[17] In each instance, legal instruments undermine the right of Indigenous Papuans to self-determination under international human rights frameworks, as national interests and imperatives trump customary rights and responsibilities.

But it is not only regional and national forces that drive hunger in Merauke today. Many women also blame the international community for turning a blind eye or remaining apathetic to the plight of West Papuans who have been forcefully incorporated into a nation to which they do not, and have never, belonged. For Vicentia, a twenty-eight-year-old member of the Samkakai clan who had recently completed higher education in Merauke City, the roots of this "betrayal" (*pengkhianatan*) and "abandonment" (*pengabaian*) can be traced back to the year 1969, when the Indonesian administration handpicked 1,026 Papuan individuals and coerced them into voting for the region's formal incorporation into Indonesia through the Act of Free Choice (Penentuan Pendapat Rakyat [PEPERA]). West Papuans' dreams of self-determination had already been undermined prior to this controversial referendum, with Indonesian military forces having entered the territory en masse since the early 1960s, large-scale logging and plantation projects being initiated without communities' consent by national and foreign corporations, and the United States signing business deals with Indonesia in 1967, guaranteeing it the rights to mine gold and copper in Papua.[18]

Throughout this fateful period, Vicentia noted, the international community remained "mute" (*bisu*) and "deaf" (*tuli*) to the theft of Indigenous Papuans' territorial, cultural, and political sovereignty and to the growing realities of aggravated food insecurity and malnutrition resulting from the conversion of forest landscapes into privatized and extractive industrial zones whose products were always intended to serve external markets rather than support local subsistence. This international community, Vicentia stressed, included not only individual nation-states—notably those that bore historical and political connections to New Guinea as former colonizers and economic allies, such as Australia, Great Britain, and the Netherlands—but also the transgovernmental institution of the United Nations, a system that historically failed West Papuans by prioritizing the appeasement of Indonesia in the Cold War context above its commitment to supporting decolonization and human rights.[19]

Historical and ongoing forms of betrayal and abandonment on the part of the international community are also read by women in the deforestation unfurling across their customary lands and territories today and in the emergent oil palm ecologies that both manifest and make possible an unequal and racist system of food production, distribution, and consumption.[20] Oil palm developments across the region, as Vicentia and many others in her village noted during our conversations around hunger's causes, are driven by a growing global demand for palm oil as food and fuel, and by policies of renewable energy use instituted in the United States and Europe. Palm oil produced from Marind soils lands on the shelves of supermarkets across the globe. Yet those who purchase it are either oblivious or indifferent to the poverty, destruction, and hunger plaguing its sites and sources of production. The emergence of commodity certification systems, such as the Roundtable on Sustainable Palm Oil, that Vicentia and others had come to familiarize themselves with through our joint advocacy efforts in the preceding years, greenwashes palm oil-containing products with a veneer of "environmental sustainability" that belies the realities of Indigenous dispossession, displacement, and disempowerment. The violence of "environmental sustainability," my friends explained, manifests not only in the vast swaths of biodiverse forest that have been cleared to make way for monocrop oil palm around their villages but also in the form of adjacent conservation areas that have more recently been established by oil palm corporations to offset the adverse environmental impacts of their industrial activities.

Sofia, a young member of the Mahuze (dog) clan and a land rights activist from Khalaoyam village, described these conservation areas as "precious sanctuaries" (*tempat suci tempat berharga*) and "rare refuges" (*tempat harta tempat khas*) in the midst of Merauke's proliferating monocrop landscapes that could offer vital sources of food and other everyday forest resources to local inhabitants. Yet they are strictly out-of-bounds to all but company personnel, environmental scientists, and sustainability auditors. Conservation zones are identified and demarcated by "foreign experts" (*ahli asing*) who originate from outside Merauke and do not understand or value Marind's relationship to the forest as a kindred being and source of food.[21] Doubly excluded from natures both exploited and preserved, Marind can no longer hunt, fish, or forage in these remaining patches of forest. Sentient ecologies turned privatized conservation zones, too, suffer from the severance of transactive relationships with the humans who once tended and fed them through previously regular but now-prohibited activities such as the scattering of seeds, the widening of waterways, the selective burning of vegetation, and the seasonal trimming of bushes and trees. As Sofia put it, "The forest and its amai become lonely and sad because they no longer share skin and wetness with anim. They go hungry. We go hungry."

For many of my companions, the generalized disregard of their rights to land, food, and cultural continuance on the part of national and international communities and their mutually enforcing capitalist and conservationist interests was most blatantly epitomized in the disappointing outcomes of their repeated formal appeals for remedy and redress in 2011, 2012, and then again in 2013. In these years, Marind villagers in the Upper Bian submitted three consecutive complaints to the United Nations Committee on the Elimination of Racial Discrimination (UNCERD) under its urgent action and early warning procedures, which I supported them in drafting and that documented in exhaustive detail the negative impacts of agribusiness developments and exclusionary conservation paradigms on Marind's food and water security, as well as on their access to customary land and their economic livelihoods.[22] These impacts were again reiterated in a formal communiqué on the violation of Marind food sovereignty and environmental justice that was presented by Marind representatives to the UN Special Rapporteur on the right to food and the UN Special Rapporteur on the rights of Indigenous peoples in Kuala Lumpur, at the Asia Regional Consultation on the Situation of Indigenous Peoples in Asia in 2013.[23]

Figure 4.3. Marind land rights activists erect a placard reading "Customary Land," 2016. Government surveillance has intensified due to Marind advocacy campaigns. Photograph by Ariana Gebze.

At the time and to date, however, the Indonesian government has neither responded to concerns raised directly with it by UNCERD on the basis of the complaints, nor addressed the Special Rapporteurs' joint statement of 2012 regarding the potentially adverse effects of MIFEE on the food security of some fifty thousand people.[24] Meanwhile, government surveillance and reprisals have intensified in response to Marind's international campaigns and grassroots land-reclaiming efforts, including in the form of arbitrary interrogations, extrajudicial incarcerations, and systemic physical and psychological intimidation (see figure 4.3).[25] Justice and remedy have yet to be delivered to Marind communities on the ground.

It is the ongoing indifference of the world to the equally ongoing violence of Indonesian settler occupation in West Papua that brings many Marind to describe themselves as targets of a genocide—one in which the international community is nothing less than complicit.[26] Here, hunger, together with poverty, disease, and population dilution and displacement, is understood as part of a broader and gradual obliteration of West Papuan cultures and communities. At once structural, spectacular, slow, and synchronous, these multiple forms of violence coalesce in the notion of *memoria passionis*, or "passionate remembrance"—an expression often deployed by West Papuans to refer to their collective experiences of territorial theft, physical and psychological abuse, cultural and demographic minoritization, and denied demands for sovereignty and self-determination.[27]

Irrespective of whether they are deemed deliberate or incidental, targeted or arbitrary, and verifiable or speculatory, discourses of genocide among Marind often operate in mutually enforcing ways. They speak to sedimented histories of violence that produce a sentiment of shared victimization among Marind men and women alike in the face of national and global forces that lie beyond their control and that also jeopardize the kindred plants, animals, and ecosystems that Marind become-with. These discourses position hunger and its raft of adverse physical, psychological, and societal effects against longer histories of colonial and capitalist incursion. They constitute and communicate embodied claims about and critiques of the fraught relationship of Papuan peoples and places to the Indonesian state and global communities. They conjure the disposability of Papuan lives and landscapes subjected to the extractive gaze and gut of an ever-hungry nation and world. They undergird an etiology that positions Marind's own hungers as the result of others, literally and symbolically, eating in their place.

Hunger as Sacrifice: Christian Virtue or Capitalist Logic?

As described earlier, many women position themselves and their communities as victims (*korban*) to the extractive violence of the nation and the world, both historically and in the present. However, this explanatory framework is complicated by women's divergent understandings of the telos of victimhood itself. Divergent interpretations of hunger's purpose or end in turn have deep-seated and conflicting implications when it comes to the question of whether hunger is a condition that should be opposed and overcome, or one that should accepted and even embraced. For individuals like Vicentia, Paolina, and other villagers who are engaged in grassroots land rights advocacy, hunger is understood as an urgent prompt to challenge and dismantle the national, legal, and structural architectures that undermine the lives, freedoms, and futures of rural Papuans to the benefit of the nation and the global community, and also the patriarchal system that positions men as the primary decision-makers when it comes to land use and management. As Paolina stressed during women's community-building gatherings in Bayau village, "Hunger is something we must fight against together—as Marind, as Papuans, but also as women. If we surrender to it, then we surrender our rights and our futures to the government, to the world, and to our men. We give in to the colonizers and we give in to the hungry world. We accept that we are always going to be the victims—both in the eyes of the nation, of the world, and of our husbands and brothers."

For women like Paolina, then, the struggle for food justice is also a struggle for Indigenous sovereignty in the face of unjust power dynamics that operate at both global and local levels, and in both political and gendered forms. Other women, however, affirm that hunger should be approached less as a symptom of West Papuans' and West Papuan women's status as "victims" and instead as a form of willing "self-sacrifice" (*pengorbanan diri*). Bendita, a young catechism instructor from Bayau, elucidated this nuanced yet important distinction to me as follows:

> If we see ourselves as victims, then we have two choices—either fight against hunger or accept it against our will. But if we think about hunger as a kind of self-sacrifice, then the suffering and pain of hunger have a reason—a point [*pu makna, pu maksud*]. It turns hunger into something useful [*berguna*]—for the greater good of the present and for our own salvation [*keselamatan*] in the future. This gives our suffering meaning [*arti*] and value [*nilai*]. Even if we cannot put an end to it, at least we can give hunger our own meanings and our own explanations. And maybe that counts as a form of empowerment [*pemberdayaan*].

The logos of suffering and its horizons of salvation in a future-to-come invoked by Bendita and other villagers is in part influenced by notions of martyrdom and sacrifice that have been instilled into Marind as adherents to the Catholic creed since the Dutch colonial period. Even as the church and its humanitarian branches were at the time of writing actively involved in supporting Marind seek remedy and redress for the theft of their lands and the violation of their right to food, local priests often described the prevalence of hunger during their sermons as a test of villagers' faith, a reminder of the importance of prayer and belief in overcoming pain and suffering, and a condition not to be explained or rationalized but rather accepted and endured. These discourses brought many community members to compare their plight to that of Jesus Christ, who willingly embraced crucifixion for the salvation of humankind. One of them was Selena, a middle-aged woman from Khalaoyam village and a regular churchgoer, who, like Bendita, worked

Figure 4.4. Two Marind women, Bendita (*center*) and Selena (*right*), with their younger relatives, 2016. Photograph by the author.

as a volunteer at the local women's catechism center (see figure 4.4). As we walked back from mass one Sunday morning, Selena shared her understanding of hunger's causes as follows:

> Hunger is a form of suffering that breaks our communities apart. But hunger also brings us closer to God across the Christian land of Papua [*tanah* Kristen Papua]—when we hunger together and pray together, we keep faith in a better future with each other and with our Christian brother and sisters across Melanesia, who also pray for us in their own lands and in their own forests. When we are hungry, we also remember the suffering of Jesus Christ, who died to save humanity. In this sense, hunger is not a punishment from <u>dema</u> arising from our wrongs. Rather, it is a test [*ujian*] of our faith and a blessing [*berkat*]. Embracing hunger brings us closer to the Lord and his Son. As the chosen people [*umat terpilih*], Papuans cannot and must not escape from suffering. If we suffer today, we will enter heaven tomorrow. If we feel the burden of hunger today, we will be blessed with abundance [*kemawahan*] tomorrow—food, forests, fortune, we will have it all and forever.

In invoking hunger as a blessing, pregnant with the promise of salvation and abundance, Selena's words point to a prevalent syncretism of Christian and millenarian epistemologies in the discursive frameworks deployed by

West Papuans to portray and explain their conditions of life under settler-colonial rule and their future-oriented identity-building projects as a Melanesian—rather than Indonesian—people and nation.[28] As Selena suggests, sustained prayer and belief in times of turmoil serve to reinstate and reaffirm Marind's connections to their Christian brothers and sisters across Melanesia, with whom Marind share creed, culture, and color. In situating themselves firmly within a Melanesian community of faith, Marind also distinguish themselves spiritually, territorially, and politically from the Indonesian state and its primarily Muslim population—a religiopolitical move that is all the more significant given West Papua's growing non-Papuan, Muslim settler community and the ongoing projects of Islamization taking place across the region.[29]

The "burden of hunger" inflicted on Marind and described here by Selena accrues heightened symbolic and moral potency in light of West Papuans' prevalent self-characterization as the "chosen people" (*umat terpilih* or *orang-orang terpilih*) and of West Papua itself as a "Christian land" (*tanah Kristen*), whose shared suffering and abuse under colonial rule are seen to be sanctioned by God as a pathway to spiritual emancipation and liberation. Such characterizations resonate with comparable ascriptions of holiness (*suci*) to West Papuan peoples and places in other parts of the region, including in the form of nationalistically inflected analogies between Papua and Israel and the identification of ancestral kinships with members of the Lost Tribes of Israel.[30] The promise of future salvation and abundance accompanying lived experiences of hunger also resonates with millenarian beliefs documented across New Guinea more broadly, wherein suffering and loss in the present herald radical societal and cosmological transformations on future horizons, including in the form of material wealth and prosperity.[31]

Hunger from this perspective comes to constitute a necessary rite of passage from the precarity of the present into the abundance of an imagined future, wherein Marind will never again lack in food, forests, or fortune. This promissory reframing of suffering in turn allows for hunger itself to be reframed from an ancestral punishment for Marind's own moral failures to a God-mandated opportunity to demonstrate and sustain Marind's moral resilience and spiritual beliefs in the face of adversity, in what might be described as an emergent form of gastroreligiosity. While the former etiology identifies human actions in the past as deterministic of ancestral retribution in the present, the latter etiology repositions human suffering and sacrifice in the present as a source of collective salvation and satiation in a redemptive, hopeful future.

But there is another side to the etiology of hunger as self-sacrifice than its religious and millenarian dimensions. Ana, whose hunger song marked the opening of this book, was one of many women who disagreed vehemently with the notion of hunger as a spiritually mandated condition of being and who understood it instead as an integral dimension of another, far more pervasive and global kind of force—capitalism (*kapitalisme*). Ana expressed this view to me one afternoon as we returned to the village after gathering tubers in the forest. During a momentary pause in the village square to breastfeed her daughter Circia, my companion brought up Selena's comment from the prior day, which she had overheard while walking behind us on the way home from mass. She asked me what I thought of Selena's explanation. I replied that it was not much different than the explanations I had heard from the local priest and several other village women, whose names I proceeded to list. Ana interrupted me, tutting loudly and gesticulating with annoyance, such that little Circia lost hold of her teat and started to whimper. My companion drew the child close to her chest and sighed, saying: "It's not about God or salvation or prayer. The truth is, we live in a world where not everyone gets to eat, or eat well. This is not particular or unique to Marind, or Papuans, or Melanesians. This is simply the way capitalism works—here, there, everywhere. Some people must go hungry in order for others to be fed."

On the one hand, Ana's statement might be understood as an internalization and reproduction of state and corporate rhetoric in West Papua, wherein oil palm and other large-scale land-based developments are endorsed and encouraged in the name of feeding the nation and feeding the world—even if it comes at the cost of the food security and well-being of those peoples whose lands foods are produced on and from. On the other hand, this statement can also be read as expressive of an acute awareness on the part of my companion of the sinister machinations of neoliberal capitalist logic itself—a logic that operates through the consumption of the bodies and futures of some groups by the hunger for profit of others.[32] As an Indigenous realpolitik, the statement communicates a recognition of Marind's own positioning within asymmetrical distributions of power, wealth, and resources that are not purely unfortunate side effects of the capitalist world system but rather that fundamentally undergird and sustain this system.

The sacrificial logic of capitalist modernity differs from the religious and millenarian epistemologies described previously. Whereas the latter are grounded in the promise of future redemption, freedom, and salvation for those sacrificed in the present, the former dictates that certain populations must *remain* in a state and slot of oppression and deprivation so that other populations can be nourished and thrive. In the unequal relations binding consumer and consumed under capitalist regimes, the hunger suffered by one party is the necessary precondition for achieving the other's satiety. Hunger, then, can be understood as a stance of selfless altruism (a willing giving up of one's needs to satisfy the other) *and* as an integral trait of capitalism itself—a force itself characterized by a relentless and unevenly portioned appetite for property, profit, and power whose continuance, as Ana put it, relies on some people going hungry in order for others to be fed. Under this logic, hunger is not just a consequence of the failure of the modern capitalist food system. It is a defining feature of capitalism's own ontology—and a symptom of its success.

Marind women's efforts to explain hunger through the divergent idioms of ancestral retribution, national and global forces, or ambiguously embraced self-sacrifice exemplify the multiple, fragmentary, and even contradictory ways in which disease and suffering are emically experienced and expressed. Such etiologies stem from diverse and overlapping arenas of life, including disease, human culpability, environmental crises, and supernatural factors, that are in turn contextually foregrounded or backgrounded by different actors, in different settings, and to different ends. As my companions often noted, discussing these etiologies with each other did not in itself remedy the suffering and pain inflicted on those vulnerable to hunger's deleterious effects. Nor were they subject to internal or gendered consensus. And yet, these emic explanatory models retain profound significance in the way they allow women to sense and make sense of hunger through their own culturally shaped and gender-inflected frameworks of meaning.

As the Australian anthropologist Jenny Munro argues in the context of alcohol consumption among West Papuan men, acknowledging and engaging with emic conceptualizations of culpability and vulnerability can bring to the surface tensions or contradictions between the blames attributed by external actors to sufferers on the basis of racial and cultural prejudices, on the one hand, and the complicity that sufferers place on themselves for the harms they experience and reproduce, on the other.[33] Attending to the creative and (self-)critical ways in which Marind women reckon with the "why" of hunger thus invites a reconsideration of meaning-making as an expression of subaltern and gendered agency—one that muddies straightforward distinctions between perpetrator and victim. Explanatory frameworks that locate the causes of hunger in geopolitical asymmetries and complicities, or that identify hunger as an unavoidable consequence and defining attribute of capitalist logic, might be relatively easy to comprehend. On the other hand, etiologies that are anchored in notions of self-blame, including those articulated by Marind women wherein responsibility for the suffering of hunger is attributed to the actions of Marind men, trouble seemingly facile classifications of the culpable and vulnerable across putatively distinct local and global scales. And yet to excise such explanations as mere expressions of false consciousness or as passive reproductions of hegemonic discourse belies their significance as expressions of epistemic sovereignty and empowering acts of protest, resistance, and testimony, that operate at once as political statements, gendered critiques, and critical self-evaluations.[34]

In Marind etiologies of hunger, culpability multiplies across diffuse scales and subjects in ways that resist reduction to any one particular entity or force. Within these messy meshworks of blame, Marind's victimization under the corrosive effects of geopolitical dynamics sits awkwardly alongside their gender-inflected self-responsibilization as targets of legitimate, if irremediable, punitive retribution on the part of ancestral spirits. Attributions of blame are further complicated by the ambivalent acceptance or embrace of hunger among those who understand it as an expression of divine mandate and a test of spiritual fortitude, or as the inescapable logos of the capitalist system itself. In each instance, Marind discourses point to hunger as a non-innocent relation between differentially situated and complicit entities and forces, whose ability to feed and to be fed is unevenly distributed yet always interconnected. This non-innocence applies as much to the dominant human and institutional processes provoking food insecurity on out-of-the-way resource frontiers as it does to the people who inhabit the shadow places of agro-industrial capitalism and whose theories of hunger, to return to Bendita's words, come to constitute a form of subaltern, epistemic empowerment, forged under otherwise profoundly disempowering conditions of life.

5

WRITING HUNGER

In late May 2018, I was invited to share a meal with the family of Barnabus, an elder of the Ndiken (white stork) clan and a resident of Khalaoyam village. A group of women prepared the food in the outdoor kitchen while Barnabus and I sat on the porch finalizing a statement on Marind food sovereignty for presentation at a government consultation in Merauke City the following week. The centerpiece of the meal, I was told, was a cut of deer, hunted by Barnabus's brothers. With forests rapidly giving way to plantations, game around Khalaoyam had become increasingly scarce. Several children in the village had never tasted it, and Barnabus himself had not eaten it for weeks. Meat, he told me, was a special treat, served only to the most honored guests. This portion had been saved especially for me.

When Nora, Barnabus's wife, began to grill the meat, a sickly sweet smell assailed my nostrils. Worried about the unpleasant odor, the women decided to boil the meat instead, but this only made things worse. The gelatinous chunks began to break apart, the broth turned milky, and the pungent steam rising from the pot stung our eyes. The meat, I realized, had been kept for too long and was thoroughly rotten. Eventually, we sat down to eat on the front porch. Holding my breath, I swallowed the viscous pieces of gray, putrid flesh placed before me, trying not to gag or wince lest I offend my hosts, who ate only rice mixed with instant noodles. Nausea and cramping took over as my stomach began to roil with discomfort.

One by one, Nora and the other women in the group proceeded to walk out, their heads bent low. After I had eaten as much as my stomach could bear of the rotten meat gifted to me, I excused myself and almost immediately went to retch behind the hut, covering my mouth to stifle the sounds so as to avoid being discovered by my hosts. Nothing came out but bile and saliva. In the distance, I glimpsed through my watering eyes the women, sitting in a circle in a patch of nearby cleared forest. When I joined them, they told me they were weeping out of anger and shame. We sat together in silence for about an hour until dusk fell and dark clouds of approaching mosquitoes forced us to return home.

By then, the men had left. The women and I sat down in a side room, where the hut's single netted window offered us the relief of an occasional breeze. Nora came over, fanning herself with a large bamboo leaf, and squatted beside me. Out of the corner of my eye, I noticed a bundle in the otherwise empty room, out of which poked what appeared to be firewood sticks. The bundle twitched. I thought I heard a faint whimper. Nora returned my questioning gaze with hesitancy. Eventually, she walked over to the bundle and untied the surrounding faded cloth, revealing an emaciated child whose frail bones jutted out of an almost translucent skin. The child's eyes were expressionless, their face sallow, fontanel sunken. Their name, Nora told me, was Mina (see figure 5.1). They were born of Nora's elder sister, Catia, who had passed away from a postpartum hemorrhage two days after delivery. It was Mina's skeletal arms and legs that I had mistaken for firewood sticks.

Nora tried to breastfeed the baby, but the infant was too weak to hold their lips to Nora's flaccid breasts. The child, Nora predicted, would not last the night. The women and I watched over Mina until the break of dawn. Some of the women cried. Those who did not told me it was because they had no more wetness left to share and were too hungry to weep. Others said they could not cry because they were too angry—with the oil palm, with the government, and with their husbands and uncles who kept selling more land and more forest to the corporations. Nora did not speak. Instead, she sang to Mina the song Mina had once sung to her.

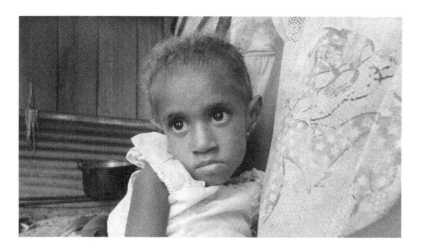

Figure 5.1. Mina, a young Marind child, 2018. Photograph by the author.

Walef, walef, *terpental dalam rumput, khei, khei, menggerutu*
   dalam hutan
Tree kangaroo, tree kangaroo, bouncing in the grass, cassowary,
   cassowary, grumbling in the forest
Mavu, mavu, *berenang dalam sungai,* dakh, dakh, *tumbuh dalam*
   rawa
Eel, eel, swimming in the river, sago, sago, growing in the swamp
Mama, mama, pangkur sagu dalam hutan, papa, papa, berburu
   dalam rawa
Mama, mama, pounding sago in the grove, papa, papa, hunting in
   the marsh
Adik, adik, memancing dalam sungai, adik, adik, bernyanyi di
   panggir sungai
Sibling, sibling, fishing in the stream, sibling, sibling, singing on
   the banks

Ketika tidak ada makanan, sa bermimpi sa makan sagu
When there is no food, I dream of eating sago
Kadang-kadang, sa pancing ikan, sa dapat buah-buah, sa makan
   nasi, sa makan supermie
Sometimes fish, sometimes fruit, sometimes rice, sometimes
   noodles
Dalam sa pu mimpi, mama bawa sagu, papa bawa daging

In my dreams, mama brings me sago, and papa brings me meat
Dalam sa pu mimpi, kelaparan terada, dalam sa pu mimpi, kelapa
sawit terada
In my dreams, there is no hunger, in my dreams, there is no oil palm

Hutan de tumbuh terus
The forest continues to grow

Tapi sa bangun lapar, lapar, lapar, selalu lapar
But then, I wake up hungry, hungry, hungry, always hungry
Suatu hari nanti, bilang mama sa akan jadi tinggi, jadi kuat
One day, mama tells me, I'll grow up tall and strong
Sa akan pigi kenal sagu, pigi dusun sagu
Then, I'll walk to find the sago, I'll walk to find the grove
Terus sa tidak lagi akan bermimpi, kelaparan de terada
Then, I will stop dreaming, then, there'll be no hunger
Yang adanya semuanya hutan, hutan yang tumbuh terus
There will only be the forest, the forest that continues to grow

When Mina drew their last breath, Nora stopped singing. After a tortuously long silence, she reached into my satchel, rummaged through its contents, and pulled out my pen and notebook. Nora handed them over to me and said, "Write it. Write it all. Write about our hunger, our sickness, and our pain. Tell these stories to the whole world. Tell them for the children, and the mothers, and the forest. Let not these deaths be in vain."[1] I was shocked that Nora would make such a request of me at this particular moment—even though it was an injunction I had heard many times before from my female companions. Pulling myself together, I reached out for the pen and notebook.

Almost immediately, Nora's mother, Paulina, pushed my hand aside and interjected: "Don't do that, sister. You must tell the stories of our lives, not our deaths. The deaths make us feel shame and guilt. They are the stories of the poor, the stories of the weak, the stories of the eaten. These are not the stories I want the world to know Marind through. Stories are treasures—some can be shared, but others cannot and should not. There is too much sorrow and too much anger."[2] "But she must, mama!" Nora interrupted. "She must tell all the stories. The anger is part of the story. The grief is part of the story. All of it—it is part of our story." Turning to me, Nora added, "We have fed you as best we can. Now, you tell the stories as best you can. This is your responsibility."[3]

A long silence followed. Paulina swatted a fly that had landed on Mina's body. The two women looked at me. I hesitatingly took the pen and notebook that had hovered in midair throughout the tense conversation. I began to write.

In this final chapter, I explore the ethical and epistemological stakes of representing the violence of hunger through the medium of writing. In doing so, I focus on a topic that was widely discussed and debated among Marind women, and that was revelatory of a profound disjuncture between those who saw in writing the promise of being known, heard, and heeded by local and global audiences; those who saw in writing the peril of divulging experiences associated with self-blame, shame, and gendered internal conflicts; and those who questioned the power of writing itself (or alone) in communicating the visceral textures of hunger as lived and localized experience.

The intertwined violence of hunger and its textual representation was brought up consistently by my female companions during fieldwork and also throughout the subsequent compilation of this work, including during iterative data validation meetings I conducted with women in the field, regular online group discussions via Facebook and WhatsApp, and sporadic telephone conversations when the signal allowed. Beyond the scope of this book, written and verbal exchanges surrounding the ethical stakes of writing the violence of hunger also shaped the production and promotion of a range of nonacademic engaged outputs related to hunger, drafts of which, like this work, I translated into Papuan creole and sent as hard copies and audiotaped recordings to my female friends prior to publication and then revised with their guidance.[4]

While I treat them separately here, it is important to note that women's perspectives on writing were far from unchanging or fixed; rather they were constantly shifting and permutating in ways that problematized not just how Marind's experiences of hunger ought to be written but also why it mattered that they be written—and, by the same token, whether and by whom they should be written in the first place. Marind women's starkly divergent perspectives on the (im)potency of writing as a mode of representation and potential avenue for redress thus illuminate the heterogeneous, rather than singular, ways in which my companions understand, imagine, and participate in the production of situated knowledge. This heterogeneity shapes not just the nature or causality of the world that Marind inhabit, as exemplified by hunger's previously described and much-disputed ecologies and etiologies, but also how and in whose words these worlds ought to be narrated and communicated—or not. In both respects, Marind women's discourses point to the troubling relationship between responsible eating and responsible writing as interconnected metabolic processes that involve the ingestion, transformation, and generation of matter and meaning across profoundly differential power divides.

In unpacking the non-innocence of ethnographic representation and attendant responsibilities on the part of ethnographers, I return in this chapter and in a different guise to a theme that has accompanied us on this foray through what Ana described in her opening hunger song as "the land of famished beings," manifest particularly in the gendered and geopolitical dynamics of culpability and victimhood that shape hunger's uneven etiologies and effects. I also engage with longer traditions in anthropology that interrogate the ethics and politics of ethnographic writing. Sustained attention to these questions of power, voice, and representation burgeoned in the 1980s with the publication of the seminal volumes *Writing Culture* and *Anthropology as Cultural Critique*, which foregrounded the inherent partiality and situatedness in space and time of anthropological writings and favored ethnography's evocative valences over its referential value.[5] Ideas presented in these works were then taken up by contributors to the volume *Women Writing Culture* (1996), who considered how feminist anthropologists have redefined the poetics and politics of ethnography.[6] The legacies of the "writing culture" movement of the 1980s and the attendant "crisis of representation" in anthropology continue to inspire more recent approaches to ethnographic writing in the context of contemporary trends and crises in the world and in academia. Central to these approaches is an embrace of different writing genres, the importance of making ethnography accessible to nonspecialist readers, and the potential of textual and multimodal experimentation in the production of ethically grounded, conceptually creative, politically engaged, and meaningfully collaborative works.[7]

In this chapter, I demonstrate how and why the equivocal ethics of ethnographic writing, alongside related questions of authorship, voice, and academic knowledge production, are topics perhaps most fruitfully approached in conversation with the people whose lives and worlds anthropologists seek to understand and convey. While these equivocal ethics are relevant across the descriptive, theoretical, and methodological dimensions and contributions of this work, I leave this reflexive account of the deeper "backstage" dynamics of researching and writing hunger until last at the request of my Marind friends who wanted the final chapter to problematize the *fact* of this book itself, in the fixed, textual form that exists before you and that you, as reader, have by now already in large part consumed.[8] The positioning of this chapter is therefore both a way of remaining faithful to my companions' wishes and also directly connected to, and representative of, the realities of non-innocence that the chapter examines and unpacks. The forms of non-innocence I trace implicate not only Marind and myself as author but also the broader anthropological endeavor and the reader themself as both audience and consumer. Much like the rotten deer meat that unsettled my stomach and senses on the fateful night of Mina's passing, this discussion and its strategic, if perhaps unexpected, positioning thus aim to enact for readers and writers alike a form of symbolic indigestion—one that destabilizes the coherency and legitimacy of the narratives that precede it by foregrounding the troubled ethics of writing hunger as a necessary yet also violent and representational act.

The chapter begins by examining why telling the(ir) story matters to those women who understand the production of this work as a form of return and responsibility for the experiences and knowledges I was entrusted with during my time in the field. I consider how the act of writing as a form of reciprocation was further compounded with the privileges and networks that my companions associated with my positionality as a foreign researcher, the potential of fleshy stories in helping readers understand and reckon with the violence wrought by capitalist consumerism across local and global scales, and the promise of an ethnographic text in rendering women's voices heard and heeded by men within their own communities. I then explore how the reticence of many women to participate in the crafting of hunger narratives relates to the dangers my companions associate with written artifacts as instruments of control and manipulation, the risks of reprisal from men in the village resulting from the divulgation and condemnation of structural inequalities between men and women in Marind society, and the question of how narratives of internal gender injustice ought to be situated and storied against a broader backdrop of Indigenous dispossession, displacement, and disempowerment across West Papua.

In this section, I also uncover how the sense of gendered solidarity that some women associated with storytelling and story writing was compounded with the trauma and pain that came with recalling and recounting the violence of hunger, the uncertainties surrounding how these stories would be interpreted by their diverse audiences, and the limitations of the textual medium itself in conveying real worlds and real lives. The final section of the chapter draws on women's conflicting perspectives to consider the non-innocence of ethnographic writing as an act of concomitantly compromised and comprising representation. I conclude by inviting a practice of "hesitant anthropology" that grapples up front with the profound dilemmas entailed in remaining accountable to those who make our writings possible, and for whom the question of *how* to write violence is indissociable from the question of whether this violence should be written at all.

Telling The(ir) Story

Nora's injunction that I pick up my pen and notebook and write about hunger, sickness, and pain—that I "write it all," in her words—communicates the sentiment of many women who repeatedly reminded me of my responsibility to "share with the world" (*bagi sama dunia*) the stories they had entrusted me with and the experiences I had been privy to during my time in the field. This sentiment was especially prevalent among women across the villages of Khalaoyam, Mirav, and Bayau who are involved in grassroots anti–oil palm campaigns in the capacity of community organizers, representative spokespersons, and consultation mediators. These women varied in age from their early twenties to their late sixties. All were married with children—some alive and others long or recently deceased. While a few among them possessed basic literacy in Indonesian and Papuan creole, most had never attended school and could not read or write—a fact that, in many cases, only enhanced the onus placed on me to document and disseminate their stories through the written medium.

Indeed, and throughout my fieldwork, the importance of directly and regularly participating in and observing Marind's everyday activities went hand in hand with that of recording their experiences and discourses, as these were lived and shared. Some stories have made their way into the world as engaged outputs in support of Marind's anti–oil palm land rights movement, including policy briefs, reports, complaints, op-eds, radio programs, and documentaries. And yet in the course of crafting these advocacy-related outputs, my companions frequently expressed dissatisfaction at the simplification of lived realities required to optimize effectiveness, intelligibility, and reach. Ethnographic writing, and particularly thick descriptions, which my companions had familiarized themselves with through my own prior works and also those of fellow and contemporary environmental anthropologists that I translated and shared in the communities, served a different but complementary use. This narrative mode, they claimed, made vital space for the granular textures and intricate complexities of people's diversely situated experiences and knowledges—a space that was valuable even if it did not serve any direct purpose in changing the worlds that the stories told within it evoked. It was this granularity that brought my companions to insist that I record and write in utmost detail what I was seeing, hearing, smelling, and learning, including at times when I felt it more appropriate to watch or listen from a distance or retreat entirely from the scene—for instance, during the wake of a deceased relative; in the midst of a heated argument about hunger's causes; upon noticing the ominous rumbling of a bulldozer approaching the forest; or, as the opening of this chapter recounts, at the untimely passing of a malnourished child.

The responsibility to tell the(ir) story was often characterized as an act of reciprocal exchange for the lived experiences and knowledges shared with and imparted on me by local women, or what the Sisseton Wahpeton Oyate science and technology studies scholar Kim TallBear describes as a form of "standing with."[9] This gamut of experiences and knowledges included the apprenticeship I received from women in traditional procurement activities such as gathering, fishing, and sago processing; the skills I developed in walking and listening to the forest with them; the shared enjoyment of encountering and preparing meals in the grove; the foods I was offered by my hosts; and the insights I acquired from women's discourses and debates surrounding the meaning and morality of hunger and satiety in their multiple, overlapping manifestations. It encompassed also the shame and resentment I witnessed when I accompanied women to the clinics, kiosks, and company headquarters to obtain food supplies or medical treatment, the deafening silences that punctuated the dull yet daily groan of empty stomachs, and the indignity and embarrassment that marked every meal that was never enough to feed everyone present. It further included the frustration, anger, and rage that women expressed in private toward their male relatives who were ceding lands to oil palm corporations, the sorrow they experienced upon encountering animals eaten by the road, and the unspeakable pain and grief shrouding the illnesses and deaths of their children and grandchildren—deaths whose gravity my companions affirmed could only be fully grasped by women, including myself, in our primary roles as mothers and child-rearers.[10]

Evocative of the Pacific-wide practice of *talanoa*, which the tangata Tiriti environmental anthropologist Trisia Farrelly and Fijian education scholar Unaisi Nabobo-Baba describe as an "empathic apprenticeship as an intentional, embodied, emotional, and intersubjective process between the researcher and the participant," the act of witnessing and its underlying subject-object distinction transformed over time into a relational "wit(h)nessing" as the

Marind women and I partook in a companionship that involved both break-ing bread in the forest and going hungry in the village.[11] Both dimensions were central to the rapport I built with my field companions, my gradual socialization and immersion into their communities and worlds, and my subsequent responsibility to write from a place of firsthand, long-term ex-perience that honored the stories and lessons learned through research.[12] As Eliana, a young mother of two and a member of the Gebze (banana) clan who hosted me during my fieldwork in her home village of Mirav, explained: "You have eaten with us and you have felt the pain of hunger with us. The government, the doctors, and the corporations—they have not experienced these things. They know our world from afar. This is why you must tell the stories, and not them. This is what you give back."

The onus to "tell the stories" as a form of reciprocity for the knowledges gifted to me invariably superseded the importance of providing food or other material goods to the communities with which I resided. In the early stages of my fieldwork, I brought as many cartons of canned meats, rice, flour, powdered milk, and vitamins and other supplements as I could to the settlements from the city, in exchange for the time and resources my friends invested in hosting me and to alleviate in what little way I could the evident food insecurity and malnutrition plaguing the villages. Soon, however, I desisted from bringing foods in light of the widespread embarrassment, shame, vexation, and disapproval that it provoked among my hosts, who associated it with the paternalistic food distribution practices undertaken by local corporations and government bodies and the diminishing experience of being seen and treated as dependent on this aid, and who reminded me that my job was not to feed them but to "share our food, share our hunger, and share our stories."

Respecting my companions' wishes in this respect was central to my enculturation within the community, as was the need to accept the gifts of food that they regularly offered me, which only further complicated the ethical stakes of the research. As poignantly exemplified by the last meal of deer meat that I shared with Barnabus and his family, community members often prioritized my satiation over that of themselves and their kin when food had to be rationed in times of extreme scarcity. I could not refuse these food gifts without vexing or offending my hosts. And yet doing so meant depriving my hosts of an already limited resource and thereby exacerbating the very condition I was investigating—hunger.

The task placed on me to document and disseminate the violence of hunger—one in which I was effectively complicit—was seen by many women as essential in enabling global audiences to understand what was happening in a seemingly out-of-the-way place whose peoples and landscapes are subjected to the violent consumption of an all-too-hungry world. These stories mattered less as solutions to the problem of hunger, which my companions knew the book in itself could not achieve, than as collectively fashioned mediums through which the lives and deaths of Marind might be remembered and commemorated—as ways, to return to Nora's words, for these deaths not to have been suffered in vain. Echoing the forms of communicative justice described by the American anthropologist Charles Briggs and the Venezuelan public health physician Clara Mantini-Briggs's Indigenous interlocutors in Venezuela, Marind women often framed their individual stories as symptoms and manifestations of broader structural injustices wrought by settler-colonial and techno-capitalist incursions that were undermining conditions of life for Marind in the present and for generations to come.[13] In the face of these entrenched injustices, storying everyday experiences of hunger came to constitute a labor of both care and critique, the former directed to hunger's victims, the latter to its manifold drivers—corporations, the government, the world, and the men of the village. Committing these oral stories to written form for future Marind generations and for global audiences, Nora often told me, might help make them "official" (*jadi resmi*), "rememberable" (*dapat diingati*), "intelligible" (*jadi jelas*), maybe even "actionable" (*dapat ditindaklanjuti*)—if not by me, then perhaps by those whose hands this book might reach.

If my long-term immersion within the Marind lifeworld constituted one source of responsibility to write and share Marind's stories, my status as a foreigner and scholar constituted another. This status came with worldly connections and networks to nonprofit organizations, educational institutions, government organs, and international funding bodies, that would in turn afford the book a broader and more diverse readership. This broader readership mattered, my friends affirmed, because it included the countries, organizations, and people whom they saw as implicated in the violence afflicting their bodies, families, and landscapes—the European Union and its biofuel policies, the Australian nation and its close geopolitical and economic ties to Indonesia, the United Nations and its human rights mechanisms, the international body of university students and scholars who would shape tomorrow's ideas, and more. Harnessing my networks and connections, as expressions of power and privilege, to raise awareness of the consequences of the world's hunger on Marind's lifeworld was often described to me as "the least I could do" (*paling tidak*) in return for the experiences I had been entrusted with during my time in the field.

In particular, sharing stories of hunger could help address what many of my companions deemed a central and burning question—namely, whether the "problem" (*masalah*) with the world is that it is too hungry, or that it no longer knows what hunger is at all. Olivia, a young woman from the Mahuze (dog) clan and a resident of Khalaoyam, explained this conundrum as follows:

> In the modern world, powerless people like us must go hungry so that powerful people can be fed. That is just how the modern world works. But these powerful people—they never seem to be satiated. They keep eating up the land, the resources, the water, the money, the coal, the wood, and more. They own phones and cars and houses and planes—even cities, islands, and soon enough, planets in outer space. Are these people never full? Are they never content? Are they never satisfied? They say Papuans are the ones who are hungry and malnourished—but in fact, they are the ones who are always hungry for more. They are the ones whose hungers are out of control. So, I wonder—is hunger a sign of progress, or poverty? Is becoming hungry the same as becoming modern? This is what we all need to ask ourselves. Maybe reading our stories will help people in the modern world think more carefully about their own hunger. Maybe then, we can talk about our hungers together, and differently.

Olivia's incisive speculation offers a powerful counternarrative to the story that the modern world tells itself about itself—namely, that it is defined and distinguished by progress, rationalism, freedom, and reason, the apex of a unilinear and universal trajectory toward material and personal fulfillment. This story finds expression in the paternalistic discourses of government, biomedical, and corporate actors in West Papua today, who invariably set the developed, progressive world of plantation modernities against the cultural backwardness and nutritional inadequacy of Marind's forest foodways. This story perpetuates longer-standing colonial discourses in the Pacific and elsewhere that, as the Sri Lankan anthropologist Gananath Obeyesekere and the Franco-American cultural critic Valérie Loichot describe, instrumentally misrepresented and reduced colonized subjects to figures evoking "pathological" or "abject" eating: the blood-thirsty cannibal, the glutton, the starved, and more.[14] This is what the scholar Tyson Yunkaporta calls "wrong story," or one that is rooted in economic models of intensive agriculture, fuel extraction, industrial mining, air, soil, and water pollution, and population extinction, each of which is driven by the attempt "to combine limitless growth and extraction with a limited resource base," and each of which contravenes the laws of the land.[15]

Instead, Olivia torques the ontology of the "modern world" as one that is itself plagued with endless and insatiable hungers—hungers of which it is by and large incognizant or ignorant.[16] Seen from this perspective, hunger multiplies further across object and subject, and cause and effect. Among people like Marind, hunger constitutes an unfortunate by-product of the material extractive logic of modernist regimes from which Marind themselves do not benefit. At the same time, hunger also constitutes a defining trait and pathology of the globalized, hungry world within which Marind and their hungers are embedded. As Olivia put it, "becoming hungry" is paradoxically both a by-product of and a precondition for "becoming modern." Her interrogative statement thus offers a powerful counterpoint to the rhetoric of development and modernization endorsed and embodied by the broader world, at the same time as it constitutes a paradoxical counternarrative *on itself*.

Olivia was one of many women who affirmed that the question of hunger is one that can only be adequately addressed, and potentially even resolved, in conversation and dialogue with faraway audiences, toward a collective reimagining of what hunger is, does, and means, across interconnected local and global contexts. A book, these women argued, could be a first step in that direction. But beyond-local hopes and expectations were by no means the only factor driving women like Olivia and others to support the project. Just as important to many was the potential of the book to act as a conduit for the expression of their grievances toward Marind men and as a catalyst for more participatory consultation and decision-making processes within their own communities.[17]

These sentiments stemmed from a widespread, if often covertly voiced, consensus that Marind women, as primary caregivers and food providers, were all too often excluded from important conversations surrounding land surrenders, negotiations with corporations and the government, and other decisions that would affect the future of Marind children and grandchildren.[18] As intimated earlier by Mirabela, a Khalaoyam resident, alongside many other women of the Upper Bian, men are invariably the ones invited to attend multistakeholder meetings in the city, where they accept compensation payments without consulting their broader collectives. They spend the money they receive from agribusiness corporations on phones and liquor while their children and wives go hungry. "Marind men forget the voices of the forest when they smell the dollar bills," Mirabela continued. "They think only of the money—not the forest, or their offspring. We try to tell them to think about the future—but they won't listen to us women. Maybe if they read our stories in a printed book—something official and public—then they will take us seriously. Maybe then, they will listen to us. Maybe then, we will be heard and heeded."

The desire for women's stories to "be heard and heeded" (*didengarin, diperhatikan*) thus operated both outwardly and inwardly for individuals like Mirabela, who identified local men as complicit in the production of local hungers and who read in the authority of a published text the possibility of being taken seriously by their male counterparts. It was this same rationale that brought many women to request that their original names be used in ethnographic accounts, and not pseudonyms, and that their self-selected photographs be included in this and other publications. Many of these women had asked to be cited under gender-altered pseudonyms in previously published articles to avoid being identified by their male relatives, but they wished to reclaim ownership of their own words and their own gendered identities within this book. Women who did opt for pseudonyms chose in lieu of their own names those of now-deceased female kin whom they claimed to have had a formative influence on their lives and whom they wished to pay tribute to. These included the names of an outspoken matriarch, renowned for her sharp wit and quick tongue; a rebellious cousin, thrice divorced for fearlessly standing up to her husbands; a wise medicine woman, enskilled in the arts of plant medicine; a respected aunt and instructor in the crafting of woven sago bags; and an adopted sister afflicted with muteness but blessed with the gift of bird call and communication. Invoking the names of women who embodied both the values of custom and its gendered contestations offered, in my companions' words, a way of "rendering present" (*jadi berada*), "commemorating" (*memperingati*), and "celebrating" (*merayakan*) within the book their meaningful ways and wisdoms, mediated through the words of their living female relatives.[19] As Nora explained: "We no longer want to have our identities as women hidden. We want the men to know whose voices they are hearing—because they will have heard them before, many times over, just like we have heard them from our sisters and grandmothers. We want them to know that the women are speaking to them—both those who are alive and those who are deceased. We want the men to know who wants things to change, and why. The stories and the truth, the rage and the sorrow—they matter just as much as the names."

The relationship between stories, truth, and names invoked by Nora and other women troubles the ethical and political stakes of pseudonym usage in academic writing. As the American Israeli anthropologist Erica Weiss and the American anthropologist Carole McGranahan note, the use of pseudonyms is about risk and the management of risk, but it is never a neutral technique. Rather, it is often revelatory of truths and of the nature of ethnographic truths.[20] Nora's words remind us that naming and being named can become an ethical prerogative when they serve to acknowledge and credit individual women as knowledge holders and knowledge producers— not just for external readers and audiences but also for men within their own community. Naming and being named also enabled women to claim ownership over, harness, and honor the affective states from which they articulated their ideas and critiques. These affective states included sorrow and grief, but also anger and rage, that together and differently responded to the injustices of exclusion, silencing, and betrayal.[21]

On the one hand, then, Nora's and Mirabela's words speak to what Unaisi Nabobo-Baba (a Fijian education scholar), Linda Tuhiwai Smith (a Māori education studies scholar), and Jo-Ann Archibald (a Sto:lo First Nation education studies scholar) and other Indigenous theorists identify as the potential of storywork in reclaiming Indigenous peoples' ability to testify to injustices and rectify the structural conditions that have historically silenced, sanitized, or stolen Indigenous voices and visions.[22] These structural conditions include the extractive violence of externally imposed settler colonialism and extractive capitalism, together with the masculinized regimes of power that have accompanied these impositions, or what Native American and Mestiza scholar and novelist M. A. Jaimes Guerrero terms "trickle down patriarchy."[23]

But these structural conditions also encompass frictions that operate internally within Indigenous societies, including gendered, culturally shaped, and precolonial norms that marginalize women from decision-making and deliberative processes—even as these processes directly affect them and their offspring, together with generations to come. For many of my companions, addressing this dual marginalization within the book was essential in conveying the entanglements of gender and food justice with the pursuit of Indigenous sovereignty.[24] As Mirabela insisted, "We cannot talk about injustices against West Papuans without talking about injustices against West Papuan women. We must talk about both of these injustices together."

It was in this context that telling and writing stories of hunger together with my female companions came to constitute an act of situated solidarity and gendered resistance in the face of dual and mutually enforcing processes of exclusion. In the process, the textual medium became pregnant with the promise of an authority and legitimacy denied to Marind women in their everyday verbal and social interactions with Marind men. But the perspectives and priorities presented here were far from the only ones shaping the contested production of this work. Just as important were the voices of those women who expressed deep-seated reservations about the promise and perils of writing the violence of hunger, which I turn to next.

Not Telling The(ir) Story

On May 28, 2021, I received a WhatsApp message from Nora's mother, Paulina. The date marked three years since her granddaughter Mina's passing, and two years since the end of her customary mourning period. That evening, Paulina's female relatives and friends from Khalaoyam, Mirav, and Mirav village had congregated in the room where Mina had drawn her last breath. Here, they had sung and wept and talked throughout the night, until the break of dawn. Paulina was writing to let me know that she was "ready" (*siap sudah*) for the book to be written and read. She and her kin had planted a bamboo sapling just outside the room where we had once sat together. The planting of this tree, she explained, marked the day when the decision was taken for this book to go ahead. Hopefully, she wrote, the plant would grow well. Hopefully, the book would be read widely. Paulina told me she had reflected many times on her actions and words since that fateful night, when she had admonished me for taking up pen and paper to write the story of Mina's death. "I am ready now for this book to exist," she wrote. "But I also want you to write *why this book shouldn't exist*. I want you to write why this book matters and why it doesn't. We want people to know *the story behind the scenes*" (emphasis in original Papuan creole).

As I corroborated with several friends via numerous individual and group discussions on WhatsApp, Facebook, and telephone conversations when a signal allowed, disclosing the "story behind the scenes" was understood by many of my female friends to be just as important as the ethnographic stories that the book itself recounts. These backstage narratives include those shared by Nora and others, whose reasons for endorsing and supporting this work I outlined in the previous section. They also include the concerns and conundrums of women like Paulina, whose reasons for opposing the book project constituted, in paradoxical ways, a central premise and nonnegotiable condition for the book to exist at all. Both are central to contextualizing the ethical and political stakes of writing violence as a representational practice. Both also raise necessarily unsettling questions surrounding the logic and legitimacy of the work before you.

Marind women's reservations surrounding this book project stemmed in part from the dangers and deceptions they associate with the textual medium itself. Many of my companions had encountered written documents primarily in the form of land contracts, surrender deals, and compensation payment forms that they had been forced to sign under duress by oil palm corporations, government bodies, and military personnel. These documents, they told me, are "official" (*resmi*)—but they are also "tools of trickery" (*alat tipuan*). Their terms are imposed on communities without prior consultation or deliberation. They are signed by individuals who often cannot read or write, and to whom the content of the documents is rarely explained in a comprehensive or timely manner. As instruments of control and coercion that have been instrumental in furthering the dispossession of Marind of their lands and livelihoods, texts are thus associated by many women with the top-down, exploitative authority of powerful, foreign agents.

The reticence of other women to participate in the production of this work, meanwhile, stemmed from their concerns over potential reprisals on the part of Marind men, who were intentionally excluded from many of the often-secretive discussions, meetings, and activities that this book draws on. Secrecy and concealment were deemed necessary by many of my female companions in creating a safe and open space to share their experiences, perspectives, and sentiments as women, beyond (and often against) the gaze of male relatives. But participating in these clandestine conversations also came laden with the risk of backlash on the part of husbands, brothers, and uncles in the private spheres of home and community. Indeed, many women worried that the book, and the process through which it came into being, might eventually become a source of internal conflict between themselves and their male relatives, including in the form of familial tensions, arguments, and sometimes even physical violence, which few of my companions were strangers to. Some were strongly in favor of the use of pseudonyms because they offered a degree of protection to female individuals from potential recriminations on the part of male relatives. Others, however, worried that concealing the identity of specific speakers would only expand the scope of women to whom these words might potentially—and wrongly—be attributed.

Alongside matters of identification, many of my companions were reluctant to portray their male kin in a negative light because it would embarrass or shame them publicly (even as they firmly believed their criticisms of men's actions and decisions were justified) and, more important, obscure the deeper factors at play: namely, Indonesian colonization and capitalist incursion.[25] For these individuals, then, hesitations surrounded not only the question of whether or not women's stories should be shared, but also *how* these stories should be presented, and what should be centered or omitted. Specifically, many of my companions worried that foregrounding women's grievances might threaten or destabilize the internal and collective unity of Marind as Indigenous West Papua people in the face of predatory and occupying state and corporate forces.

One such woman was Stefania, a member of the Kavzum (eel) clan and a mother of three from Khalaoyam village, who vehemently affirmed that stories should sustain and nurture solidarity among Marind themselves, regardless of gender divides, in the face of what she called the "bigger enemies." "We are already fighting with the oil palm companies and the government," Stefania explained. "We don't need more fights within our own villages. We need to put our differences as men and women aside and stand strong together in the face of our bigger enemies." For women like Stefania, then, storying hunger demanded what the Indian feminist critic Gayatri Chakravorty Spivak terms a practice of "strategic essentialism" wherein centering collective experiences of Indigenous dispossession and disempowerment took precedence over uncovering internal gendered inequalities that, while integral to women's lives and discourses, had to be situated and understood first and foremost in the context of West Papuans' ongoing pursuit for sovereignty as colonized Indigenous Peoples.[26]

Yet for other women, writing (and, subsequently, reading) the stories recounted in this book was experienced less as an empowering activity than as a deeply traumatic event because it meant having to repeat, remember, and relive the harrowing shame, grief, anger, and self-blame associated with the experience and witnessing of hunger. As I described previously, many of my female companions see themselves as responsible for the plight of their children and grandchildren, whose hunger testifies to their inability to fulfill their duties as carers and providers. Rather than serving a cathartic or remedial purpose, sharing stories of hunger reignited in violently vivid ways these women's memories of the frail bodies of malnourished infants, the jutting bones of toddlers, and the dull, gray skin of newborns, in which they read their own failures as mothers and nourishers. For some, writing the book together continued to haunt them in their sleep in the form of harrowing nightmares in which appeared the corpses of children, the burned remains of cleared forests, and the trampled bodies of kin-turned-roadkill. The deeply anxiogenic effects of these nightly experiences only exacerbated the lived pain of hunger in the waking world, in a cumulative buildup of shame that some women deemed profoundly disempowering. One such woman was Bernardina, a young mother of three and a member of the Ndiken clan, who initially participated actively in discussions surrounding the drafting of the book but eventually decided to withdraw from the process because of its emotional toll. "To write and read these stories," she explained, "is to be punished and shamed all over again. It is to relive the sadness and the guilt. It is all too much to bear."

For Bernardina's elder sister, Katarina, the problem with writing had less to do with its affective toll on those involved in its crafting than with how the book might be interpreted by its disparate and largely unknown audiences. Katarina justified her apprehension as follows: "Before the book is in the world, we have control over what stories we tell. But once the book is in the world, we lose control over how our stories are understood by others. We have seen this happen before—with the government, companies, even researchers and anthropologists. We have seen our stories used against us many times."

Katarina's concern that Marind's stories might be misinterpreted by outsiders was echoed by many of my female companions who spoke of their male relatives having undergone similar experiences in the context of land rights negotiations with state and corporate actors.[27] In these interactions, Marind's attempts to communicate their cultural and spiritual values, knowledges, and aspirations for their peoples and forests were frequently met with condescension, derision, and paternalism. For instance, their understanding of satiety as a condition distributed across human and forest life-forms, their characterization of plants and animals as intimate and ancestral kin, and their attribution of hunger to other-than-human entities and infrastructures were often dismissed by state and corporate actors as symptomatic of Marind's primitivism and backwardness. Such perceptions were in turn and at times conveniently invoked and instrumentalized by these actors to further legitimate the need for top-down development projects like oil palm plantations that could help uplift Marind from their retrograde way of life and worldviews.

Meanwhile, women who had spent time working or studying in Merauke City, Jayapura, or Jakarta noted that the damaging consequences of (mis)representation were by no means restricted to the context of land rights advocacy and negotiations. These women identified a similar dynamic stemming from bodies of literature produced by European colonial figures—

Figure 5.2. Karolina, a Marind woman, 2018. Photograph by the author.

anthropologists, missionaries, administrators, and explorers—and also by contemporary Indonesian scholars, that were said by many to portray Marind and other Papuan peoples in a deprecatory and diminishing light.

One among these women was Karolina, a woman in her late twenties from the Balagaize (crocodile) clan and a resident of Bayau village (see figure 5.2). During her studies toward a nursing diploma at Cendrawasih University in Jayapura city, Karolina had become acquainted with translated extracts from ethnographic sources produced by the Dutch anthropologists Jan van Baal and Jan Boelaars and also by Indonesian anthropologists, including Kanjeng Pangeran Haryo Koentjaraningrat (the so-called founding father of anthropology in the country) and Sarlito Sarwono, among others.[28]

Many of these texts, Karolina affirmed, are problematic because they emphasize aspects of Papuan lives and cultures that then became instrumental to the civilizational agendas of consecutive colonial orders—from the ritualized sodomization of Marind novices and the headhunting and warfare traditions of Marind clans as described in European writings, to the superstitious, lazy, sexually promiscuous, alcoholic, and violent attributes of Papuan peoples more generally, as described in Indonesian texts. "These works," Karolina stressed, "make us sound like savages and drunkards, whose ancestors spent all their time killing other tribes, stealing their children, and raping their offspring. These works don't talk about our forests, or our skin, or pride and dignity. They leave out the things that matter."

Katarina's and Karolina's concerns bring to mind the condemnation by the Solomon Islander and political theorist Tarcisius Kabutaulaka and the Papua New Guinean philosopher Bernard Mullu Narokobi of the prevalent racist tropes of savagery and darkness that haunt colonial and anthropological representations of Melanesian peoples.[29] They point to an acute awareness on my companions' part of the consequential role of national and global actors and audiences in the shaping of Papuan representations and attendant forms of (dis)empowerment—one that has also been identified as central to the relational construction of West Papuan identities in the context of local and transnational West Papuan political and religious movements.[30] They further identify in stories the possibility and the imperative of reclaiming forms of dignity, desire, and pride that persist in ways that should not be framed solely or primarily against the violence of settler-colonial occupation.[31]

In tandem with critiquing the primitivist representation of Marind and other Papuan Peoples in anthropological scholarship, Karolina also worried that telling stories of hunger and suffering only within this book would occlude the positive, generative, and life-sustaining dimensions of Marind's everyday existences—dimensions that, Karolina emphasized, persist despite the devastating impact of hunger on Marind bodies, lands, and relations. Sharing "the things that matter" (*apa yang penting*), in my companion's words, meant sharing stories of eating together in the grove, of exchanging skin and wetness with one's kith and kin, and of immersing oneself within the sentient ecology of the forest. It meant including the sensory and affective textures of the feeding marshes and swamps, the sounds and voices of their resident birds and mammals, and the gustatory pleasures afforded by sago meals, collectively prepared and shared under the welcoming shade of sago palms.

Incorporating these facets of the Marind lifeworld within the book was seen by many women as essential in countering single-sided narratives that would portray their people solely as passive victims and subjects of injustice, or relying purely on what Paulina called "the stories of the poor, the stories of the weak, the stories of the eaten." Instead, narratives of hunger had to be accompanied by contrapuntal epistemologies of satiety and nourishment, as these arise from reciprocal relations of eating and being eaten across species lines. "Our stories cannot only be about death and pain," Karolina affirmed. "They also have to be about hope, continuity, courage and struggle—about the things that make life possible, and worthwhile."

Karolina's stance resonates with the strategies of survivance of West Papuan women interviewed by the anthropologist Julian Smythe who "break the silence" by sharing stories of suffering but also by celebrating Papuan women's ongoing capacity to care for family and community—to sing, to laugh, and to struggle.[32] In a similar vein, my companion's insistence on incorporating stories of joy, pleasure, and enjoyment within the book marked a refusal to reduce life to pain and loss alone, and Indigenous Marind communities to the problematic trope of what the American anthropologist Joel Robbins terms the "suffering subject."[33] Instead, Karolina invited a practice of narrative "plotting" that enacts in epistemic terms the kinds of resilience and resistance that the Black American critical race theorist Sylvia Wynter identifies as central to the literal "plots" cultivated by the enslaved on the periphery of colonial plantations.[34] Akin to food provision grounds that nourished oppositional forms of Black life through practices of more-than-human care and continuance, Karolina called for counter–plantation narrative plots that recognized and celebrated the multiple forms of ongoingness and continuance that make life worth living and, in doing, empower those invested in their crafting.

And yet for many women, nourishing narrative plots alone proved sorely inadequate in communicating the complex and ongoingly transforming textures of the world as lived. Justina, a young woman from the Kaize (cassowary) clan who was renowned across the Upper Bian for her skills in composing songs and telling stories, often pointed out after reading my drafts that "much was lost" (*banyak de hilang*) in the conversion of lived experience to written word. This included the scents of the grove, the caress of the wind, and the violent pangs of hungers unquelled. It encompassed the tonality, pitch, and rhythm of words both storied and sung. It included also the muffled weeping of infants in their cribs, the sighs and tears of tired parents, and the anger and shame eating away at the hearts of mothers and grandmothers. "Writing," Justina told me, "cannot make readers feel all of this—in their skin, in their wetness, in their gut. They can understand it with their minds—but they are unable to experience it in their bodies. For when it comes to hunger, where else can one start but one's own body?"

The limits of the textual medium in enabling readers to know hunger by "starting from one's body" (*mulai dari kitorang pu badan*) were compounded with the equally problematic question of endings. A book, Justina noted, must end (*selesai*)—somewhere and somehow. But conclusions, as endings of sorts, occlude the fact that experience continues, lives on, and transforms over time, in the image of the unendingness and inconclusiveness of the hungers described in this work. In inscribing dynamic lifeworlds with the veneer of fixity and finality, conclusions thus come to constitute a form of representative violence—one that, for individuals like Justina, only heightened the importance of being there. "To really know our hunger," she insisted, "people must come here and experience it for themselves. They must feel it in their skin and their gut and their wetness. They must eat and be eaten—just like you have. Only then can the reality of hunger come to life."

But even the experience of being there is fraught with temporal, affective, and relational limits when one is not from the place or people one immerses oneself in and with. The eighteen months I spent living among Marind represented a significantly longer period of immersion than the short stints of visiting NGO activists, government actors, and corporate representatives. It allowed me to incorporate within this book vital insights into the granularities of the everyday Marind lifeworld and its constitutive transformations. And yet, as my companions frequently reminded me, this field experience still came nowhere close to a life lived in, with, and from Marind lands and forests. As Paulina put it, "Your experience matters, but it is just the beginning. Your skin and wetness are not of this earth. Even though you have eaten and gone hungry with us, you can never really or fully know our hungers—just like we can never really or fully know yours. There is still a gap there—a distance."

The impossibility invoked by Paulina of "knowing each other's hungers" (*pahami saling pu kelaparan*) in their entirety and intricacy was often in turn accompanied by an acute awareness on the part of my companions that my experiences in the Upper Bian were already set against a precondition of safety and escape that Marind do not enjoy—namely, my ability and freedom to return to the comforts and stability of my home in Australia whenever I wished. For me, unlike for them, the possibility of being *there* was never untethered from the privilege of getting *out*. Vulnerabilities shared in the field—enduring hunger, experiencing shame, losing wetness, and ingesting rotten meat—enabled the creation of particular kinds of intimacies, trust, and understanding between my friends and me. But these were always, and always would be, unevenly shared vulnerabilities—the one sought after and evadable, the other imposed and evading control.

Ethnographic writing, as the Black American poet-anthropologist Irma McClaurin writes, comes with the momentous responsibility of "hold[ing] in our words, real people's lives."[35] Living up to this responsibility, in the eyes of my companions, demanded a disclosure of the debates and disagreements that shaped—and for many years, preempted—the production of this book. This reflexive mode of avowal helps to temper presumptions of internal unity, finality, or consensus with regard to the findings presented therein. It pushes against the heroism of ethnographic fieldwork and of the fieldworker as "discoverer-hero" by foregrounding the moral quandaries of narrating violence in ways that do justice to our interlocutors' own divergent desires and demands.[36] It problematizes the capacity of textual narratives to codify the brutally nonverbal—and often unspeakable—realities of hunger, shame, and suffering, alongside the equally nonverbal realities of care, pleasure, and nourishment.[37] It brings into question the right and responsibility of ethnographers to document forms of violence that are associated by their interlocutors with self-blame and shame.[38] It draws attention also to the representational risks of "doomed" or "fatal impact" narratives that represent Indigenous Peoples solely through their experiences of loss, suffering, and disempowerment and, in so doing, obscure Indigenous forms of survivance, continuance, and desire.[39] As the Fijian (Lauan) historian Tracey Banivanua Mar notes, doom-centered narratives elide Pacific peoples' ongoing insistence and persistence in the face of colonization and its regimes of imposed invisibility.[40] They gloss over Pacific peoples' ongoing efforts to "be themselves and hold together" in the face of seemingly unsurmountable odds.[41]

Just as important, perhaps, this reflexive foray troubles the very existence of a work that seeks to pay tribute to the lives and knowledges of Marind women whose active participation in and contribution to the shaping of the book's content were accompanied by an equally meaningful resistance to its textual crafting and public dissemination. In these and other respects, this account follows Audra Simpson's injunction to "take up refusal in generative ways" in order to speak more broadly to the non-innocence of ethnographic representation as a figurative and fraught metabolization of others' lived experience and in order to reckon explicitly with the difficult relations of responsibility, reciprocity, and refusal that knowing and writing others' lived experience entails.[42]

Staying with the truths and troubles of compromise, as they shape the practice of ethnographic writing, means acknowledging and engaging with the generative expectations and counterexpectations we receive from the peoples whose stories we seek to communicate through our words and writings. Thinking of the ambiguous gift of rotten deer meat offered to me that evening at Barnabus's home, this acknowledgment and engagement entail cultivating what the Moroccan-Canadian theorist Kyla Wazana Tompkins pertinently describes as a counterhegemonic practice of "indigestion," wherein we open space for our interlocutors to push back against their metaphoric consumption through acts of representation and interpretation that may be unsettling or unsavory, but that tell us something vital about the power systems and structures within which these acts of epistemic sovereignty are embedded and to which they are responding.[43] Embracing such indigestions in turn calls for an overt problematization within ethnographic narratives of the challenges involved in "standing with" our interlocutors and their concerns and worldviews when these concerns and worldviews are internally at odds with one another, when they require the exclusion of certain voices within the collective consciousness of the broader community, and when they muddy the seemingly straightforward nature of and relation between principles and practices of respectful, responsible, and reciprocal research.[44]

In both respects, the "behind-the-scenes" dynamics of research and representation disclosed in this chapter uncover the profound if often unspoken debts and dilemmas that accompany ethnographic writing as a way of "taking up the speech and silence of others, and then giving those elements the reach of another world."[45] These dynamics draw attention to the lure and limits of texts in communicating and affecting the realities and relations they describe; the entangled sentiments of frustration and shame shrouding the experience of hunger; the asymmetrical dynamics of power, privilege, and vulnerability between multiply situated researchers and their equally multiply situated interlocutors; the potential redress and reprisals accompanying the telling of stories; and the always-present yet beyond-reach possibilities of misrepresentation, misreading, and misappropriation.

In doing so, they raise unsettling but vital questions surrounding the why, the who, the what, and the whether of ethnographic knowledge production.

More broadly, these questions invite a pairing of attention to hesitation in two, interrelated forms. The first entails approaching hesitation as an object of anthropological inquiry—one that animates in often conflictual ways how people conceptualize, theorize, and rationalize the nature and causality of the worlds they inhabit, together with what they want said or unsaid, written or unwritten, and for whom, or what the Italian anthropologist Alessandra Gribaldo calls an "anthropology of hesitations."[46] The second entails approaching hesitation as a method of anthropological inquiry—one that engages explicitly with the ethical, political, and practical conundrums of remaining accountable and responsible to those who make our writings possible, or what one might call a practice of "hesitant anthropology."

Centering hesitation as method draws attention to its meaningful valences not solely as an empirical reality of the field and its protagonists but also and importantly, as an epistemic and moral conundrum for the ethnographer themself, bound as they are in complex intersubjective relations of trust and accountability to both their interlocutors and their disciplines. It brings into productive dialogue the hesitations people face *in* everyday life with the hesitations anthropologists face *from* the field, and what anthropologists should or should not do *with* these hesitations in their representational craft. It points to hesitation not necessarily or always as an "either-or" between writing or not writing but also as a collaborative and iterative process of thinking through *how* people's discourses and experiences ought to be described and analyzed.

Taken together, an anthropology of hesitations and a praxis of hesitant anthropology heighten and haunt the ethical stakes of scholarly knowledge production. They demand that we stay with the trouble, rather than eschew or be paralyzed by the productive confusions shaping the lives of those whose worlds we seek to understand, and the limits to which we can achieve this in experiential and representational terms. They complicate the ethical imperative to unveil violence and suffering by revealing the differing ways in which what counts as ethical and responsible in the first instance is understood by those who live with violence directly and daily. As empirical object, research methodology, and conceptual analytic, hesitation thus offers a possible pathway toward reckoning with the non-innocence of ethnographic writings as always already compromised texts—both in terms of the compromises that must be made in their crafting and in terms of their potentially compromising consequences for those whose stories these texts recount.

Engaging in dialogue with Marind throughout the production of this book and long prior on questions of non-innocence and hesitation, as they are distributed across real worlds and representational writs, was challenging, destabilizing, and at times paralyzing. But it was also productive. It opened spaces for difficult yet vital conversations among us about power asymmetries writ small and large—between Marind men and women in the villages; between colonizing regimes and Indigenous Peoples; and also between foreign researchers, their audiences, and the communities they claim to speak about, with, or for. It uncovered the necessity and challenge of navigating the temporal pressures of academic knowledge production while respecting calls for slowness stemming from communities in the field that are themselves struggling to reconcile the urgency of getting their stories *out* with the importance of getting these stories *right*. These conversations have radically changed the tempo and tenor of the book's transmutations, together with the social and intellectual relations and frictions that make it possible and meaningful.

To write about ethnographic non-innocence can nourish modes of critically engaged scholarship that enrich our understandings of contemporary life. It directs attention to the responsibilities and failures that accompany the process of ethnographic writing as a "way of participating in the activity of the world, a making and remaking of instances of life entangled with moments of thought."[47] It points to the potential of hesitation as a method for creating points of productive if always partial cocreation, connection, contention, and conversation, across differently situated anthropologists and anthropologies.[48]

Yet as the Unangax̂ scholar Eve Tuck and the diasporic settler of color Wayne Yang remind us in the context of decolonization, avowing of ethnographic non-innocence in a hesitant mode does not, in and of itself, absolve our writings of their constitutive impurities. The importance of this reminder is only amplified when considered within/against the economy of knowledge, prestige, and cultural capital that anthropology and academia more broadly find root in and reproduce.[49] While not a topic invoked by my companions in the field, it is here that hesitant anthropology shows its potential to act as a cultural critique not only of the ethnographic settings we study *in* but also of the institutional worlds we study these settings *from*.[50] Within these institutional worlds, as the Indian American anthropologist Kirin Narayan and others note, the inherently collaborative nature of research as a process unfolding in dialogue across disciplinary fields and ethnographic field sites is too often belied by the unyielding benchmarks of "professional survival and success"—even if these benchmarks are not known to or deemed relevant by the communities whose stories anthropologists are entrusted with and recount.[51]

I am thinking here of the primacy given to individual authorship and attribution when it comes to publication and promotion metrics; the conventions of genre, outlets, and form that pose limits to creative experimentation and multimodal expression; and the pressures on early career researchers in particular to produce high theory and (re)new(ed) jargon in order to carve out and secure their niche in the academic job market.[52] I am thinking also of the strategic invisibilization of hiatuses, paralysis, failures, and breakdowns—in fieldwork relationships, the writing process, institutional recognition, individual mental and physical health, and more—that must often remain unsaid in order to establish oneself as a legitimate high-impact researcher on an accelerating and upward trajectory, and therefore as someone worthy of funding and citing. Alongside precarity, I have in mind certain academic infrastructures of privilege—for instance, the privilege of retrospective avowal, or confessional memoir writing, that seems to come only with the achievement of seniority and (advanced) tenure, and also the privilege of the stance of hesitation that I frame here as an ethical prerogative but that, not unlike the countermovement of "slow academia," is also a symptom of the ability to afford (sometimes literally) to think/read/write slowly in the first place. Expressive of the material, economic, and cultural infrastructures of academia as institution, these dictates, as the Spanish anthropologist Paloma Gay y Blasco writes, often come to shape the possibilities of ethnographic writing and dissemination as much as (if not more than) the field-based experiences, relationships, and protagonists that make this research possible and meaningful from the outset.[53] The author of this work and this work itself are no exception to such rules.

At the same time, the admittedly limited reach and impact of ethnographic texts, of disciplines like anthropology, and of institutions like academia beyond the confines of their own communities and circles offer a sobering reminder of the humble parameters of possibility that even the most ethically driven of scholarly writing can provide in fostering effective and meaningful transformation in the worlds these works describe.[54] As Marind women themselves convey, there is only so much a book can encompass *of* the world, let alone achieve *in* that world. Acknowledging non-innocence through an active and engaged stance of hesitation, as such, will require a lot more in pragmatic and institutional terms to become more than an end in itself and instead a means to something else—even if that something else might not materialize in the form one might in some instances hope for, and in others depend on.

Impurity heightens and haunts the craft and content of the text before you in many other ways—from the single authorship of a work that belies its multiple and equivocal chorus of voices, to the inclusion of photographs and real names that puts my companions at risk of reprisal, to the terminology of "companionship" that glosses over the various and varying relationships that together shape both field and fieldworker. Yet if you are reading these words, then a choice has, in the end, been made—one shaped as much by my attempt to do justice to my companions' wishes as by the pursuit of my own intellectual interests, the institutional expectations of scholarly knowledge production, the temporal demands of academic publishing, and the voices of many others who will have fed into and nourished the text-to-be: colleagues, reviewers, editors, students, and more. Just as deliberations surrounding the politics and poetics of writing formed an integral part of my fieldwork, so too this book may fuel other kinds of generative debates and disagreements among those whose stories it seeks to retell—and also among the situated audiences who may animate its "public afterlife" through their own, situated acts of ingestion and interpretation.[55] In the process, books, too, may inflect in their own partial and pharmakonic ways, and through their fortitudes and failures, the nature of the worlds they world and are worlded by.

CONCLUSION

This book has examined how hunger shapes the alimentary and affective lives of an Indigenous Papuan community on a nascent agribusiness frontier, where entrenched colonial-capitalist regimes and emergent ecological rifts are reconfiguring relations of eating and being eaten within and across species lines. Drawing primarily on the experiences and theories of Marind women, the work has sought to push against the framing of hunger as a human-only, biologically determined, and individually experienced condition of being by uncovering its dispersed and disputed ontology as meaningful event, everyday affect, gendered critique, and cultural idiom through which my companions in the field understand, critique, ingest, and ultimately reproduce capitalist modernity's uneven relations of feeding and being fed. In the process, hunger's etiologies and effects reveal themselves to be distributed across the realms of the human and more-than-human, real and representational, fleshly and figurative, and somatic and substantive. They center the bodily mediated and gendered violence of colonial racial capitalism, the rapacious logics of dispossession undergirding corporate neo-natures, and the heterogeneous discourses of Indigenous communities caught in the teeth of imposed gastrocolonial regimes. They point to the indissociability of Indigenous food sovereignty from broader questions surrounding Indigenous territorial sovereignty and political self-determination, and from the environmental, social, and racial dimensions of food (in)justice as these undermine Indigenous Peoples' collective capacity to maintain their cultural integrity, physical health, and intimate and ancestral relations to kindred beings, entities, and ecosystems.[1] They also reveal the challenges of achieving food justice among peoples and in places subjected to the consuming violence of the "colonial mouth," or imperialist political and epistemological machines that ingest, disfigure, and dissolve the worlds and subjects exposed to their excessive greed.[2]

Taking seriously the "slipperiness" of hunger as lived experience, moral metaphor, and social critique, as this work has attempted to do, is critical in overcoming the reduction of foods to nutrients and calories as supposedly neutral and universal determinants of human health, anchored in the scientification of human experience as quantifiable data and of the body as a machine in need of fuel.[3] As the British historian Tom Scott-Smith notes, how one conceives of the "empty stomach" is a crucial determinant in how one then proceeds to treat it.[4] Expanding the scope of what hunger does to people and what people do with it, beyond the dominant idioms of malnutrition and food insecurity, sheds vital light on the political, sensual, cultural, moral, and affective dimensions of food and hunger that are routinely elided in scientific, policy, and poverty discourses, together with the more-than-human sociality of consumption as a mutualistic relation of eating and being eaten. Such an approach foregrounds what is lost or obscured through the metrification, medicalization, individualization, and rationalization of hunger as a purely technical concern, best quantified, addressed, and solved by scientists and policymakers as experts. It helps counter the prevalence of deficit-centered approaches to Indigenous diets within nutritional scholarship and its lack of attention to the ravaging effects of (settler) colonization on Indigenous food-based identities, ecologies, and socialities. It further points to frictions and hesitations among the hungry themselves over what a good diet entails; what subsistence is (un)desirable; how nutrition relates to nourishment, appetite, and satiety; and what foods can best sustain human, intergenerational, and ecological well-being across local and global scales.

Reckoning with the interconnectedness of hungers across local and global scales, as the Marind women whose stories this book recounts themselves do, raises what the French philosopher Jacques Derrida describes as the moral question of how one should eat well (*bien manger*) in an increasingly vulnerable and always more-than-human world.[5] This question brings us to consider what powers and forces dictate what goes into which bodies, what counts as food, when food means life, and who or what becomes eater and eaten.[6] It centers the complex entanglements of the cultural, colonial, culinary, and corporeal in the situated signification of hunger. Grappling with these entanglements can be confronting—especially for those among us who care about the shared futures of the planet's diverse and variably vulnerable communities of life, yet who may feel paralyzed by the seemingly impossible or inchoate horizons of real action and change in what the American historian Julie Livingston aptly describes as an age of "self-devouring growth."[7] And yet hunger offers a potent entry point in the urgent task of reimagining contemporary struggles for social, environmental, racial, and multispecies justice as mediated and moved by the pursuit of what one might term *metabolic justice*.[8]

In naming metabolic justice, I do not seek to (super)impose a conceptual frame atop the theories articulated by my companions in the Upper Bian. Rather, I offer this language as a way of crystallizing a philosophy, practice, and politics of coexistence that ripple throughout many of the narratives presented in this book. Metabolic justice manifested in the Marind ethos of becoming good food for nonhuman kin in the forest; in their understandings of different hungers as diagnostic of individuals' moral, material, bodily, and social relations; and in their framing of eating and being eaten as a process that is always already distributed across more-than-human landscapes, lifeforms, and lifetimes. Ruptures and violations in metabolic justice, or what one might term metabolic *in*justice, meanwhile, surfaced in the subjection of Marind bodies and ecologies to the predatory logics of colonial-capitalist infrastructures and institutions; the racialized and imposed introduction of alien and commodified foodways as poor substitutes for intimately cherished forest foodways; the hungers experienced by Marind's nonhuman kin in the face of habitat destruction and plantation expansion; the unevenly distributed responsibilities and impacts of hunger among Marind men and women; and the roots of these disparate yet interconnected vulnerabilities within longer histories of occupation, dispossession, and assimilation.

In these and other respects, metabolic justice as analytic draws attention to the material and physiological dynamics of absorption, ingestion, and transmutation that alternately sustain or undermine organismic well-being across individuals and collectives. Metabolism centers distributed processes of conversion and connection that draw into their fold the bodies of the eaters (their organs, cells, and tissues) and the bodies of those eaten (the plants, animals, and ecosystems whose own metabolic activity makes food for humans possible). Beyond the realm of food, metabolism also encompasses the corporeal transformations and vulnerabilities wrought by exposures to sensory stimuli and environmental toxins. It is an in-betweenness of body and environment that, in its in-betweenness, challenges the very boundedness and separability of bodies and beings from their constitutive environments.[9]

To approach justice in metabolic terms, then, invites us to attend to the uneven intersections and interactions of biopolitical and social life, the human and more-than-human, and the material and metaphoric, as these are mediated by differently situated and privileged guts. It opens space for considering how hungers are experienced, understood, and explained; whom they position as privileged or vulnerable across interconnected local and global settings; and what they expose about the power systems determining who must go hungry in order for others to be fed. It prompts us to interrogate the interface between bodies and worlds across scales, as these shape life, living, and livability across different domains and degrees of metabolic exposure, absorption, and porosity. It expands our understanding of metabolism as an embodied, transformative process, distributed across foods, environments, and bodies that are themselves historically constituted, socially shaped, symbolically charged, affectively mediated, and representationally refracted.

As the central topic of this book, hunger might seem a counterintuitive starting point for theorizing metabolic justice. Hunger, in many ways, is an expression of the limits of metabolism and the capacity to metabolize. To be hungry, in its simplest meaning, is to lack the nutrition necessary for metabolic transformation. When hunger reaches an extreme degree, or starvation, the body begins to consume its own internal energy stores, in a process known as autophagy—first carbohydrates, then fats, proteins, and eventually muscle and then brain. The body eats itself. And yet at the same time, hunger is a form of pain. Like all other forms of physiological pain, it is a signal to do something—it is the impulse that keeps us alive. As a corporeally mediated call to action, hunger responds to injustice, absences, damages, and debilities in individual and not-always-human bodies that in turn diagnose social dis-ease within broader geopolitical anatomies of power, domination, and extraction.

The potential of metabolic justice in reimagining relations of feeding and being fed within broader anatomies of power accrues heightened significance in an epoch of intensifying capitalist extraction. In this epoch, biodiverse landscapes and lifeworlds across the tropics and elsewhere are giving way to radically simplified, homogenized, and privatized monocrops of plants and animals whose proliferation is legitimated by the food and fuel needs of a growing human population. The pursuit of ever-greater and ever-more-concentrated economic gains is undoing ecosystems at local and planetary scales. In the process, industrial activities are increasingly "uncoupling life from death, diminishing death's capacity to channel vitality back to the living."[10]

Lest this framing be read as overly abstract or removed from the reader's own everyday world, consider for a moment how industrial capitalism's ghostly hauntings manifest in palm oil—the product of the cash crop taking over Marind's nourishing forests, that is present in over half of all supermarket goods globally, and that is still largely produced from stolen or otherwise sacrificed lands and exploited human and nonhuman bodies in West Papua and well beyond.[11] This ubiquitous (if often camouflaged) commodity nourishes the skin and infiltrates the pores of many of us on a daily basis through the myriad cosmetics and cleaning goods it is found in—our soaps, shampoos, toothpastes, detergents, and washing powder. It penetrates our flesh and metabolisms through the myriad foods it is also an ingredient of—from ice cream and french fries, to chocolate bars and cereals. Beyond human metabolisms, palm oil's by-products, including meal and kernel, feed our cherished pets at home, alongside the livestock and dairy animals in industrial farms that then become food for us. With oil palm biomass now increasingly being used as a raw material for paper production, the substance may literally be within the reach of your fingers right now as your read this text.

In these and so many other ways, the consumption of oil palm as an omnipresent product connects the cosmopolitan "us" to peoples and ecologies who find themselves pulled into amplified patterns of death and suffering, whose skin, wetness, and hunger we may never know, yet whose bodies nonetheless pay the price for "progress." Indigenous Peoples like the Marind might literally live in the shadow of the oil palms on remote agribusiness frontiers like West Papua. But no matter where we call home or whom we call kin, all of us live *in the shadow of the plantation*—a material formation and enduring ideology whose extractive and racializing logic constitutes a crucible of colonial-capitalist regimes past and present.

And yet at the same time, the world that many of us inhabit is also one in which what we have vastly outweighs what we need, or indeed want.

Profit and property, rather than need or accessibility, constitute the central operatives of capitalist (il)logic. When this logic fails or falters, technology and science are often heralded as solutions to the suboptimal productivity of natures-turned-capital. A "techno-fix" mentality remains the dominant drive behind efforts to mitigate and remedy environmental harms and to achieve sustainable food production, but in ways that often leave technocapitalist logics unquestioned. Even as metabolic processes that sustain life on Earth are breaking down and generating potentially irremediable metabolic rifts, reified imaginaries of anthropocentrism and human exceptionalism, compounded with impossibly limitless consumerism, continue to obscure and obstruct the interdependent webs of relations needed to sustain human and more-than-human life. In the process, we lost sight of the importance of becoming and remaining obligated to, and by, the many beings whose metabolic trajectories intersect with our own.[12]

Thinking with metabolic justice thus demands that we chew on the question that my companions in the field themselves ask of the worlds consuming them—namely, whether the modern condition is one of excessive and insatiable hunger, or whether the material overabundance of the worlds we inhabit in fact preempts us from knowing hunger and the lessons that hunger as a relation might usefully teach us—about ourselves, and about others.[13] This speculative provocation, articulated succinctly by my companion Olivia, brings us to rethink the modern world as one afflicted by two seemingly contradictory yet coexistent pathologies. On the one hand, this is a world characterized by an uncontrollable hunger for goods and gains that no amount of consumption can ever satiate and that is fueled by the normalization of material overabundance. It entails the sacrifice of ecologies, socialities, foodways, and identities of communities like Marind whose lands are appropriated and exploited by the agro-industrial food system. And yet even as the modern global world is plagued by endless hungers, it is also an impoverished world in that hunger no longer constitutes a meaningful—or productive—event and experience. This is a world that relies on the invisibilization of the peoples and places that feed it, and of the environmental, social, and ethical relations that nourish it. This is a world, to borrow Marind terms, of "plastic foods" whose rampant commodification obscures the communities of life implicated for better and for worse in their production and proliferation.

Audra Simpson and Andrea Smith argue that attending to Indigenous theories of change from the grassroots allows us to attune ourselves to forms of analysis that "take up political issues in ways that have important consequences for communities of every sort"—our own included.[14] In a similar spirit, and as a philosophical and political provocation, Marind's interrogation of the broader world orders within which they are embedded offers a powerful intersubjective framing for the Indigenous theories of hunger recounted in this work. These theories invite us to reimagine ethics and justice by considering how acts of eating shape our relationships with human and other-than-human beings, and with the structures of food production and distribution that our eating relies on and sustains.[15] They constitute a resounding critique and a call for responsibility, reckoning, and repair in the face of a global industrial food system that perpetuates the cannibalistic logic of colonial racial capitalism as, in the words of Grace Dillon, an Anishinaabe cultural critic, "the consumption of one people by another."[16] In a world where every meal is connected but not every meal is shared, Marind theories of hunger thus implicate all of us who are in one way or another invested in impure, metabolic relations as situated earthly dwellers and as everyday global consumers.[17]

Craig Santos Perez, a close friend, colleague, and early reviewer of this book, once told me that ethnographic works can be heartbreaking without necessarily being hopeless.[18] Craig's words stay with me as I reflect on the violences recounted in this work, and the violence of recounting them in itself. They stay with me because for all the suffering and loss that exist on out-of-the-way extractive frontiers, Marind theories of hunger are also animated by hope, creativity, and possibility. These theories draw attention to nourishment as a potentially more capacious ways of envisioning what we feed and what feeds us—and, by extension, how we, too, might become good food for others within more-than-human processes of metabolic justice. Much like hunger, which is irreducible as an experience to the quantitative metrics of calories or the scientific classification of food groups and nutrients, nourishment operates well beyond the narrowly defined scope of nutrition in that it is as much about food and feeding as it is about broader imaginaries and relations of cherishing, valuing, and nurturing.[19] Nourishment encompasses the diverse affects, relations, ethics, practices, ideologies, and socialities that together imbue foods with sensory, aesthetic, cultural, and political meaning. It speaks to hunger and satiety as phenomena that transcend the biological imperative to keep a body alive, and that reveal instead what it takes for a life to be worth living. In an epoch of intensifying natural resource exploitation, thinking with nourishment brings us to consider critically not just what we eat but what is eating us—to whose benefit, and at whose cost.[20] It demands that we collectively fashion foodways that are grounded in the premise and promise of more-than-human metabolic justice—a justice not reliant on relentlessly consuming each other up but rather on willingly carrying each other on toward more equitable futures and relations of feeding and being fed.

As the last chapter of this work conveyed, metabolic justice also extends beyond the realm of literal foods and eating to encompass relations of consumption, transformation, and (in)digestion at the heart of ethnographic writing and representation as a practice shaped as much by those whom we attempt to co-story with as by those who claim authorship and those who consume others' hungers in reading works like the one before you. At this other yet related level, then, rethinking writing as processes of metabolization invites us to ask: What forms of non-innocence animate the object of our inquiries as anthropologists, and what forms of hesitation do these inquiries demand? What hungers drive us to write what we write, and whose desires and appetites are satiated or stimulated in writing's craft and consumption? What imaginaries and possibilities for metabolic justice do ethnographic narratives of violence alternately enable or elide? How do we do justice through our words and our writs to the multiple different demands placed on us by those on whose lifeworlds we build our careers and our capital?

These matters bring us back to questions of power, ethics, representation, and politics that are by no means new to anthropology, but that Marind exhort us to reckon with and revisit—through their own idioms, experiences, and theories. This exhortation stems from an out-of-the-way plantation frontier, seemingly far removed from our everyday lives as scholars—but it also comes at a critical and timely juncture, when calls are growing from within and beyond academia to decolonize (if at all possible) a discipline that continues to propel us along on a professional track that is often profoundly individualistic, heroic, and hierarchical, even as we might try to write against that very individualism, heroism, and hierarchism.[21] This is an exhortation that, even if heeded and put into practice, does not in and of itself exonerate us as ethnographers of our conflictual responsibilities toward the peoples and worlds we learn from, nor remedy the fact that even the most well-meaning attempts to dismantle academic structures of power and privilege can unwittingly dissolve into tokenistic gesturing or performative posturing, ultimately entrenching, rather than unsettling, the status quo. This is an exhortation that, as Mina sings in the coda to this book, we must nonetheless learn to keep safe, store well, and hold on tight to—in the manner of a cherished cassowary feather, a bag of nourishing sago starch, or an arrow to the bow—as we navigate sites and stories of violence and vulnerability that are cause for rightful outrage but also invitations to collectively and carefully put that outrage to work.[22]

In early 2022, during the final write-up of this book, a new actor had taken to the stage in the Upper Bian. Via an extensive series of Facebook and WhatsApp messages sent by her niece between February 2 and February 21 that year, Nora informed me that cases of COVID-19 had for the first time been detected in her home village of Khalaoyam. Several local men had contracted the disease while visiting Merauke City or working on nearby plantations and then brought it back to the villages, where their wives and children had subsequently become infected.

The virus, Nora wrote, was "eating up" (*makan habis*) the bodies of its victims, weakening the skin and wetness of people whose health and immunity were already compromised by everyday food insecurity and rampant malnutrition and to whom access to vaccines and treatment was prohibited by both cost and availability. Isolated from their kin to prevent further contagion, these individuals could no longer participate in collective hunting and foraging expeditions or walk the forest in the company of their other-than-human siblings and ancestors. Their bodies were turning ever more gray and dry. Their families were overcome with worry and fear. Most disturbing of all, according to Nora, was the fact that the coronavirus appeared to rob people of their sense of appetite, together with their capacity to taste and smell. No matter what or how much they ate, the diseased could not seem to recognize the flavors, scents, or even textures of the foods they consumed—whether instant noodles or rice, or fresh cassowary flesh or riverine fish. As Nora reported in one of her Facebook messages: "People who have been eaten by the virus tell us that everything they eat has become bland and without flavor. Everything has become like plastic—the sago, the game, the fruits. Everything tastes like nothing [*semuanya terada rasa apa-apa*]. This virus—we cannot see it, but we know that it is hungry. It eats people's bodies—and it also eats their hunger. It, too, now inhabits this land of famished beings."

The spread of the coronavirus constituted the latest manifestation of Marind's subjection to the destructive effects of parasitic human and other-than-human others within unevenly distributed dynamics of contagion, consumption, and contamination. The fears and anxieties provoked by its arrival among many Upper Bian residents stemmed both from the fact that it was new and unknown *and* from the fact that it conjured memories of the devastating impacts of the donovanosis and influenza epidemics that almost eradicated their people in the first half of the twentieth century. It testified in palpable ways to the inseparability of local realities from global forces whose agents, much like the virus, may be invisible to the human eye, but whose deleterious effects are nonetheless felt through the immediacy of one's wetness and skin. At once novel threat and all-too-familiar déjà vu, the virus was reanimating debates and deliberations surrounding hunger among the Indigenous dwellers of the West Papuan plantation frontier, for whom the matter at stake today, as in the past, remains just as much to eat or not to eat, as to eat or be eaten. How, whether, and by whom this story will be told remains to be seen.

CODA

*Kulit aku hitam, kulit kamu putih, rambut aku keriting, rambut
  kamu lurus*
My skin is black, your skin is white, my hair is curly, your hair is
  straight
Tanah aku hutan, tanah kamu kota
My land is the forest, your land is the city

Jagalah lagu ini dengan baik, macam bulu burung cendrawasih
Keep this song safe, like a bird of paradise plume
Simpanlah lagu ini dengan baik, macam tepung-tepung sagu
Store this song well, like freshly rasped sago
*Peganglah lagu ini dengan baik, macam anak panah ke busur, kan
  sa mau tahu ini*
Hold this song tight, like an arrow to the bow, for this, I want to know

Ketika kau makan sa pu dusun, kau rasa sa pu nafas kah?
When you eat my groves, can you feel my breath?

Ketika kau makan sa pu rawa, kau rasa sa pu kulit kah?
When you eat my swamps, can you feel my skin?
Ketika kau makan sa pu danau, kau rasa sa pu keringat kah?
When you eat my lakes, can you feel my sweat?
Ketika kau makan sa pu hutan, kau rasa sa pu lapar kah?
When you eat my forests, can you feel my hunger?

Mina's hunger song, January 2, 2018, Khalaoyam village

Introduction

1   In this work, *oil palm* refers to the plant known in Linnean scientific taxonomy as *Elaeis guineensis Jacquin*, and *palm oil* to the edible oil that is
obtained from the fruits and kernels of the oil palm plant.

2   The terms *companion* and *friend* gloss a range of different and changing
relationships that I entertained with Marind individuals and groups in
the field—colleague, apprentice, and teacher, sister, aunt, adopted pig-
daughter, and more. Inspired by the Australian anthropologist Melinda
Hinkson's characterization of her friendship with the Warlpiri woman
Nungarrayi as a form of dynamic, generative, if never friction-free "jour-
neying," I choose these terms to honor the many forms of accompaniment
that shaped my research with the women of rural Merauke. These include
literal accompaniments in the forests, villages, and plantations but also
intellectual and affective companionships that undergirded the writing
process and that sustained and challenged in meaningful ways the tenor
of our intersubjective relationships and the substance and structure of the
text before you. I reserve the term *interlocutor* for broader statements on
the researcher–research subject dynamic, in recognition of its contextually shaped and situated forms across time and place, and individual and
collective. Hinkson, *See How We Roll*, 21.

3   In this work, *more-than-human* and *other-than-human* serve as qualifiers
for native plants, animals, and elements, as well as ancestral creator spirits,

whom Marind refer to collectively as <u>amai</u> and <u>dema</u>, respectively. The terms also encompass an array of introduced or foreign entities, forces, and infrastructures that participate in shaping the Marind lifeworld—cities, roads, plantations, corporations, oil palm, and others. With a few exceptions, I favor *more-than-human* over *multispecies* to make space for beings who do not fit comfortably within dominant scientific frameworks of *bios*. In doing so, I align my analysis with Indigenous Marind ways of classifying beings, relations, and matter that do not necessarily or primarily find anchorage in the Western, taxonomic concept of "species." Chao, "Thinking Beyond Bios"; Price and Chao, "Multispecies"; TallBear, "Interspecies Thinking"; Winter, "Unearthing the Time/Space/Matter."

4   As I describe elsewhere, sugarcane, oil palm, and timber companies operating in Merauke are systematically failing to respect the right of the Marind to withhold their consent to land conversion, and communities often give their consent based on deceptive information and restricted freedom of choice. Where provided to villagers, details about the design, implementation, and anticipated impacts of planned projects (both positive and negative) tend to be insufficient or partial, terms of compensation unilaterally imposed, and contracts vague or nonexistent. National and local regulations stipulating the right of communities to give or withhold their consent are also rarely implemented, interpreted to suit the interests of corporations and the government, or trumped by national interest priorities. Forest Peoples Programme, PUSAKA, and Sawit Watch, *"Sweetness Like unto Death"*; see also Colchester and Chao, *Conflict or Consent?*; Chao, "Cultivating Consent."

5   Food Security Council, Ministry of Agriculture, and World Food Programme, *Food Security and Vulnerability Atlas of Indonesia, 2015*, xvi.

6   These violations were most recently documented in a statement published in January 2021 by the United Nations special rapporteur on the rights of Indigenous Peoples, the special rapporteur on extrajudicial, summary, or arbitrary executions, and the special rapporteur on the human rights of internally displaced persons, which called for urgent humanitarian access to West Papua as well as a full and independent investigation into abuses committed against Indigenous Papuans, including the violation of their right to food and to health. Office of the United Nations High Commissioner for Human Rights, "South-East Asia/Agrofuel."

7   These include the Roundtable on Sustainable Palm Oil, the Office of the Compliance Advisor Ombudsman of the International Finance Corporation, the Indonesian National Human Rights Commission, the United Nations Committee on the Elimination of Racial Discrimination, the United Nations special rapporteur on the right to food, and the United Nations special rapporteur on the rights of Indigenous Peoples.

8   According to the British anthropologist Michael Young, the prevalent perception of hunger as a primarily biological condition partly explains its relatively sporadic treatment as a topic of ethnographic inquiry. This stands in contrast to food and eating, whose sociocultural dimensions have long constituted staples of anthropological analysis. Young, "'Worst Disease,'" 111; see also Scheper-Hughes, "Hungry Bodies," 232.

9   The condition of hunger was in fact central to the original formulation of "geopolitics," a term coined by the Brazilian physician and geographer Josué de Castro in his seminal but underacknowledged work, *Geografia da Fome* (The geography of hunger). This foundational text lay the conceptual ground for a vast body of scholarship in political economy that theorizes food insecurity and famine as products of world systems dynamics and geopolitical inequities, rather than outcomes of biological or environmental factors alone. De Castro, *Geografia da Fome*; see also Devereux, *Theories of Famine*; Drèze and Sen, *Political Economy of Hunger*; Nally, *Human Encumbrances*; Sen, *Poverty and Famines*; Watts, *Silent Violence*.

10   Scheper-Hughes, "Madness of Hunger," 433; Hastrup, "Hunger," 727. On the medicalization, technocratization, and depoliticization of "hunger" in modern food security, nutritional science, and humanitarian discourse and practice, see de Waal, *Famine That Kills*; Edkins, *Whose Hunger?*; Kwiatkowski, *Struggling with Development*; Nally, "Against Food Security"; Nott, "'How Little Progress'?"; Sanabria and Yates-Doerr, "Alimentary Uncertainties"; Scott-Smith, *On an Empty Stomach*; Scrinis, *Nutritionism*; Tallis, *Hunger*; Yates-Doerr, "Opacity of Reduction."

      A word on citations. In *Pollution Is Colonialism*, Max Liboiron, a Red River Métis/Michif geographer, critiques the tendency in scholarly works to introduce Indigenous authors with their nation/affiliation while leaving settler and white scholars unmarked. This approach, Liboiron points out, is problematic because it "re-centers settlers and whiteness as an unexceptional norm, while deviations have to be marked and named." In this work, I adopt and adapt Liboiron's citational methodology in identifying all scholars cited by their cultural or ethnic background and by their primary disciplinary affiliation. Where such information was not readily or publicly available and given I could not consult all works both published and in progress, I contacted scholars directly to explain my citational approach and seek out how they wished to be identified. One individual chose to be identified only by discipline and not by cultural heritage or land relations, so I have added the qualifier "unmarked" following their field of expertise. I thank all the individuals who responded to my query (and most did). I extend particular gratitude to those who took this opportunity to initiate a broader and deeper conversation with me around the importance and imperfections of attempting to encompass in any one digestible statement the multiple factors that shape one's sense of being and belonging—from the cultural, gendered, and national, to the racial, religious, regional, and more. Liboiron, *Pollution Is Colonialism*, 3n10.

11 Cousins, "Antiretroviral Therapy," 434; Yates-Doerr, "Intervals of Confidence," 230.

12 Ishiyama and TallBear, "Nuclear Waste," 200–201; see also Giraud, *What Comes after Entanglement?*; Govindrajan, *Animal Intimacies*.

13 Ulijaszek, Mann, and Elton, *Evolving Human Nutrition*, 18; see also Chappell, *Beginning to End Hunger*, 53.

14 Kanem and Norris, "Examination of the Noken and Indigenous Cultural Identity"; Whyte, "Food Sovereignty"; Fresno-Calleja, "Fighting Gastrocolonialism"; Coté, "'Indigenizing' Food Sovereignty"; Washburn, "'No Page Is Ever Truly Blank'"; Wilson, *Postcolonialism*.

15 Nichter, "Idioms of Distress Revisited," 404–5; Hardin, *Faith and the Pursuit of Health*, 54; Mendenhall, *Rethinking Diabetes*, 10.

16 Goldstein, "Ground Not Given," 101; Winchester, *Land*.

17 Das, *Life and Words*; K. Stewart, *Ordinary Affects*. On the importance of attending to the everydayness of hunger as mundane reality rather than spectacular event, see Essex, "Idle Hands," 195; Messer and Shipton, "Hunger in Africa," 230; Phillips, *Ethnography of Hunger*; Singh, "Hunger and Thirst," 576–78.

18 I borrow the term "gastrologies" from the American anthropologists Frederick Errington and Deborah Gewertz to describe how Indigenous Marind foodways shape and are shaped by culturally mediated and intersecting gastrogeographies (who eats what, where), gastropolitics (who gets what food, from whom, under what circumstances, and with what consequences), and gastro-identities (who becomes what by virtue of what is or is not eaten). Errington and Gewertz, "Pacific Island Gastrologies," 591.

19 Santos Perez, "Facing Hawai'i's Future"; Appadurai, "Gastro-Politics."

20 Holland, Ochoa, and Tompkins, "On the Visceral," 395; see also Hardin, *Faith and the Pursuit of Health*; Solomon, *Metabolic Living*.

21 Roy, *Alimentary Tracts*, 23–24. While beyond the ambit of this particular work, hunger's ethicopolitical valences as a form of protest have also been extensively explored in the context of hunger strikes, which constitute expressions of bodily and metabolically mediated refusal, dissent, and resistance to dominant institutional orders. See, for instance, Aretxaga, *Shattering Silence*; Gómez-Barris, "Mapuche Hunger Acts"; P. Anderson, *So Much Wasted*; Grant, *Last Weapons*.

22 hooks, *Black Looks*, 21; see also Ahenakew, *Towards Scarring*, 37–38; Bartolovich, "Consumerism," 234.

23   In this respect, the work before you complements ethnographic accounts
     that examine hunger, malnutrition, food insecurity, and eating disor-
     ders from perspectives situated in the "Global North" and that attend to
     late capitalist economies' relationship to food excess, waste, scarcity, and
     inequality in Anglo, European, or settler-American contexts. See, for in-
     stance, Boarder Giles, *Mass Conspiracy*; Caldwell, *Not by Bread Alone*;
     Dickinson, *Feeding the Crisis*; Garthwaite, *Hunger Pains*; Guthman, *Weigh-
     ing In*; Mendenhall, *Rethinking Diabetes*; Warin, *Abject Relations*; Warin
     and Zivkovic, *Fatness, Obesity, and Disadvantage*.

24   Here, I follow David Welchman Gegeo in approaching "Indigenous epistemol-
     ogy" as "a cultural group's ways of thinking and of creating and reformulat-
     ing knowledge using traditional discourses and media of communication . . .
     and anchoring the truth of the discourse in culture." Like all epistemolo-
     gies, Indigenous epistemology constitutes, in the Lenape Indigenous studies
     scholar Joanne Barker's terms, "an active hermeneutic, a politics of interpre-
     tation and representation, [that is] contingent upon the historical contexts,
     political systems, and social relationships in which they are articulated." It
     includes the fact of Indigenous knowledge itself but also how that Indigenous
     knowledge is theorized and constructed, and how it is then applied, or, as the
     Native Hawai'ian cultural practitioner Manulani Aluli-Meyer puts it, "what
     one knows, how one knows, and what is worth knowing in a changing world."
     Gegeo, "Indigenous Knowledge," 311; Gegeo and Watson-Gegeo, "Whose
     Knowledge?," 381–403; Barker, "Indigenous Feminisms"; Aluli-Meyer, "Our
     Own Liberation," 125; see also Semali and Kincheloe, *What Is Indigenous
     Knowledge?*, 24; Tuhiwai Smith, *Decolonizing Methodologies*, 39.

25   Parreñas, "Ethnography after Anthropology," 456. Parreñas's invitation
     brings to mind the Australian anthropologist Michael Taussig's critique of
     academic writing as "agribusiness writing," or an institutionalized mode
     of production that conceals the means of production, prioritizes mastery
     over wonder, and approaches writing as a means, rather than a source, of
     experience for readers and writers alike. Taussig, *Corn Wolf*, 5–6.

26   Jobson, "Case for Letting Anthropology Burn"; joannemariebarker and
     Teaiwa, "Native Information"; see also the contributions to the *American
     Ethnologist* fiftieth anniversary special issue of 2024, edited by Susanna
     Trnka, Jesse Hession Grayman, and Lisa L. Wynn and themed around
     the question "What Good Is Anthropology?" and their 2023 forum in the
     same journal, "Decolonizing Anthropology: Global Perspectives."

27   Ethics approval for fieldwork was sought and obtained from my university,
     the application for which was drafted jointly with Marind community mem-
     bers to center local principles and protocols of responsible, respectful, and
     reciprocal research. Customary rituals, hosted by village elders in each of
     the three villages at the onset of my fieldwork, were integral to formalizing

my welcome to and extended stay within these settlements. These rituals were complemented with additional ceremonies performed at regular intervals throughout my research, during which decisions were revisited and validated regarding my participation in everyday village life, the use of the data collected, and the ways in which these data would be communicated to outside audiences in the form of scholarly and engaged outputs. In an effort to comply with national laws, additional fieldwork permits were sought from the Indonesian government through the then Ministry of Research and Technology. The almost-immediate rejection of these applications by the government in light of "security and safety concerns" for my well-being as a foreign visitor was widely understood by communities as symptomatic of a broader trend in restrictions to freedom of movement and expression in West Papua, where access to researchers and journalists remains tightly controlled. This broader political context only heightened the importance of conducting the proposed research in the eyes of many of my companions, the vast majority of whom had in any case voiced strong opposition in the first place to the pursuit of formal permission from what is widely perceived as a colonizing and occupying nation-state. For further details on my relationships with Marind communities and the political and practical stakes of my research in Merauke, see Chao, *In the Shadow of the Palms*, 3–4, 22–27.

28 Chao, *In the Shadow of the Palms*.

29 Goodyear-Kaʻōpua, "Indigenous and Decolonizing Studies," 88. Goodyear-Kaʻōpua's invitation also resonates with the call by the Cree/Saulteaux political scientist Gina Starblanket to center everyday personal relationships as a "primary site of political action" in the pursuit of Indigenous and gender sovereignty. Starblanket, "Being Indigenous Feminists," 37.

30 These activities took place alongside a formal workshop I organized in August 2019 with the support of a Wenner-Gren Engagement Grant, titled "Oil Palm Expansion in West Papua: Multi-stakeholder Workshop on Sustainability in the Agribusiness Sector." Attended by Indonesian government, corporate, and not-for-profit organizations, as well as Marind representatives, the workshop offered a platform for Marind to communicate the adverse impacts of oil palm developments on their livelihoods, land rights, cultural well-being, food security, and physical environment. The workshop resulted in a set of recommendations for achieving rights-based, culturally sensitive, and environmentally sustainable palm oil production in rural West Papua, including "the development of binding and verifiable safeguards, standard operational procedures, and protocols to protect Indigenous communities' food and water security and cultural food sovereignty." Chao, "Engaged Anthropology."

31 On the gendered dimensions of globalization and modernization in the Pacific, see Jolly and Macintyre, *Family and Gender*; Macintyre and Spark, *Transformations of Gender*; Wardlow, *Wayward Women*.

32   Nickel, "'I Am Not a Women's Libber,'" 299.

33   Kahaleole Hall, "Strategies of Erasure," 274–79; see also Barker, "Introduction: Critically Sovereign," 21; Ross, "From the 'F' Word," 45. On colonial racial capitalism, see Koshy et al., *Colonial Racial Capitalism*.

34   On speaking truth to power, see Zinn, "Speaking Truth"; Rutherford, "Kinky Empiricism." The gendered dynamics of food insecurity, hunger, and famine, and the particular burdens of care, shame, and responsibility placed on women as food providers and child-bearers, have been extensively explored in anthropology and consonant disciplines. See, for instance, Biehl, *Vita*; M. A. Carney, *Unending Hunger*; Kelleher, *Feminization of Famine*; van Houten, "Gendered Political Economies"; Kimura, *Hidden Hunger*; Kwiatkowski, *Struggling with Development*; Mendenhall, *Rethinking Diabetes*; Scheper-Hughes, *Death without Weeping*; Tappan, *Riddle of Malnutrition*; Vaughan, *Story of an African Famine*; Weismantel, *Food, Gender, and Poverty*.

35   Mohanty, "Under Western Eyes," 62–63; see also Visweswaran, *Fictions of Feminist Ethnography*; Spivak, "Can the Subaltern Speak?"

36   Mohanty, "Under Western Eyes," 62.

37   On scholarly debates surrounding Indigenous, Pacific, and transnational feminisms, see Arvin, "Indigenous Feminist Notes on Embodying Alliance," 335; Blackwell, Briggs, and Chiu, "Transnational Feminisms Roundtable"; Dhamoon, "Feminist Approach to Decolonizing Antiracism"; Gifort, "Show or Tell?"; Green, "Introduction—Indigenous Feminism"; Kahaleole Hall, "Navigating Our Own 'Sea of Islands,'" 16; Karides, "Why Island Feminism?," 31; Lin, "An Introduction: 'Indigenous Feminisms,'" 10; Moura-Koçoğlu, "Decolonizing Gender Roles," 242–44; Shanley, "Thoughts on Indian Feminism"; Spark, Cox, and Corbett, "'Keeping an Eye Out for Women,'" 86; Yoneyama, "Liberation under Siege," 889–904. On the risks of characterizing entire populations of women or even an educated intellectual class of women as "feminist" or "antifeminist," see also Jolly, "Beyond the Horizon?," 150; Weiner, *Women of Value*.

38   This understanding among many Marind women resonates with a rebuttal by the Māori (Waitaha ki Waipounamu iwi) scholar in education studies Makere Stewart-Harawira of strands of Western feminism that sever womanhood from the environment and land itself as the basis for many Indigenous Peoples' claims to self-determination. Accusations that "the linking of land and women functions to re-inscribe Indigenous women as passive and subordinate," Stewart-Harawira notes, elide the intimate and often sacral relationship between women and land and the ascription of the feminine to the earth itself, thus evidencing "the ongoing inscribing of colonial interpretations onto Indigenous societies." Stewart-Harawira, "Practicing Indigenous Feminism," 128. On Indigenous and Black critiques of feminism

as a Western, middle-class import and of gender inequality as a product of Western imperial culture, see Allen, "Who Is Your Mother?"; Allen, *Sacred Hoop*; Banivanua Mar, "Focussing on the Margins of Rights," 59; hooks, *Ain't I a Woman*; hooks, *Talking Back*; Kahaleole Hall, "Strategies of Erasure," 277; Liboiron, *Pollution Is Colonialism*, 41n11; Moreton-Robinson, *Talkin' Up*; Trask, "Feminism and Indigenous Hawaiian Nationalism."

39 The largely implicit or unnamed nature of feminist thought and practice among my companions in rural Merauke stands in contrast to peri-urban and urban areas of West Papua and other regions of the Pacific, where women's organizations, alliances, research bodies, and other collective institutions and movements self-identify under the rubric of Indigenous feminism or Indigenous gender empowerment. See Spark, Cox, and Corbett, "'Keeping an Eye Out for Women'"; Ginoza, "Archipelagic Feminisms"; Underhill-Sem, "Contract Scholars"; Souder, "Feminism and Women's Studies."

40 On dual marginalization, see Huhndorf and Suzack, "Indigenous Feminism," 3; see also Kanem and Norris, "Indigenous Women"; Crenshaw, "Demarginalizing the Intersection of Race and Sex."

41 Feedback received from the manuscript's two reviewers, together with guidance offered by my editor, Ken Wissoker, was translated from English into *logat* Papua and discussed with my friends in the field during sessions held via Facebook video on September 7 and 12, 2023, and then again on February 1, 4, and 10, 2024. These formal discussions were supplemented by iterative and ad hoc conversations over WhatsApp that together fed directly into the revision of this text. Speaking back directly to reviewer requests and to elements of the peer review process, as I do in this section, fits a broader desire of this work to illustrate how the often-hesitant practices of knowledge-making are integral to the knowledge that is eventually produced.

42 Moore, *Comparing Impossibilities*, 25–26. The anecdotes that open each chapter were chosen in consultation with the individuals featured within them, thereby marking a departure from Moore's understanding of diagnostic events as selected primarily by the ethnographer in light of their understanding of their relevance to their object of inquiry and research trajectory.

43 I borrow the term "hidden transcripts" from the American political scientist James Scott to describe discourses that "[take] place offstage, beyond direct observation by powerholders." This encompasses "speeches, gestures, and practices that confirm, contradict, or inflect" what appears in the realm of public social performance, and that speak to the particular constraints of domination and power experienced by those who alternately enact, endure, and resist them. Scott, *Domination and the Arts of Resistance*, 4–5.

44 My use of the expression "slow reading" draws on Deborah Bird Rose's call for "slow writing" as a way of being "called forth by events within the living world" and of responding to "our impossible position as participants in

and witnesses to catastrophes beyond our comprehension." Slow writing, Rose continues, is anchored in "slow encounters," which are anchored in events we participate in and share, imaginatively or otherwise, and that "promote understandings of embodied, relational, and contingent ethics" in an age of multiple, overlapping crises. Rose, "Slowly," 2, 9.

45   As Coburn et al. write, such a contrapuntal reading also demands that we critically consider who gets to make accusations of romanticization in the first place and who is spared such condemnation. This point is conveyed in a statement that merits quoting in full:

> Our affirmations are no more romantic than a naïve celebration of the often-dubious "achievements" made possible by Western social science, ranging from the atomic bomb to species-threatening climate change. Moreover, the charge of romanticization is not an equal one, since romanticizing the dominant social science paradigm does not have the same political effect as idealizing Indigenous knowledges that historically and up to the present day have been excluded and stigmatized. In fact, given widespread belief in the impoverished nature of Indigenous knowledge claims, any claims that Indigenous research is a useful, even powerful way of doing social science may appear "romantic," while romanticism about mainstream research paradigms appears as commonsense rather than idealism.

Coburn et al., "Unspeakable Things," 331. On the strategic valences of Indigenous discourses of resistance and vulnerability, as they are enacted and reflected on by Marind male land rights activists, see Chao, "Tree of Many Lives."

46   Hailing from South Sumatra, Albertus Vembrianto (who goes by the pen name Vembri Waluyas) grounds his creative practice in an ethos of sustainable storying and photographing that seeks, in his words, to uncover "the complexity and diversity of the problems, to ignite the facts that humans live together, relying on the sincerity of nature, as well as to remind the importance of collective responsibility over what has been damaged." Waluyas's photographs have featured in investigative reports on West Papua published by the British Broadcasting Corporation, Al Jazeera, the *Jakarta Post*, and the Gecko Project, and in exhibitions including World Press Photo, Jakarta International Photo Festival, and Biennale Jogja. In 2022, he received an Indigenous Photographers Award from the Pulitzer Center in recognition of his contributions to journalist activism. To find out more about Waluyas's work, see https://www.albertus-vembrianto.com/.

47   Leon-Quijano, "Why Do 'Good' Pictures Matter in Anthropology?," 591, 573.

48   Decisions around which stories to tell and not to tell included not only those experienced and recounted by my companions but also those that I underwent during my fieldwork. One story in particular stands out here.

It is the story of a miscarriage I have alluded to in fleeting ways in previous works. It is a story that brought Marind women and me into a very particular and intimate kind of relationship, born through an experience that has become all too prevalent in the Upper Bian as a result of growing malnutrition and its particular impacts on women's reproductive health, and that is gendered in ways few other experiences can ever be. It is a story that my companions believed should be told but that I, unlike so many of them, have yet to find the courage to properly tell—here or elsewhere. It is a story that I invoke—again, in brief, in the spirit of literal and figurative passing—to convey to the reader how respect for necessary silences worked in both directions throughout the intersubjective process of composing this book.

49 My use of the term *persistence* is inspired by the American transnational feminist scholar Kenna Neitch's critique of the language of "resistance" that frames Indigenous actions primarily as reactions against Euro-American colonialism. Closely tied to the notions of "resurgence" and "survivance" articulated by the Michi Saagiig Nishnaabeg scholar and artist Leanne Betasamosake Simpson and the Chippewa/Anishinaabe scholar Gerald Vizenor, respectively, the idiom of persistence pushes against the naturalized positioning of Indigenous agency as "contingent on its opposition to a dominant power." Instead, it draws attention to modes of Indigenous continuance and creativity that long predate and also transcend or exceed the effects of colonial incursion. Neitch, "Indigenous Persistence," 428–29; L. B. Simpson, "Indigenous Resurgence"; Whyte, "Food Sovereignty"; Vizenor, *Manifest Manners*. Here and elsewhere, I capitalize "Indigenous People" to distinguish *people* (with a lower case *p*) denoting individual human beings from *People* (with capital *P*) denoting social, cultural, and political groupings of people. The latter use is most commonly found in the form "Indigenous Peoples" referring to a socio-cultural-political identification and proper noun. See Winter, "Sand as Subject of Multispecies Justice."

50 Tuhiwai Smith, *Decolonizing Methodologies*, 37–40; see also hooks, *Teaching to Transgress*, 61; McGranahan, "Theory as Ethics," 289.

51 Durutalo, "Anthropology and Authoritarianism," 207–8; T. K. Teaiwa, "Analogies," 75; see also K. M. Teaiwa, *Consuming Ocean Island*, xv.

52 Gegeo, "Indigenous Knowledge"; see also Gegeo and Watson-Gegeo, "Whose Knowledge?," 403; Trask, "Feminism and Indigenous Hawaiian Nationalism," 911.

53 Vunibola and Scobie, "Islands of Indigenous Innovation," 6. As a culturally Melanesian world region under Indonesian occupation since the early 1960s, West Papua occupies an ambiguous position within the geopolitical sphere "Asia-Pacific." My decision to situate this work within a Pacific context is driven by a desire to engage with West Papua's violent and volatile history of settler colonization while also respecting my companions' self-

identification as Melanesian people—rather than Indonesian or Southeast Asian people—and their social, cultural, ecological, and spiritual ties to Marind and other Papuan ethnic groups across the border in Papua New Guinea. In doing so, I refrain from reproducing in representational terms the positioning of West Papua and West Papuans solely or primarily in relation to colonial forces, and instead make space for culturally shaped modes of Indigenous persistence, continuance, and survivance that are equally central to Marind ways of being and knowing.

54 Vesperi and Waterston, "Introduction: The Writer in the Anthropologist," 10.

55 T. K. Teaiwa, "Ancestors We Get to Choose," 46, 52–53; Arvin, Tuck, and Morrill, "Decolonizing Feminism," 12.

56 Ahmed, *Living a Feminist Life*, 3, 8.

57 A. Simpson and Smith, "Introduction," 7; see also Diaz and Kēhaulani Kauanui, "Native Pacific Cultural Studies," 318; Nickel, "Introduction," 9.

Chapter 1. Satiation and Hunger in the Forest

1 Original: *Kalo dong mau paham kelaparan di kampung, dong mesti paham kekenyangan di hutan.*

2 Chao, *In the Shadow of the Palms*, 16, 21.

3 In anthropological literature, dema has been alternately translated as "mana," "spirit," "totem-ancestor," and "spiritual being." Van Baal, *Dema*, 178.

4 Marind social organization is structured around nine major clans (boan) that sit in turn within a four-phratry system. Each Marind village must include members of all nine boan in order to ensure that feasts, rituals, and mythical reenactments of cosmological rejuvenation are representative of the totemic affiliations and origins of the four phratries. Knauft, *South Coast New Guinea Cultures*, 137–209. For a detailed taxonomy of Marind clans and their respective totemic affiliations, see van Baal, *Dema*, Annex IV A–D.

5 I follow the American anthropologist Barrett Brenton in using the term "ethnonutrition" to refer to the ways in which social groups "recognize, categorize, and explain the impact of their diet and foodways in maintaining or restoring order in natural, social, or spiritual realms." Brenton, "Piki, Polenta, and Pellagra," 37; see also Messer, "Anthropological Perspectives on Diet," 205–10.

6 Articulated by Schaeffer in the context of Native American epistemologies, the concept of "sacredscience" pushes against the alienation of science from the sacred within Western knowledge paradigms. Instead, it draws attention to how Indigenous knowledge systems integrate biological knowledge and spiritual cosmologies in ways that account for "the lively presence and knowledge of wind patterns, animal habits and behaviors, the edible parts of

animals and plants, plant growth, star patterns, and what all life forces need to survive, propagate themselves, and thrive." It is this refusal to segregate science from the sacred, Schaeffer notes, that fosters responsibilities to "respect the relational web and life force that holds us all together." Simpson offers a similar articulation of Indigenous epistemologies in describing Nishnaabeg "intelligence" as anchored in "the commingling of emotional and intellectual knowledge combined in motion or movement, and the making and remaking of the world in a generative fashion within Indigenous bodies that are engaged in accountable relationship with other beings." Schaeffer, *Unsettled Borders*, 22, 17–18; L. B. Simpson, *As We Have Always Done*, 21.

7   Hau'ofa, *We Are the Ocean*, 74–75; see also Kēhaulani Kauanui, *Paradoxes of Hawaiian Sovereignty*, 200; Nabobo-Baba, *Knowing and Learning*; Ravuvu, *Vaka i Taukei*; Waiko, "Komge Oro," 16–19.

8   This more-than-human relational ethos is prevalent across Melanesian and other Indigenous Pacific onto-epistemologies. For examples, see Aluli-Meyer, "Our Own Liberation"; Gegeo and Watson-Gegeo, "'How We Know'"; Matapo and Enari, "Re-imagining the Dialogic Spaces"; Nabobo-Baba, *Knowing and Learning*; Stewart-Harawira, "Returning the Sacred"; Winter, "Seat at the Table."

9   The French philosopher Corine Pelluchon deploys the concept of milieu to reframe nourishment not simply in terms of the foods that sustain us but also in terms of the environments wherein foods are procured, prepared, and consumed. To think about nourishment as milieu, Pelluchon notes, helps push against the naturalization of nature as a resource by bringing into the fold the diverse activities, organisms, environments, and relations that make sustenance possible and meaningful. Pelluchon, *Nourishment*, 10.

10   Elsewhere, I describe this ethos of interspecies engagement as one of "restrained care," or a form of care wherein Marind actively refrain from overly influencing or controlling the movements, growth, and reproduction of nonhuman beings, in recognition and respect of their inherent wildness (*liar*) and freedom (*bebas*). Care manifests instead in human actions that sustain nonhuman flourishing through the indirect enhancement of habitats and environments in the course of everyday forest activities, such as the clearing of waterways, the scattering of seeds, and the distribution of food resources to the benefit of forest organisms. Taken together, restraint and/in care takes as its central focus the preservation of nonhuman beings' species-specific modalities of being, as these are embedded within and generative of broader and relational socioecological networks. Chao, *In the Shadow of the Palms*, 100–101.

11   On the cosmological significance of skin and wetness among Marind, see Chao "Children of the Palms," 248–52; Chao, "Sago," 321; Chao, "Wetness," 96–97; and Chao, *In the Shadow of the Palms*, 77–94. I translate <u>igid</u>

as "skin" in line with its translation by Marind into Indonesian as *kulit*. I translate dubadub more loosely as "wetness" to capture and convey the myriad manifestations that Marind identify for a concept they say cannot be translated into any single word. These manifestations range from the moistness of forest soils to the juiciness of forest fruit, the liquidity of rivers and streams, the succulence of plants and animal flesh, and the cosmological flows of literal and symbolic fluids that enable reciprocal nourishment within the Marind lifeworld.

12 On the centrality of bodily fluids, surfaces, and exchanges in the construction of personhood in other Melanesian societies, see Becker, *Body, Self, and Society*; Eves, *Magical Body*; Goldman and Ballard, *Fluid Ontologies*; P. Stewart and Strathern, *Humors and Substances*.

13 On transcorporeality, see Alaimo, *Bodily Natures*, 4, 20, 22.

14 Here, I follow the lead of Indigenous scholars who critique "multispecies" approaches for excluding beings that do not sit comfortably within dominant secular scientific understandings of life as *bios*. TallBear, "Indigenous Reflection"; Stewart-Harawira, "Returning the Sacred"; Wooltorton, Poelina, and Collard, "River Relationships."

15 In this respect, Marind philosophies of "skinship" differ from psychoanalytical approaches that understand the autonomy of the individual to require the breaking off or tearing of a skin shared in common with their parents, or that posit the evolution of humans to involve a shift in sensory development from touch to hearing, and culminating in sight. Anzieu, *Skin-Ego*, 45–46; Montagu, *Touching*; Gregory, "Skinship," 180–81.

16 West, "Translation, Value, and Space," 633.

17 These bodily, more-than-human socialities bring to mind the characterization among Trobriand Islanders of laboring for and feeding their kin as "giving them their sweat" (*kepwe'isi*). Mosko, *Ways of Baloma*, 192–93. On the socialization of unborn children though mediated encounters between women's wombs and forest skins, see also Chao, "Children of the Palms," 245–6, 248–52.

18 On the sharing of bodily substances and the creation of social relations through the medium of food in Melanesia, see Eves, *Magical Body*, 37; Halvaksz, "Taste of Public Places," 144–49; von Poser, "Bosmun Foodways"; Strathern, "Melpa Food-Names," 504; Weiner, *Inalienable Possessions*, 27.

19 von Poser, *Foodways and Empathy*, 1.

20 Nabobo-Baba, *Knowing and Learning*, 94; see also Aluli-Meyer, "Our Own Liberation."

21 On the relationship between food, memory, and the body in Melanesia, see Battaglia, *On the Bones of the Serpent*; Eves, "Remembrance of Things Passed."

22   The importance of complementing primary starch foods with a diversity of accompanying dishes including meat and vegetables is a recurring motif within emic food classifications and attendant notions of satiety across the central and eastern Pacific. See Pollock, *These Roots Remain*.

23   TallBear, cited in Nickel, "Introduction," 2; see also Wāhpāsiw and Halfe, "Conversations on Indigenous Feminism," 227.

24   Mol, *Eating in Theory*, 30; see also Paxson, *Eating beside Ourselves*, 6–7.

25   Plumwood, "Tasteless," 324; see also Pratt, "Care, Toxics and Being Prey," 444.

26   Rose, *Nourishing Terrains*, 7, 23.

27   Fujikane, *Mapping Abundance*, 8; see also Aikau et al., "Indigenous Feminisms Roundtable," 87. For comparable analogies between the condition of land and its human and other-than-human dwellers in Melanesia, see A. Anderson, *Landscapes of Relations*, 97–99; Becker, *Body, Self, and Society*, 56, 85; Leach, *Creative Land*, 30–31.

28   Comparable coping strategies are documented by the British anthropologist Audrey Richards in her seminal works on land, labor, and diet in Northern Rhodesia (present-day Zimbabwe) and also elsewhere in the African continent. See Richards, *Hunger and Work in a Savage Tribe*; Richards, *Land, Labor, and Diet*; Campbell, "Strategies for Coping"; de Waal, *Famine That Kills*; Morell-Hart, "Foodways and Resilience"; Shipton, "African Famines."

29   The American anthropologist Jessica Hardin identifies a similar dynamic in Samoa, where discourses surrounding hunger, satiety, and bodily and metabolic disorders act as "metacommunication" for the state of one's social and moral relationships. Hardin, *Faith and the Pursuit of Health*, 54; see also Kalofonos, "'All I Eat Is ARVs,'" 363; Mendenhall, *Rethinking Diabetes*, 10.

30   Young, *Fighting with Food*, 177, 188; Young, "'Worst Disease,'" 126.

31   Among the Kalauna and the Massim, hunger is objectified as disease inflicted on communities by spirits and by ritual leaders who have the power to regulate food supplies but also to provoke insatiable hunger (*tufo'a* or *loka*) as a sanction and punishment. Among the Yagwoia-Angan, the malignant power of *womba* is said to penetrate victims' bodies, drink their blood, and consume their vital organs, while also afflicting people's souls with an insatiable craving for pig meat and human flesh. A similar phenomenon exists among the inhabitants of New Ireland in the form of famine sorcery, which makes people experience hunger despite the abundance of food. Young, "'Worst Disease,'" 113–19; Mimica, *Of Humans, Pigs, and Souls*, 27–31; Eves, "Remembrance of Things Passed," 275. On the attribution of disease to malignant acts of sorcery in Melanesia, see also W. Anderson, *Collectors of Lost Souls*; Lindenbaum, *Kuru Sorcery*.

32   A comparable danger arises among adults in the context of skin-changing (*ganti kulit*), wherein Marind men who adopt the bodies and behaviors

of forest creatures in the context of hunting may become captive to their animal habitus and unable or unwilling to return to their human form. Chao, *In the Shadow of the Palms*, 87–94.

33   For comparable examples of food taboos intended to prevent a transference of undesired physical or behavioral traits to children in Melanesia, see Bonnemère, *Acting for Others*, 113–16; Jolly, "Gifts, Commodities, and Corporeality," 55. The observation of dietary restrictions on the part of Marind mothers and fathers during pregnancy and postpartum bears comparison to the practice of couvade documented among Indigenous Peoples of lowland South America, among whom taboos on the consumption of particular foods serve in part to prevent newborns from acquiring animal-like, rather than human, characteristics. Rival, "Androgynous Parents"; Vilaça, "Making Kin."

34   Hatley, "Blood Intimacies," 73–74; Derrida, *Gift of Death*, 69.

35   Tynan, "What Is Relationality?," 599.

36   Tuana, "Viscous Porosity," 200–201.

37   Ginn, Beisel, and Barua, "Flourishing," 113; Butler, *Precarious Life*, 26; Govindrajan, *Animal Intimacies*.

38   Despret and Meuret, "Cosmoecological Sheep," 27–28; see also Despret, *What Would Animals Say*, 86–87; Stengers, "Cosmopolitical Proposal."

39   This relational and more-than-human understanding of hunger is central to what Ahenakew terms "Indigenous notions of wellness" that are anchored in "balance, steadiness, resilience, and smoothness of physical and spiritual relations in order to enable reciprocal flows and the integration of human and non-human relations within a larger land-metabolism." Nicole Redvers, a member of the Deninu K'ue First Nation and an Indigenous health expert, and her colleagues make a similar point in their call for "molecular decolonization" through the recognition and protection of humans' "tempered patterns of consumption in reciprocity with the land to maintain balance." Ahenakew, *Towards Scarring*, 20, 26; Redvers et al., "Molecular Decolonization."

Chapter 2. Hungers That Never Go Away

Portions of this chapter draw on my "Eating and Being Eaten: The Meanings of Hunger among Marind," published in *Medical Anthropology: Cross-Cultural Studies in Health and Illness* (2021); and my "Gastrocolonialism: The Intersections of Race, Food, and Development in West Papua," published in the *International Journal of Human Rights* (2022).

1   Chao, *In the Shadow of the Palms*, 167–82.

2   The mnemonic functions of hunger in structuring historical periods and events among Marind find resonance with similar temporal classifications

among inhabitants of the African continent, notably in Uganda, Kenya, Tanzania, and Sudan. See Willerslev and Meinert, "Understanding Hunger," 830–32; Ogoye-Ndegwa and Aagaard-Hansen, "Famines," 237–40; Phillips, *Ethnography of Hunger*, 6; de Waal, *Famine That Kills*, 71–72.

3   Vernon, *Hunger*, 3.

4   On headhunting and fertility and initiation rites in precolonial Marind society, see van Baal, *Dema*, 471–764; Baxter Riley, *Among Papuan Headhunters*; Knauft, *South Coast New Guinea Cultures*, 137–209; Serpenti, *Cultivators in the Swamps*.

5   For a comprehensive historical account of the donovanosis epidemics and their impacts on Marind communities in Merauke, see Richens, *Tik Merauke*; Vogel and Richens, "Donovanosis."

6   On racism as structural violence in West Papua, see Karma, *Seakan Kitorang Setengah Binatang*; Chao, "We Are (Not) Monkeys"; Eichhorn, "Resource Extraction"; Munro, "Global HIV Interventions"; Webb-Gannon, "#Papuanlivesmatter."

7   *Kompas*, "Merauke Diharapkan Jadi Lumbung Padi Nasional"; Maulia, "Indonesia Pledges to 'Feed the World.'" On *lumbung*, or the "traditional rice barn," as a recurring metaphor within Indonesian food security discourses, see MacRae and Reuter, "Lumbung Nation." Large-scale agroindustrial food estates such as MIFEE have long been central to Indonesian food security policy and practice. Such estates were first established during Sukarno's presidency, which saw the beginnings of industrial agricultural expansion across the archipelago's outer islands of Sumatra, Kalimantan, Sulawesi, and West Papua (known as Irian Jaya at the time), together with state-sponsored transmigration schemes (*transmigrasi*) to supply the local labor force. This expansion was actively pursued by Sukarno's successor, Suharto, as exemplified by the Mega Rice Project in Central Kalimantan. This program aimed to convert a staggering 1.4 million hectares of peat swamp forest into rice paddies but was eventually abandoned due to poor environmental conditions and failed economic policies. Neilson and Wright, "State and Food Security Discourses"; McCarthy, Vel, and Afiff, "Trajectories of Land Acquisition"; Li and Semedi, *Plantation Life*, 14–16; McCarthy, "Tenure and Transformation"; Galudra et al., "Hot Spots of Confusion."

8   WALHI Papua et al., *Swallowing Indonesia's Forests*, 15–19.

9   I was involved in five participatory mapping expeditions during my fieldwork in Khalaoyam, Mirav, and Bayau. These activities sat within a broader and ongoing struggle by Marind activists to secure formal recognition of their customary rights to lands and forests through the production and use of maps in court cases as evidence of traditional ownership and use. For

further details on the politics of Marind cartography as cultural practice and land reclaiming strategy, see Chao, *In the Shadow of the Palms*, 51–74; Chao, "There Are No Straight Lines."

10   Similar trends in nutritional decline have been identified among communities inhabiting areas converted from forests to oil palm plantations in other regions of West Papua and across the Indonesian archipelago. See Nurhasan et al., "Toward a Sustainable Food System"; Purwestri et al., *From Growing Food to Growing Cash.*

11   As the Japanese American feminist science and technology studies scholar Aya Kimura notes, the biofortification of processed foods with iron, zinc, calcium, magnesium, phosphorus, potassium, vitamins, and folic acid is often invoked in the government's promotion of "healthy foods" in Indonesia—even as it obscures these foods' high sodium, preservative, additive, oil, sugar, and salt content. Kimura, *Hidden Hunger*, 101.

12   Syah, "Ini Kata Bupati Merauke." For local media coverage documenting rising rates of malnutrition in Merauke, see Prasetyo and Harthana, "Suku Marind"; Razaki, "Delapan Kasus Gizi Buruk"; Suriyanto, "20 Persen Balita Merauke Kurang Gizi"; *Seputar Papua*, "2021, Kasus Stunting di Merauke."

13   The British anthropologist Alice Street deploys the concept of the "clinical gaze" in her analysis of hospital infrastructures in Papua New Guinea as places where patients become acutely aware of their marginality and invisibility in the course of their interactions with doctors. A similarly diminishing experience is documented by Jenny Munro in her ethnographic study of West Papuan students who have come to know or learn the feeling of shame (*malu*) through their encounters with the Indonesian state and the national educational system. Street, *Biomedicine in an Unstable Place*, 224; Munro, "'Now We Know Shame,'" 169–70.

14   On the social, racial, and technocratic stigma associated with the HIV/AIDS epidemic in West Papua, see Butt, "Local Biologies"; Butt, "'Lipstick Girls'"; Butt, "'Living in HIV-Land'"; Kirsch, "Rumour"; Munro, "Global HIV Interventions."

15   Yates-Doerr, "Opacity of Reduction," 294; Deer et al., "Rage," 1061; see also McLennan et al., "Problem with Relying on Dietary Surveys"; Pollock, *These Roots Remain.*

16   Choudhury, "Making of the American Calorie," 16.

17   The concept of food sovereignty was first articulated by the international farmers organization La Via Campesina at the World Food Summit in 1996 and defined as "the peoples', Countries' or State Unions' RIGHT to define their agricultural and food policy, without any dumping vis-à-vis third countries." Central to food sovereignty are the prioritization of local agricultural production to feed local people; access to land, water, seeds,

and credit for farmers and landless communities; the institution of land reforms; and the recognition of women farmers' rights as major contributors to agricultural production. Representing a grassroots-driven, self-determined, and human rights–based alternative to neoliberal food policies, food sovereignty is often understood to mark a departure from definitions of food security articulated by intergovernmental institutions like the Food and Agriculture Organization, and that tend to center the securement of food availability, access, utilization, and stability, notably through international trade and markets. La Via Campesina, "Food Sovereignty"; Food and Agriculture Organization, *Food Security*; Canfield, *Translating Food Sovereignty*. On the relationship between food sovereignty and food security as principles and as practice, see Schanbacher, *Politics of Food*; Agarwal, "Food Sovereignty"; Edelman et al., "Introduction."

18 Fischler deploys the concept of "gastro-anomie" to describe and critique the multiple and contradictory demands and pressures placed on consumers by the modern industrial food system. The sense of freedom of choice created by this system, Fischler argues, is accompanied by an "anxious tugging" (*un tiraillement anxieux*) as individualized decisions around food become untethered from socially shaped structures and categories of meaning. Fischler, "Gastro-nomie et gastro-anomie," 206.

19 For comparable examples of the synecdochic uses of "food" and "sago," as well as other staple root vegetables in Melanesia, see Glazebrook, *Permissive Residents*, 97; MacCarthy, "Playing Politics with Yams," 140; Schieffelin, *Sorrow of the Lonely*, 31; Stasch, *Society of Others*, 169.

20 For comparable examples of bodily deterioration as symptomatic of broader societal and ecological decline in Melanesia, see Clark, *Steel to Stone*, 119–43; Lattas, "Sorcery and Colonialism," 71; van Oosterhout, "Scent of Sweat," 25.

21 Throop, "Sacred Suffering," 84.

22 Holtzman, "Food and Memory," 367.

23 Fajans, "Shame, Social Action, and the Person," 175; Fajans, *They Make Themselves*, 119.

24 As I explore elsewhere, analogous and antagonistic indexicalities between humans and other-than-humans are central to Marind theories of socio-environmental and cosmological change. These include indexicalities identified by Marind in their relationships with sago palms, oil palms, domesticated animals, plantation parasites and mutualists, and the racialized figure of the monkey. See Chao, "Children of the Palms"; Chao, "Tree of Many Lives"; Chao, *In the Shadow of the Palms*; Chao, "Plastic Cassowary"; Chao, "The Beetle or the Bug?"; Chao, "We Are (Not) Monkeys."

25 Chao, "Plastic Cassowary," 839–40.

26 Bourdieu, *Distinction*, 6.

27 On the ambivalent association of rice with modernity and dependency in West Papua, see Chao, "Gastrocolonialism"; Nerenberg, "Terminal Economy," 117–20.

28 As I discuss elsewhere, disparaging comments about sago-based diets and sago societies stemming from government representatives and biomedical practitioners are prevalent in contemporary West Papua and sit within longer histories of colonial discourses and stereotypes in both Melanesia and Southeast Asia. Within these discourses, the ad hoc procuration by communities of semiwild or wild sago was often associated with native laziness and opportunism and contrasted with the disciplined and cultured activities of formal agriculture and agricultural crops, notably rice paddy farming. Chao, *In Shadow of the Palms*, 259–60.

29 Santos Perez, "Facing Hawai'i's Future."

30 Original: *Orang Papua kulitnya hitam. Sayang sekali, tapi ya sudah. Warna kulit orang Papua tidak bisa kami mengubah. Tapi kita bisa mengangkat mereka ke dunia modern dengan membawakan mereka makanan modern. Bagi orang Papua, kemajuan itu mulai bukan di kulit, tapi mulai di perut.*

31 On the dichotomization of native and foreign foods as nourishing and strong versus empty and weak in Melanesia, see Bashkow, *Meaning of Whitemen*, 179–246; Halvaksz, "Taste of Public Places," 150; Jolly, "Gifts, Commodities and Corporeality," 48; Kahn, "'Men Are Taro,'" 42–44.

32 The Amungme feminist theorist and Christian theologian Josina Wospakrik documents a similar rejection of "modern foods" among women in the West Papuan regency of Mimika, who associate the consumption of imported commodities with poor maternal and child health. Wospakrik, "Transculturation," 167–69; see also Kahn and Sexton, "The Fresh and the Canned"; van Eeuwijk, *Small but Strong*.

33 While no means universal or unitary across their regional manifestations, the gendered dynamics of land-based developments have been documented in a range of other Melanesian settings. For instance, the Vanuatu gender specialist Anna Naupa, Australian anthropologist Martha Macintyre, and Australian political ecologist Simon Foale describe how women in Vanuatu and Papua New Guinea tend to be more critical of extractive projects like logging and mining but are often marginalized from negotiations surrounding land developments and land reform. Women are also rarely the beneficiaries of payments from corporate and government bodies, with compensation often received and spent by local men. Similar dynamics have been identified in the Artic and Canadian contexts by the Sámi political scientist Rauna Kuokkanen and the Mi'kmaw legal scholar Sherry Pictou, respectively, who note how colonial constructions of masculinity are perpetuated through the stratification of gender in

economic activities, wherein Indigenous men are privileged as income earners and beneficiaries of profits derived from extractive industries, to the neglect of Indigenous women's material and social well-being. Naupa, "Making the Invisible Seen"; Macintyre and Foale, "Global Imperatives"; Kuokkanen, "From Indigenous Economies," 276; Pictou, "Decolonizing Decolonization," 377. For comparable examples in other Pacific settings, see Burton, "Knowing about Culture"; Bolabola, "Fiji"; Fairbairn-Dunlop, "Gender, Culture and Sustainable Development"; Monson, "Politics of Property"; Kabutaulaka, "Rumble in the Jungle"; Stewart-Harawira, "Practicing Indigenous Feminism."

34   For examples of "eating money" as expressive of individualistic, materialistic, and wasteful behaviors in other parts of Melanesia, see Dyer, "Eating Money," 88–89; Eräsaari, "'Wasting Time,'" 322; Jacka, *Alchemy in the Rainforest*, 240; Sexton, "'Eating' Money," 119–20.

35   While not nearly as prominent as hunger within Marind women's discourses, the consumption of alcohol (*miras*) is also gendered in that it is associated primarily with men and sometimes described in tandem with "bad hunger" as "bad thirst" (*kehausan buruk*). See Munro, "Indigenous Masculinities."

36   The loss of freedom attributed to plantation workers is also invoked by Marind in describing the fate of animals that are now seeking shelter in their villages following the destruction of their native habitats. Described by Marind as "orphans" (*anak yatim*) and "refugees" (*pengungsi*), village-bound animals are pitied by their keepers because they are severed from their kin in the forest and deprived of their autonomy and wildness. In both instances, village animals conjure to Marind their own loss of freedom and self-determination as coerced citizens of the Indonesian nation-state. Chao, "Plastic Cassowary."

37   Kahn, *Always Hungry*, 151.

Chapter 3. Of Roads and Other Hungry Beings

Portions of this chapter draw on my "Gastrocolonialism: The Intersections of Race, Food, and Development in West Papua," published in the *International Journal of Human Rights* (2022); and my "Multispecies Mourning: Grieving as Resistance on the West Papuan Plantation Frontier," published in *Cultural Studies* (2022).

1   Mrázek, *Engineers of Happy Land*.

2   Chao, *In the Shadow of the Palms*, 39–41. On the ambiguous significance of roads in West Papua as promissory conduits for economic and social advancement and as threatening infrastructures of state and military control, see Ballard, "Signature of Terror"; Kusumaryati, "Great Colonial Roads"; Martinkus, *The Road*.

3   Yunkaporta, *Sand Talk*, 76.

4   Fajans, *They Make Themselves*, 120. The Australian anthropologist Diana Glazebrook identifies a similar association among West Papuan refugees living in Australia, whose songs point to the relationship between experiences of hunger and the isolation and loneliness arising from ruptured ties to their native environment and community. Glazebrook, *Permissive Residents*, 95–105.

5   As I describe elsewhere, a comparably rapacious kind of hunger to that of roads is attributed by many Marind male activists to the cash crop of oil palm itself, which is often described as an insatiable and self-interested plant that saps the water from rivers, eats the soils and forests on which it grows, and devours time by rupturing the shared temporalities of growth, reproduction, and senescence of Marind and their plant and animal kin. The hunger of oil palm also manifests in dreams that many Marind describe as "being eaten by oil palm" (*dimakan sawit*), in which sleeping villagers witness and experience their death repeatedly from the point of view of forest animals and plants whose lives and futures are also threatened by agribusiness expansion. Chao, *In the Shadow of the Palms*, 143–200.

6   Rose, "Multispecies Knots," 128.

7   To "re-member," writes the Yesáh (Occaneechi) sociologist Marshall Jeffries, involves "not just collectively remembering and taking back traditions but also recreating a shared sense of membership and belonging in [*sic*] a community." It speaks to the socially and politically empowering work of memory in "restoring cultural and historical knowledge, tradition, and language." Jeffries, "Re-membering," 163, 189n13.

8   Hobart and Kneese, "Radical Care," 2–3.

9   Butler, *Frames of War*, 42–43.

10 Stasch, "Singapore, Big Village of the Dead."

11 The Indonesian term *jaya* can be translated as "victorious," "prosperous," "glorious," or "triumphant."

12 Irian Jaya ("Irian victorious") is an acronym of the Indonesian slogan "Ikut Republik Indonesia Anti-Netherlands" (follow Indonesia against Holland) and *jaya* ("victorious"). It was used during the Indonesian takeover in the 1960s and persisted after the renaming of the western half of New Guinea as Papua in the 1970s.

13 Ananta, Utami, and Handayani, "Statistics on Ethnic Diversity"; Elmslie, "Great Divide."

14 Karma, *Seakan Kitorang Setengah Binatang*; see also Chao, "We Are (Not) Monkeys."

15   Sexual violence constituted what Louise Halfe, a Cree poet and social worker, and Omeasoo Wāhpāsiw, a nehiyaw iskwew living in Anishinaabe territory, call a "hush-hush topic" for many of my companions in the field. These experiences, which I understood implicitly to occur both in the city and in the villages, were considered too private or shameful to discuss and were often also associated with disparaging representations of Marind as primitive and savage in light of their precolonial ritualized fertility cults, which reportedly involved both collective heterosexual and homosexual intercourse. Both factors explain my limited treatment of these topics within the book. Wāhpāsiw and Halfe, "Conversations on Indigenous Feminism," 211.

16   See, for instance, Brown, "Eating the Dead," 117–19; Gould, *To Lead as Equals*, 29; Nash, *We Eat the Mines*, ix; Peña, *Terror in the Machine*, 3; Stoler, *Capitalism and Confrontation*, 197–98; Bayart, *State in Africa*, xvii; Mbembe, *On the Postcolony*, 160–66; Phillips, *Ethnography of Hunger*, 111–12; de Waal, *Famine That Kills*, 12; Lattas, "Sorcery and Colonialism," 61–62. The cannibalistic logic invoked by Marind also brings to mind the German-born philosopher Karl Marx's likening of capitalist production in a class-based context to the operations of the "vampire, werewolf, or parasite forever feeding off the lifeblood of the proletariat." Marx cited in Lefebvre, "Conspicuous Consumption," 48.

17   On the various meanings of *suanggi* across Indonesia, see Bubandt, *Empty Seashell*.

18   On the notion of "imported" modes of sorcery as more efficacious than local variants in other Melanesian regions, see Stasch, "Giving Up Homicide"; Zelenietz, "Sorcery and Social Change," 12.

19   Césaire, *Notebook of a Return*; Chamoiseau, *Creole Folktales*.

20   Scheper-Hughes, *Death without Weeping*, 32–33; Gordillo, "Breath of the Devils," 39–42.

21   Originally developed in the context of war zone trauma and primarily deployed within the fields of mental health and clinical psychology, the concept of moral injury has more recently been activated to consider how climate change and ecological destruction undermine individuals' and communities' sense of psychological and moral well-being, as they find themselves perpetrating, witnessing, or failing to prevent acts that contribute to environmental degradation. Litz et al., "Moral Injury"; Henritze et al., "Moral Injury."

22   The American-born philosopher Janna Thompson describes this condition as one of "temporal vulnerability," or the kind of vulnerability that "people possess in respect to their position in time and their relationship to preceding and succeeding generations." Thompson, "Being in Time," 164.

Portions of this chapter draw on my "Wrathful Ancestors, Corporate Sorcerers: Rituals Gone Rogue in Merauke, West Papua," published in *Oceania* (2019); and my "Eating and Being Eaten: The Meanings of Hunger among Marind," published in *Medical Anthropology: Cross-Cultural Studies in Health and Illness* (2021).

1   Here and elsewhere, and in line with Marind custom, I refer to children of the age of approximately five and under with the pronoun *they*. These children are identified with neutral pronouns in Marind language because they are not considered to be fully human yet and because their gender is as of yet uncertain. See Chao, "Children of the Palms," 4.

2   Mimica, *Of Humans, Pigs, and Souls*, 47.

3   Farmer, AIDS *and Accusation*, 165.

4   Some of these feasts marked the growth and transition of children across age-grades while others served to celebrate marriages, intertribal reconciliations, or female and male initiations. Yet other feasts marked successful headhunting expeditions and the capture of children from neighboring tribes. Angai generally entailed the ceremonial killing of a pig, the consumption of a sago dish (sago sep), the building of a feast house, together with collective dancing, singing, the performance of dema's past undertakings, and the wearing of intricate costumes and headdresses fashioned from bird of paradise feathers, boar tusks, cassowary casques, sago bark, and other forest-derived materials.

5   Van Baal, *Dema*, 828–62.

6   Chao, *In the Shadow of the Palms*, 143–51.

7   MacCarthy, "Playing Politics with Yams." The Belgian anthropologist Filip de Boeck documents a similar perception among the aLuund of southwestern Zaire, who read in the physical condition of hunger both an effect and a source of social and cosmological disintegration. De Boeck, "'When Hunger Goes Around the Land,'" 257; see also Mendenhall, *Rethinking Diabetes*, 10. For psychocultural approaches to hunger as a trigger of social anxiety and disintegration, see DuBois, *People of Alor*; Firth, *Social Change in Tikopia*; Holmberg, *Nomads of the Longbow*; Shack, "Hunger, Anxiety, and Ritual"; Turnbull, *Mountain People*.

8   The American anthropologists Mary Howard and Ann Millard describe a comparable situation among the Chagga of Mount Kilimanjaro in Tanzania, who widely interpret hunger less as a consequence of their political disempowerment and historical marginalization than as a consequence of their own internal fallibilities and failures, notably those of parents who bear children in quick succession, in violation of customary norms.

These forms of self-culpabilization have been exacerbated by introduced Christian, biomedical, and humanitarian discourses that attribute hunger to irresponsible parenting practices, and particularly those of women and mothers. Howard and Millard, *Hunger and Shame*; see also Kwiatkowski, *Struggling with Development*.

9   Sahlins, "What Kinship Is," 2.

10   Similar notions of ancestral punishment have been documented in North Efate, Vanuatu, where men who claim or lease lands to corporations over which they have no rights become subject to the curse of "being eaten by the land" (*graon hemi kaekae vu*). In both instances, spirits embedded within the landscape exert retribution on those within the community who do not follow the path of custom (*kastom*). McDonnell, "'The Land Will Eat You,'" 151, 157.

11   Bateson et al., "Toward a Theory of Schizophrenia."

12   Stasch, "Giving Up Homicide," 33.

13   Barker, "Introduction: Critically Sovereign," 21.

14   Neilson and Wright, "State and Food Security Discourses," 134–36.

15   The phrase "feed Indonesia and then the world" is the official translation of *Indonesia berswasembada pangan, agar bisa mengatasi krisis pangan dunia*, meaning "make Indonesia self-sufficient in food in order to overcome the world food crisis." A historically central motif within Indonesian corporate and state discourses surrounding the promotion of oil palm expansion, the phrase was first used in relation to the MIFEE project by President Susilo Bambang Yudhoyono in 2008, and then reiterated at the Indonesian Chamber of Commerce conferences "Feed Indonesia, Feed the World" in 2010 and 2012. Ito, Rachman, and Savitri, "Power to Make Land Dispossession Acceptable," 39–42; see also Li and Semedi, *Plantation Life*, 2.

16   Papuan civil society organizations have on several occasions symbolically "returned" Otsus to the central government in light of its unfulfilled promises of self-determination for West Papuan peoples. In August 2005, for instance, 13,000 Papuans led by the Papuan Customary Council (Dewan Adat Papua) carried a coffin to parliament to symbolize the failure of the law, and again in June 2010, when the Papuan Democracy Forum (Forum Demokrasi Papua) organized a collective march protesting against the law and demanding a referendum. More recent protests took place in July 2021, when the Indonesian government announced the renewal of an amended Otsus law, which, among other revisions, now excludes the right of Papuans to establish local political parties and the right of Papuan political parties to participate in local elections. Beo da Costa and Lamb, "Indonesia Parliament Passes Revised Autonomy Law"; Bertrand, "Autonomy and Stabil-

ity"; Myrtinnen, "Under Two Flags"; Strangio, "Protests Greet Indonesia's Renewal of Papuan Autonomy Law"; Widjojo, *Papua Road Map*.

17   Povinelli, *Cunning of Recognition*, 16–17.

18   Leith, *Politics of Power*.

19   Kluge, "West Papua." Still today, governments across the world continue to disregard the claims and demands brought to them by exiled West Papuan activists and organizations in favor of maintaining geopolitical and economic alliances with Indonesia. Examples cited by Vicentia and others included the controversial Lombok Treaty of 2006, which guarantees no interference on matters of "internal affairs" or "sovereignty" between Indonesia and Australia; the New Zealand parliament ban on Benny Wenda, the leader of the United Liberation Movement for West Papua, in 2013; the military training and equipment contract signed between the French warship combat systems corporation Thales and Indonesia in 2014; and, most recently, the rejection of a petition for a referendum signed by 1.8 million Papuans by the United Nations' decolonization committee in 2017.

20   Hatch, Sternlieb, and Gordon, "Sugar Ecologies," 595.

21   Milne, *Corporate Nature*; see also West, *Conservation Is Our Government Now*; Runtuboi et al., "Oil Palm Plantations."

22   Forest Peoples Programme, "Request for Consideration"; Forest Peoples Programme, "Request for Further Consideration" (2012); Forest Peoples Programme, "Request for Further Consideration" (2013).

23   Sawit Watch and Forest Peoples Programme, "Joint Statement."

24   Kemal, "UN CERD Formal Communication"; Office of the United Nations High Commissioner for Human Rights, "South-East Asia/Agrofuel"; Avtonomov, "UN CERD Formal Communication."

25   Hadiprayitno, "Behind Transformation."

26   On Indonesian occupation as a driver of genocide in West Papua, see Banivanua Mar, "'Thousand Miles'"; Elmslie and Webb-Gannon, "Slow-Motion Genocide"; Kirsch, "Rumour"; Manufandu, "Land Grabbing"; Ondawame, "West Papua"; Wing and King, *Genocide in West Papua?*

27   Hernawan and van den Broek, "Dialog Nasional Papua."

28   See, for example, Giay, "Zakheus Pakage"; Kamma, *Koreri-Messianic Movements*; Ondawame, *One People, One Soul*; Rutherford, "Nationalism and Millenarianism"; Timmer, "Return of the Kingdom."

29   On Islamization in West Papua, see Slama, "Papua as an Islamic Frontier."

30   Timmer, "Papua Coming of Age." For comparable discourses documented in Papua New Guinea, Fiji, and the Solomon Islands, see Dundon, "DNA, Israel and the Ancestors"; Newland, "Lost Tribes of Israel"; Timmer, "Straightening the Path."

31 On millenarianism and cargo cults in Melanesia, see Rutherford, *Raiding the Land of the Foreigners*; Lawrence, *Road Belong Cargo*; Burridge, *Mambu*; *New Heaven, New Earth*; Lindstrom, *Cargo Cult*; Oosterwal, "Cargo Cult"; Robbins, "Secrecy"; Worsley, *Trumpet Shall Sound*.

32 Gordillo, "Breath of the Devils," 42.

33 Munro, "Indigenous Masculinities," 52–54.

34 On the importance of attending to Indigenous discourses of self-responsibilization in the context of climate change and attendant socio-environmental and cosmological changes, see also Smith, *Mountains of Blame*; Rudiak-Gould, *Climate Change and Tradition*.

Chapter 5. Writing Hunger

Portions of this chapter draw on my "To Write or Not to Write? Towards a Hesitant Anthropology," published in *American Ethnologist* (2023).

1 Original: *Tulislah. Tulis semuanya. Tulislah kitorang pu kelaparan, pu penyakit, pu sakit. Ceritakan ini sama seluruh dunia. Buatlah untuk kitorang pu anak-anak, pu ibu, pu hutan. Jangan biarkan kematian ini jadi sia-sia.*

2 Original: *Jangan begitu. Kau harus cerita kitorang pu kisah hidup, jangan cerita kematian. Kematian itu, bikin kitorang jadi malu dan rasa bersalah. Itu kisah orang miskin, kisah orang lemah, kisah orang yang dimakan. Itu kisah penuh kesedihan dan kemarahan.*

3 Original: *Dong harus, mama. Dong harus menceritakan kisah-kisah semua. Kitorang telah memberi kau makanan sebaik mungkin. Sekarang, kau harus menceritakan kitorang pu kisah-kisah sebaik mungkin. Inilah kau pu tanggung jawab.*

4 For examples of such engaged outputs, see, inter alia, Chao and Smolker, "West Papua"; Chao, "Culture, Food and Environment"; Chao, "Hunger in the Rubble"; Chao, "Is Hunger Culture-Bound?"; Chao, "Hunger and Culture"; Chao and Pearson, "Culture, Food and Environment"; Chao, "'In the Plantations'"; Chao and Beta, "Talking Indonesia"; Chao, "They Grow and Die"; Chao, "Pluralizing Justice"; Chao, "Forest Foodways."

5 Clifford and Marcus, *Writing Culture*; Marcus and Fischer, *Anthropology as Cultural Critique*.

6 Behar and Gordon, *Women Writing Culture*.

7 For recent key sources on ethnographic writing and its relationship to power, voice, authorship, and representation, see Starn, *Writing Culture*; McGranahan, *Writing Anthropology*; Wulf, *Anthropologist as Writer*; Waterston and Vesperi, *Anthropology Off the Shelf*; MacClancy, *Exotic No More*; Ballestero and Winthereik, *Experimenting with Ethnography*; Narayan,

Alive in the Writing; Pandian and McLean, *Crumpled Paper Boat*; Pandian, *Possible Anthropology*.

8   Kirsch, *Engaged Anthropology*, 49.

9   TallBear describes the practice of "standing with" as a willingness on the part of the researcher to be "altered, to revise her stakes in the knowledge to be produced." Standing with, TallBear notes, finds root in a broader praxis of "feminist objectivity," or an objectivity grounded in an experience-near enmeshment in the lives, knowledges, and priorities of one's research subjects. TallBear, "Standing with and Speaking as Faith," 2, 6.

10   The association made by many of my companions between womanhood and motherhood brings to mind what the nehiyaw iskwew education scholar Omeasoo Wāhpāsiw and the Cree poet and their mother Louise Halfe describe in the Native American context as "womb-an-hood," or the centrality of motherhood within Indigenous women's diverse political strategies, alliances, and identities. Wāhpāsiw and Halfe, "Conversations on Indigenous Feminism," 211–21; see also August, "Māori Women," 120; Nickel, "'I Am Not a Women's Libber,'" 300.

11   Farrelly and Nabobo-Baba, "Talanoa as Empathic Apprenticeship," 320; see also Halapua, "Talanoa in Building Democracy," 1–6. I borrow the term "wit(h)nessing" from the Australian ecologist and interdisciplinary artist Louise Boscacci to describe the affective and sensory relations of encounter and exchange that are enabled by intersubjective relations of observing and bearing testimony. I draw on the American science and technology studies scholar Donna Haraway's theorization of "companionship" from the Latin *cum panis* as a relation of "breaking bread together." Boscacci, "Wit(h)nessing"; Haraway, *When Species Meet*, 208.

12   McGranahan, *Writing Anthropology*, 10.

13   Briggs and Mantini-Briggs, *Tell Me Why My Children Died*, 16–19; see also Kalofonos, "All I Eat Is ARVs," 363–64.

14   Obeyesekere, *Cannibal Talk*; Loichot, *Tropics Bite Back*, viii, 38–39. On the representation of colonized subjects as "abject eaters," see also Bartolovich, "Consumerism"; Githire, *Cannibal Writes*; Herrmann, *To Feast on Us*; Macura-Nnamdi, "Alimentary Life"; Roy, *Alimentary Tracts*.

15   Articulated by Yunkaporta in the context of Aboriginal Australian philosophies and practices, "wrong story" is the counterpoint to "right" or "proper story," which encompasses ways of being and knowing that "regenerate every entity of the landscape in perpetuity, including our own." Yunkaporta, "All Our Landscapes Are Broken."

16   This torquing resonates with the wiindigoo/windigo poetics animating Algonquian figurations of hunger in the novels *Ledfeather* and *The Round House*. Marking the intersection of Native and First Nations art, these

novels push against colonial representations of "Native hunger," personified in the figures of the starved Indian and archetypal Indigenous cannibal, by associating the cannibalistic figure of the wiindigoo/windigo instead with settler occupation and the consumption of Native life in the form of reservations, national parks, and other extractive and dispossessory infrastructures. In doing so, the novels repurpose the wiindigoo/windigo to articulate "an analysis of the institutional racism that informed settler food policy as well as the discursive strategies that Native people continue to use to subvert it." Miner, "Consuming the Wiindigoo," 231–32, 248; see also Forbes, *Columbus and Other Cannibals*.

17 The British historian Megan Vaughan documents a similar potency in women's songs and stories about the Malawi famine of 1949–50 that act as veiled critiques of the changing realities of gender, kinship, and marital relations within their social settings. Vaughan, *Story of an African Famine*, 121.

18 Similar grievances have also been voiced by West Papuan women in recent films, including independent shorts produced by Papuan Voices (a grassroots video advocacy initiative aiming to support Papuans to bring their everyday stories and concerns to a wider audience through visual ethnographic narration) and in the Indonesian journalist Asrida Elisabet's documentary *Tanah Mama* (2015), which centers on West Papuan women's limited access to land and the precarity of their lives in the face of changing gender roles and expectations within the modern cash economy. Kadir, "Women's Grievances"; Spark, "'Food Is Life,'" 78–81.

19 Alongside decisions around the use of pseudonyms or real names, the women cited in this work also selected the descriptors that accompany their words and that often involved a combination of village affiliation, clan, age, profession, and children birthed.

20 Weiss and McGranahan, "Rethinking Pseudonyms."

21 The importance placed by Nora and other women on writing and owning rage brings to mind the Black American feminist and civil rights activist Audre Lorde's framing of rage as a cogent and meaningful response to racial discrimination in their seminal essay "The Uses of Anger." Drawing on Lorde's work in the context of Indigenous education pedagogies, Muscogee (Creek) Nation legal scholar Sarah Deer, Chickasaw literary scholar Jodi Byrd, and colleagues identify in rage and anger vital components of anticolonial action. Rage and anger, they write, must be honored, made space for, and recognized as "intellectual tools for analyzing the contours of injustice." Lorde, "Uses of Anger"; Deer et al., "Rage," 1058–59; see also Flowers, "Refusal to Forgive," 33.

22 Nabobo-Baba, "Research and Pacific Indigenous Peoples"; Tuhiwai Smith, *Decolonizing Methodologies*; Archibald, *Indigenous Storywork*; see also Coburn et al., "Unspeakable Things."

23 Jaimes Guerrero, "'Patriarchal Colonialism,'" 58.

24 The mutually enforcing relationship between sovereignty and gender justice identified by Mirabela resonates with similar positions adopted by some Indigenous and feminist theorists, who argue that nationhood and race should not be privileged over gender inequalities in the pursuit of Indigenous self-determination. For instance, the Kānaka Maoli anthropologist J. Kēhaulani Kauanui calls for attention to both colonial and precolonial gender oppression as crucial to an "engaged politics of decolonization" in the Hawai'ian context, noting that contemporary forms of gendered oppression should not be treated as secondary to the restoration of political sovereignty. Makere Stewart-Harawira, a Māori (Waitaha ki Waipounamu iwi) scholar in education studies, argues that in the context of corporatized postsettlement enterprise deals and the global economic imperative of imperialism, the decolonization of Māori society demands "a recognition of and return to the role and function of Maori women within political and spiritual leadership." In a similar vein, Emma LaRocque, a Cree and Métis Native American studies scholar, and Fay Blaney, a Xwemalhkwu educator and activist, affirm that patriarchy within precolonial Indigenous traditions and social organizations should not be exempt from critical scrutiny in the struggle for social justice. Kēhaulani Kauanui, "Native Hawaiian Decolonization," 285; Stewart-Harawira, "Practicing Indigenous Feminism"; LaRocque, "Colonization of a Native Woman Scholar," 14; Blaney, "Aboriginal Women's Action Network," 158; see also Kahaleole Hall, "Navigating Our Own 'Sea of Islands,'" 16; Kuokkanen, *Restructuring Relations*, 221; Pictou, "Decolonizing Decolonization"; Ross, "From the 'F' Word," 50.

25 The reluctance of many women to blame their men for injustices suffered brings to mind the Salish and Kootenai women's studies scholar Luana Ross's experiences of discussing "the 'f' word" (feminism) with Native American women in Montana and Oregon. The fact that Native women were often fiercely protective of Native men, Ross notes, must be viewed in the context of colonialism and the oppressive and discriminatory nature of the white criminal justice system. It is this colonial backdrop that made discussions surrounding the responsibilities of Native men and the uncovering of gendered and sexual violence difficult, and often shrouded in silence. Ross, "From the 'F' Word," 45; see also Nickel, "'I Am Not Women's Libber,'" 302; Stewart-Harawira, "Practicing Indigenous Feminism"; Deer et al., "Rage," 1064.

26 Spivak, "Subaltern Studies." The precedence given by Stefania to Indigenous solidarity over gendered asymmetries in the face of colonial invasion brings to mind the Native Hawai'ian activist and scholar Haunani-Kay Trask's critique of feminisms that focus exclusively on women and, doing so, neglect the historical oppression of all Hawai'ians within the larger force field of

Western imperialism. When considered within and against this larger force field, Trask argues, Indigenous women's experiences must be understood as a matter of nationalism and sovereignty, and not a feminist problem. Trask, "Feminism and Indigenous Hawaiian Nationalism," 909, 911.

27   Chao, "Tree of Many Lives," 522–23.

28   Sources referred to by Karolina over the course of our conversations included Indonesian translations of the Dutch anthropologist Jan van Baal's *Dema: Description and Analysis of Marind-Anim Culture (South New Guinea)* (1966); the Dutch anthropologist Jan Boelaars's *Head-Hunters about Themselves: An Ethnographic Report from Irian Jaya, Indonesia* (1981); the British explorer Edward Baxter Riley's *Among Papuan Headhunters* (1925); and the British explorer Alfred Haddon's *The Tugeri Head-Hunters of New Guinea* (1891). They also included source language versions of works produced by Indonesian anthropologists, such as Kanjeng Pangeran Haryo Koentjaraningrat and Daniel C. Ajamiseba's "Reaksi Penduduk Asli Terhadap Pembangunan Dan Perubahan" (Native inhabitants' reactions to development and change; 1994); Koentjaraningrat and Harsja Bachtiar's *Penduduk Irian Barat* (Inhabitants of West Irian; 1963); and Sarlito Sarwono's *Teori-Teori Psikologi Sosial* (Social psychology theories; 1998).

29   Kabutaulaka, "Re-presenting Melanesia"; Narokobi, "Art and Nationalism"; see also Morauta et al., "Indigenous Anthropology." Similar critiques have been voiced by Epeli Hau'ofa, who notes that anthropological representations of Melanesian Peoples have historically capitalized on copulation, sorcery, and violence, to the exclusion of people's sentiments, systems of morality, ideas of the good and the bad, and philosophies of life. These incomplete and distorted representations, Hau'ofa writes, perpetuate egregious stereotypes of Melanesian Peoples and, in doing so, deny them "important aspects of their humanity." Hau'ofa, *We Are the Ocean*, 6.

30   See Mote and Rutherford, "From Irian Jaya to Papua"; Rutherford, *Laughing at Leviathan*; Webb-Gannon, *Morning Star Rising*.

31   Akibayashi, "Okinawa Women Act against Military Violence," 52.

32   Smythe, "Laughter That Knows the Darkness"; see also Munro and Baransano, "From Saving to Survivance." I borrow the term *survivance* from Gerald Vizenor to refer to the continuous and active presence of Indigenous Peoples through stories and narratives that enact conjoined survival and resistance while also exceeding their respective confines. Survivance challenges the imposition of absence, victimry, and nihility characteristic of what Vizenor terms "manifest manners," or the "course of dominance, the racialist notions and misnomers sustained in archives and lexicons as 'authentic' representations of Indian cultures," and that are perpetuated both in historical colonial discourses and in contemporary discourses of resilience. Vizenor, *Manifest Manners*, vii, x, 17; see also Wilbur and Gone, "Beyond Resilience."

33 Robbins, "Beyond the Suffering Subject."

34 In juxtaposing literal and narrative plots, I invoke a formation that has been extensively theorized by critical race, history, and literary scholars since Sylvia Wynter's original engagement with the term in 1971. Within this scholarship, the plot is recognized as a space of Black liberation and empowerment, in contrapuntal relation to the plantation as a space of Black death and dehumanization. Writing in the context of Caribbean societies, for instance, the Haitian anthropologist Michel-Rolph Trouillot describes how food plots "provided a space quite distinct from the plantation fields sown with sugarcane, coffee, and cotton—space where one learned to cherish root crops, plantains, and bananas; space to raise and roast a pig, to run after a goat, or to barbecue a chicken; space to bury the loved ones who passed away, to worship the ancestors, and to invent new gods when the old ones were forgotten." As sites of subaltern refusal and counterplantation resilience, plots offered forms of literal and spiritual nourishment that were integral to surviving plantation slavery itself. Wynter, "Novel and History"; Trouillot, "Culture on the Edges," 203; see also Davis et al., "Anthropocene"; J. A. Carney, "Subsistence in the Plantationocene"; Goffe, "Reproducing the Plot"; Sapp Moore, "Between the State and the Yard."

35 McClaurin, "Walking in Zora's Shoes," 123.

36 Arif, "We Don't Need Another Hero"; Douglas-Jones et al., "Trial by Fire."

37 Hastrup, "Hunger," 733.

38 Smith, *Mountains of Blame*; Wentworth, "Public Eating."

39 McNamara and Farbotko, "Resisting a 'Doomed' Fate," 18; Santos Perez, *Navigating CHamoru Poetry*, 18.

40 Banivanua Mar, *Decolonisation and the Pacific*, 225.

41 Hau'ofa, *We Are the Ocean*, 65.

42 A. Simpson, "On Ethnographic Refusal," 78.

43 Tompkins, *Racial Indigestion*, 117. In pointing to how the significance of metaphors is shaped as much by the metaphor itself as by the positionality of the agents who craft and deploy them, I complement the American philosopher Susan Sontag's critique of the dangers of metaphors when deployed to attribute blame to and stigmatize those subject to illness and suffering. Specifically, I suggest that metaphors can come to constitute forms of grassroots epistemic sovereignty and resistance when articulated and harnessed by disempowered communities themselves in interrogating and critiquing the broader world orders within which they are situated. Sontag, *Illness as Metaphor*; see also W. Anderson, "Virus on the March?"

44   TallBear, "Standing with and Speaking as Faith," 2; Tuhiwai Smith, *Decolonizing Methodologies*, 89; Archibald, Lee-Morgan, and De Santolo, *Decolonizing Research*, 7; Archibald, *Indigenous Storywork*, 1.

45   Paper Boat Collective, "Introduction: Archipelagos," 23–24.

46   Gribaldo, *Unexpected Subjects*, 112, 129–31.

47   Paper Boat Collective, "Introduction: Archipelagos," 14; see also Pandian, *Possible Anthropology*, 61.

48   I borrow the term "cocreation" from the Indigenous community-based arts collective Miyarrka Media's book, *Phone and Spear: A Yuta Anthropology*, a unique and unprecedented exemplar of what genuinely experimental, collaborative, and world-(re)making anthropology can achieve across difference.

49   Tuck and Yang, "Decolonization Is Not a Metaphor"; see also Ticktin, "World without Innocence"; Shotwell, *Against Purity*; Visweswaran, *Fictions of Feminist Ethnography*, 100.

50   Marcus and Fischer, *Anthropology as Cultural Critique*.

51   Narayan, *Alive in the Writing*, 60; see also Gay y Blasco, "Uncertainty."

52   The individualism of academic authorship works hand in hand with anthropocentrism, whereby nonhuman actors are rarely acknowledged as coproducers of knowledge. For notable exceptions in the form of publications coauthored by Indigenous and non-Indigenous scholars and by the landscapes they collectively story, see Martuwarra RiverofLife et al., "Recognizing the Martuwarra's First Law"; Bawaka Country, Wright, and Suchet-Pearson, "Co-becoming Bawaka."

53   Gay y Blasco, "Uncertainty," 133–34.

54   Starn, "Introduction," 9.

55   Fassin, "Public Afterlife"; Pandian, *Possible Anthropology*, 61.

Conclusion

1   Whyte, "Food Sovereignty," 12.

2   Loichot, *Tropics Bite Back*, viii.

3   Vernon, *Hunger*, 8.

4   Scott-Smith, *On an Empty Stomach*, 10.

5   Derrida, "'Eating Well,'" 115; see also Probyn, *Eating the Ocean*, 163.

6   Hobart, "Food, Work, and Radical Care"; Solomon, *Metabolic Living*, 5, 227.

7   Livingston, *Self-Devouring Growth*, 5.

8   Chao, "Metabolic (In)justice."

9 Landecker, "Food as Exposure"; Paxson, *Eating beside Ourselves*, 11; Solomon, *Metabolic Living*; Yates-Doerr, *Weight of Obesity*, 11; see also Kelley, *After Eating*; Mol, *Eating in Theory*.

10 Kirksey and Chao, "Introduction," 16.

11 Shanahan, "Palm Oil."

12 Despret and Meuret, "Cosmoecological Sheep," 27.

13 Coveney, "In Praise of Hunger."

14 A. Simpson and Smith, "Introduction," 7. The Swedish anthropologist Don Kulick makes a similar argument in contending that for all its ethical, representational, and political pitfalls, the anthropological endeavor nonetheless matters in the way it allows people who are different from us to teach us something not just about them but also about ourselves. Powerful, privileged people, Kulick writes, should bear responsibility for, rather than eschew, engaging with those less advantaged than themselves—even where that engagement "restricts itself simply to knowing that those other people exist somewhere else in the world, and that they have their own viewpoints about their existence—viewpoints that may confound, complicate, and challenge *our own*." Kulick, *Death in the Rainforest*, 269 (my emphasis).

15 Pelluchon, *Nourishment*, 1, 156, 346.

16 Dillon, "Foreword," 19.

17 Shotwell, *Against Purity*. I thank the anthropologist Philippa Barr (unmarked) for inviting me to think about metabolic (in)justice through the lens of meals always connected but not always shared.

18 This was but one of countless insights offered by Craig as expert commentator and other participants of an ultimate peer review of this monograph held at the University of Sydney in September 2022, each of which has made its way into this work in different forms and places.

19 Burnett et al., "Anthropologists Respond."

20 Probyn, *Carnal Appetites*, 2–3.

21 Thomas and Clarke, "Can Anthropology Be Decolonized?"

22 I thank Danilyn Rutherford for inviting me to think more deeply about outrage as a meaningful response to ethnographic narratives and also about the imperative on the part of anthropologists and (other) audiences to put this outrage to work. Rutherford, "Book Review," 200.

Agarwal, Bina. "Food Sovereignty, Food Security and Democratic Choice: Critical Contradictions, Difficult Conciliations." *Journal of Peasant Studies* 41, no. 6 (2014): 1247–68. https://doi.org/10.1080/03066150.2013.876996.

Ahenakew, Cash. *Towards Scarring: Our Collective Soul Wound*. Ontario: Musagetes, 2019.

Ahmed, Sara. *Living a Feminist Life*. Durham, NC: Duke University Press, 2017.

Aikau, Hokulani K., Maile Arvin, Mishuana Goeman, and Scott Morgensen. "Indigenous Feminisms Roundtable." *Frontiers: A Journal of Women Studies* 36, no. 3 (2015): 84–106. https://doi.org/10.5250/fronjwomestud.36.3.0084.

Akibayashi, Kozue. "Okinawa Women Act against Military Violence: An Island Feminism Reclaiming Dignity." *Okinawan Journal of Island Studies* 1 (March 2020): 37–54. https://riis.skr.u-ryukyu.ac.jp/publications/5007/.

Alaimo, Stacy. *Bodily Natures: Science, Environment, and the Material Self*. Bloomington: Indiana University Press, 2010.

Allen, Paula G. *The Sacred Hoop: Recovering the Feminine in American Indian Traditions*. Boston: Beacon Press, 1986.

Allen, Paula G. "Who Is Your Mother? Red Roots of White Feminism." *Sinister Wisdom* 25 (Winter 1984): 34–46.

Aluli-Meyer, Manulani. "Our Own Liberation: Reflections on Hawaiian Epistemology." *Contemporary Pacific* 13, no. 1 (Spring 2001): 124–48. https://www.jstor.org/stable/23718511.

Ananta, Aris, Dwi Retno Wilujeng Wahyu Utami, and Nur Budi Handayani. "Statistics on Ethnic Diversity in the Land of Papua, Indonesia." *Asia and the *Pacific Policy Studies* 3, no. 3 (2016): 458–74. https://doi.org/10.1002/app5.143.

Anderson, Astrid. *Landscapes of Relations and Belonging: Body, Place and Politics in Wogeo, Papua New Guinea.* New York: Berghahn, 2011.

Anderson, Patrick. *So Much Wasted: Hunger, Performance, and the Morbidity of Resistance.* Durham, NC: Duke University Press, 2010.

Anderson, Warwick. *The Collectors of Lost Souls: Turning Kuru Scientists into Whitemen.* Baltimore: Johns Hopkins University Press, 2019.

Anderson, Warwick. "Virus on the March? Military Model and Metaphor in the COVID-19 Pandemic." *Health and History* 25, no. 1 (2023): 42–60. https://doi.org/10.1353/hah.2023.a904708.

Anzieu, Didier. *The Skin-Ego.* Translated by Naomi Segal. New Haven, CT: Yale University Press, 2016.

Appadurai, Arjun. "Gastro-Politics in Hindu South Asia." *American Ethnologist* 8, no. 3 (August 1981): 494–511. https://www.jstor.org/stable/644298.

Archibald, Jo-Ann. *Indigenous Storywork: Educating the Heart, Mind, Body, and Spirit.* Vancouver: University of British Columbia Press, 2008.

Archibald, Jo-Ann, Jenny Lee-Morgan, and Jason De Santolo. *Decolonizing Research: Indigenous Storywork as Methodology.* New York: Zed Books, 2019.

Aretxaga, Begoña. *Shattering Silence: Women, Nationalism, and Political Subjectivity in Northern Ireland.* Princeton, NJ: Princeton University Press, 1997.

Arif, Yasmeen. "We Don't Need Another Hero." *Commoning Ethnography* 3, no. 1 (2020): 117–22. https://doi.org/10.26686/ce.v3i1.6651.

Arvin, Maile. "Indigenous Feminist Notes on Embodying Alliance against Settler Colonialism." *Meridians: Feminism, Race, Transnationalism* 18, no. 2 (October 2019): 335–57. https://www.muse.jhu.edu/article/746123.

Arvin, Maile, Eve Tuck, and Angie Morrill. "Decolonizing Feminism: Challenging Connections between Settler Colonialism and Heteropatriarchy." *Feminist Formations* 25, no. 1 (Spring 2013): 8–34. https://www.jstor.org/stable/43860665.

August, Wikitoria. "Māori Women: Bodies, Spaces, Sacredness and Mana." *New Zealand Geographer* 61, no. 2 (August 2005): 117–23. https://doi.org/10.1111/j.1745-7939.2005.00025.x.

Avtonomov, Alexei. "UN CERD Formal Communication to the Permanent Mission of Indonesia regarding the Situation of the Malind and Other Indigenous People of the Merauke District Affected by the MIFEE Project." Geneva: Chairperson of the Committee on the Elimination of Racial Discrimination. August 30, 2013. http://www.forestpeoples.org/topics/un-human-rights-system/publication/2013/un-cerd-formal-communication-permanent-mission-indone.

Ballard, Chris. "The Signature of Terror: Violence, Memory and Landscape at Freeport." In *Inscribed Landscapes: Marking and Making Place*, edited by Bruno David and Meredith Wilson, 13–26. Honolulu: University of Hawaiʻi Press, 2002.

Ballestero, Andrea, and Brit Ross Winthereik, eds. *Experimenting with Ethnography: A Companion to Analysis.* Durham, NC: Duke University Press, 2021.

Banivanua Mar, Tracey. *Decolonisation and the Pacific: Indigenous Globalisation and the Ends of Empire*. Cambridge: Cambridge University Press, 2016.

Banivanua Mar, Tracey. "Focussing on the Margins of Rights: Human Rights through the Lens of Critical Race Theory." *Just Policy: A Journal of Australian Social Policy* 43 (2007): 55–63. https://opal.latrobe.edu.au/articles/journal _contribution/Focussing_on_the_margins_of_rights_human_rights_through _the_lens_of_critical_race_theory/22201354.

Banivanua Mar, Tracey. "'A Thousand Miles of Cannibal Lands': Imagining Away Genocide in the Re-colonization of West Papua." *Journal of Genocide Research* 10, no. 4 (2008): 583–602. https://doi.org/10.1080/14623520802447743.

Barker, Joanne. "Indigenous Feminisms." In *The Oxford Handbook of Indigenous People's Politics*, edited by Dale Turner, Donna L. VanCott, and Lucero A. Jose, 1–17. Oxford: Oxford University Press, 2013. https://doi.org/10.1093/oxfordhb /9780195386653.013.007.

Barker, Joanne. "Introduction: Critically Sovereign." In *Critically Sovereign: Indigenous Gender, Sexuality, and Feminist Studies*, edited by Joanne Barker, 1–44. Durham, NC: Duke University Press, 2017.

Bartolovich, Crystal. "Consumerism, or the Cultural Logic of Late Cannibalism." In *Cannibalism and the Colonial World*, edited by Francis Barker, Peter Hulme, and Margaret Iversen, 204–37. New York: Cambridge University Press, 1998.

Bashkow, Ira. *The Meaning of Whitemen: Race and Modernity in the Orokaiva Cultural World*. Chicago: University of Chicago Press, 2006.

Bateson, Gregory, Don D. Jackson, Jay Haley, and John Weakland. "Toward a Theory of Schizophrenia." *Behavorial Science* 1, no. 4 (1956): 251–64. https://doi .org/10.1002/bs.3830010402.

Battaglia, Deborah. *On the Bones of the Serpent: Person, Memory, and Mortality in Sabarl Island Society*. Chicago: University of Chicago Press, 1990.

Bawaka Country, Sarah Wright, and Sandie Suchet-Pearson. "Co-becoming Bawaka: Towards a Relational Understanding of Place/Space." *Progress in Human Geography* 40, no. 4 (2015): 455–75. https://doi.org/10.1177/0309132515589437.

Baxter Riley, Edward. *Among Papuan Headhunters*. Philadelphia: Lippincott, 1925.

Bayart, Jean-François. *The State in Africa: The Politics of the Belly*. Translated by Mary Harper. London: Longman, 1993.

Becker, Anne E. *Body, Self, and Society: The View from Fiji*. Philadelphia: University of Pennsylvania Press, 1995.

Behar, Ruth, and Deborah A. Gordon, eds. *Women Writing Culture*. Oakland: University of California Press, 1996.

Beo da Costa, Agustinus, and Kate Lamb. "Indonesia Parliament Passes Revised Autonomy Law for Restive Papua." *Reuters*, July 15, 2021. https://www.reuters .com/world/asia-pacific/indonesia-parliament-passes-revised-autonomy-law -restive-papua-2021-07-15/.

Bertrand, Jacques. "Autonomy and Stability: The Perils of Implementation and 'Divide-and-Rule' Tactics in Papua, Indonesia." *Nationalism and Ethnic Politics* 20, no. 2 (2014): 174–99. https://doi.org/10.1080/13537113.2014.909157.

Biehl, João G. *Vita: Life in a Zone of Social Abandonment*. Berkeley: University of California Press, 2013.

Blackwell, Maylei, Laura Briggs, and Mignonette Chiu. "Transnational Feminisms Roundtable." *Frontiers: A Journal of Women Studies* 36, no. 3 (2015): 1–24. https://doi.org/10.5250/fronjwomestud.36.3.0001.

Blaney, Fay. "Aboriginal Women's Action Network." In *Strong Women Stories: Native Vision and Community Survival*, edited by Kim Anderson and Bonita Lawrence, 156–72. Toronto: Sumach Press, 2003.

Boarder Giles, David. *A Mass Conspiracy to Feed People: Food Not Bombs and the World-Class Waste of Global Cities*. Durham, NC: Duke University Press, 2021.

Boelaars, Jan H. M. C. *Head-Hunters about Themselves: An Ethnographic Report from Irian Jaya, Indonesia*. The Hague: Martinus Nijhoff, 1981.

Bolabola, Cema. "Fiji: Customary Constraints and Legal Progress." In *Land Rights of Pacific Women*, edited by University of the South Pacific, 1–66. Suva: University of the South Pacific, 1986.

Bonnemère, Pascale. *Acting for Others: Relational Transformations in Papua New Guinea*. Chicago: HAU Books, 2018.

Boscacci, Louise. "Wit(h)nessing." *Environmental Humanities* 10, no. 1 (May 2018): 343–47. https://doi.org/10.1215/22011919-4385617.

Bourdieu, Pierre. *Distinction: A Social Critique of the Judgement of Taste*. Translated by Richard Nice. Cambridge, MA: Harvard University Press, 1984.

Brenton, Barrett P. "Piki, Polenta, and Pellagra: Maize, Nutrition, and Nurturing the Natural." In *Nurture: Proceedings of the Oxford Symposium on Food and Cooking*, edited by Richard Hosking, 36–50. Bristol: Footwork, 2004.

Briggs, Charles L., and Clara Mantini-Briggs. *Tell Me Why My Children Died: Rabies, Indigenous Knowledge, and Communicative Justice*. Durham, NC: Duke University Press, 2016.

Brown, Vincent. "Eating the Dead: Consumption and Regeneration in the History of Sugar." *Food and Foodways* 16, no. 2 (2008): 117–26. https://doi.org/10.1080/07409710802085973.

Bubandt, Nils. *The Empty Seashell: Witchcraft and Doubt on an Indonesian Island*. Ithaca, NY: Cornell University Press, 2014.

Burnett, Diana, Megan A. Carney, Lauren Carruth, et al. "Anthropologists Respond to the *Lancet* EAT Commission." *Revista BioNatura* 5, no. 1 (2020): 1023–24. https://doi.org/10.21931/RB/2020.05.01.2.

Burridge, Kenelm. *Mambu: A Melanesian Millennium*. London: Methuen, 1960.

Burridge, Kenelm. *New Heaven, New Earth: A Study of Millenarian Activities*. New York: Schocken, 1969.

Burton, John. "Knowing about Culture: The Handling of Social Issues at Resource Projects in Papua New Guinea." In *Culture and Sustainable Development in the Pacific*, edited by Antony Hooper, 98–110. Canberra: Australian National University E-Press and Asia Pacific Press, 2005.

Butler, Judith. *Frames of War: When Is Life Grievable?* London: Verso, 2010.

Butler, Judith. *Precarious Life: The Powers of Mourning and Violence*. London: Verso, 2004.

Butt, Leslie. "'Lipstick Girls' and 'Fallen Women': AIDS and Conspiratorial Thinking in Papua, Indonesia." *Cultural Anthropology* 20, no. 3 (August 2005): 412–42. https://www.jstor.org/stable/3651598.

Butt, Leslie. "'Living in HIV-Land': Mobility and Seropositivity among Highlands Papuan Men." In *From 'Stone Age' to 'Real-Time': Exploring Papuan Temporalities, Mobilities and Religiosities*, edited by Martin Slama and Jenny Munro, 221–42. Canberra: Australian National University Press, 2015.

Butt, Leslie. "Local Biologies and HIV/AIDS in Highlands Papua, Indonesia." *Culture, Medicine, and Psychiatry* 37, no. 1 (March 2013): 179–94. https://doi.org/10.1007/s11013-012-9299-2.

Caldwell, Melissa L. *Not by Bread Alone: Social Support in the New Russia*. Berkeley: University of California Press, 2004.

Campbell, David J. "Strategies for Coping with Severe Food Deficits in Rural Africa: A Review of the Literature." *Food and Foodways* 4, no. 2 (1990): 143–62. https://doi.org/10.1080/07409710.1990.9961976.

Canfield, Matthew C. *Translating Food Sovereignty: Cultivating Justice in an Age of Transnational Governance*. Stanford, CA: Stanford University Press, 2022.

Carney, Judith A. "Subsistence in the Plantationocene: Dooryard Gardens, Agrobiodiversity, and the Subaltern Economies of Slavery." *Journal of Peasant Studies* 48, no. 5 (2021): 1075–99. https://doi.org/10.1080/03066150.2020.1725488.

Carney, Megan A. *The Unending Hunger: Tracing Women and Food Insecurity Across Borders*. Berkeley: University of California Press, 2015.

Césaire, Aimé. *Notebook of a Return to the Native Land*. Translated by Clayton Eshleman and Annette Smith. Middletown, CT: Wesleyan University Press, 2001.

Chamoiseau, Patrick. *Creole Folktales*. Translated by Linda Coverdale. New York: New Press, 1994.

Chao, Sophie. "The Beetle or the Bug? Multispecies Politics in a West Papuan Oil Palm Plantation." *American Anthropologist* 123, no. 2 (September 2021): 476–89. https://doi.org/10.1111/aman.13592.

Chao, Sophie. "Children of the Palms: Growing Plants and Growing People in a Papuan Plantationocene." *Journal of the Royal Anthropological Institute* 27, no. 2 (June 2021): 245–64. https://doi.org/10.1111/1467-9655.13489.

Chao, Sophie. "Cultivating Consent: Challenges and Opportunities in the West Papuan Palm Oil Sector." *New Mandala*, August 26, 2019. https://www.newmandala.org/cultivating-consent/.

Chao, Sophie. "Culture, Food and Environment: Indigenous Experiences of Hunger in West Papua." Sydney Environment Institute. June 12, 2019. https://www.researchgate.net/publication/333773682_Culture_Food_and_Environment_Indigenous_Experiences_of_Hunger_in_West_Papua.

Chao, Sophie. "Engaged Anthropology: Sophie Chao." *Wenner-Gren Foundation for Anthropological Research* (blog). August 6, 2019. http://blog.wennergren.org/2019/08/eag_schao/.

Chao, Sophie. "Forest Foodways in West Papua." *E-Flux Journal* 128 (June 2022). https://www.e-flux.com/journal/128/470561/forest-foodways-in-west-papua/.

Chao, Sophie. "Gastrocolonialism: The Intersections of Race, Food, and Development in West Papua." *International Journal of Human Rights* 26, no. 5 (2022): 811–32. https://doi.org/10.1080/13642987.2021.1968378.

Chao, Sophie. "Hunger and Culture in West Papua." *Inside Indonesia*, October 30, 2019. https://www.insideindonesia.org/hunger-and-culture-in-west-papua.

Chao, Sophie. "游荡在印尼马老奇森林废墟里的饥饿感." [Hunger in the rubble of the forest]. *The Paper*, August 9, 2019. https://www.thepaper.cn/newsDetail_forward_4070953.

Chao, Sophie. "'In the Plantations There Is Hunger and Loneliness': The Cultural Dimensions of Food Insecurity in Papua (Commentary)." *Mongabay*, July 14, 2020. https://news.mongabay.com/2020/07/in-the-plantations-there-is-hunger-and-loneliness-the-cultural-dimensions-of-food-insecurity-in-papua-commentary/.

Chao, Sophie. *In the Shadow of the Palms: More-Than-Human Becomings in West Papua*. Durham, NC: Duke University Press, 2022.

Chao, Sophie. "Is Hunger Culture-Bound?" *Somatosphere*, June 7, 2019. http://somatosphere.net/2019/is-hunger-culture-bound.html/.

Chao, Sophie. "Metabolic (In)justice." *Backchannels*, April 5, 2023. https://4sonline.org/news_manager.php?page=30028.

Chao, Sophie. "The Plastic Cassowary: Problematic 'Pets' in West Papua." *Ethnos* 84, no. 5 (2019): 828–48. https://doi.org/10.1080/00141844.2018.1502798.

Chao, Sophie. "Pluralizing Justice: Indigenous Perspectives from the West Papuan Oil Palm Frontier." Struggles for Sovereignty: Land, Water, Farming, Food. 2021. https://strugglesforsovereignty.net/the-west-papuan-oil-palm-frontier/.

Chao, Sophie. "Sago." In *The Mind of Plants: Narratives on Vegetal Intelligence*, edited by Patrícia Vieira, Monica Gagliano, and John C. Ryan, 317–25. Santa Fe, NM: Synergetic Press, 2021.

Chao, Sophie. "There Are No Straight Lines in Nature: Making Living Maps in West Papua." *Anthropology Now* 9, no. 1 (2017): 16–33. https://doi.org/10.1080/19428200.2017.1291014.

Chao, Sophie. "They Grow and Die Lonely and Sad." *Fieldsights*, January 26, 2021. https://culanth.org/fieldsights/they-grow-and-die-lonely-and-sad.

Chao, Sophie. "Thinking Beyond Bios in an Age of Planetary Undoing." In *Beyond Bios: The Life of Matter and the Matter of Life*, edited by Sophie Chao, Christine Winter, and David Schlosberg. Durham, NC: Duke University Press, forthcoming.

Chao, Sophie. "A Tree of Many Lives: Vegetal Teleontologies in West Papua." *HAU: Journal of Ethnographic Theory* 10, no. 2 (Autumn 2020): 514–29. https://doi.org/10.1086/709505.

Chao, Sophie. "We Are (Not) Monkeys: Contested Cosmopolitical Symbols in West Papua." *American Ethnologist* 48, no. 3 (August 2021): 274–87. https://doi.org/10.1111/amet.13023.

Chao, Sophie. "Wetness." *Art+Australia* 8, no. 57 (2022): 94–97.

Chao, Sophie, and Annisa Beta. "Talking Indonesia: Papua, Food and Racism." *Talking Indonesia* (podcast). September 30, 2021. https://indonesiaatmelbourne.unimelb.edu.au/talking-indonesia-papua-food-and-racism/.

Chao, Sophie, and Natali Pearson. "Culture, Food and Environment: Indigenous Experiences of Hunger in West Papua—Dr Sophie Chao." *SSEAC Stories* (podcast). March 18, 2020. https://podcasts.apple.com/au/podcast/culture-food-and-environment-indigenous-experiences/id1514290750?i=1000475132725.

Chao, Sophie, and Rachel Smolker. "West Papua: Depths of Loss and Heights of Resistance." *Forest Cover* 62 (2019): 10–11. https://globalforestcoalition.org/forest-cover-62/#fc6204.

Chappell, Jahi M. *Beginning to End Hunger: Food and the Environment in Belo Horizonte, Brazil, and Beyond*. Berkeley: University of California Press, 2018.

Choudhury, Athia N. "The Making of the American Calorie and the Metabolic Metrics of Empire." *Journal of Transnational American Studies* 13, no. 1 (2022): 15–44. https://doi.org/10.5070/T813158578.

Clark, Jeffrey. *Steel to Stone: A Chronicle of Colonialism in the Southern Highlands of Papua New Guinea*. Edited by Chris Ballard and Michael Nihill. New York: Oxford University Press, 2000.

Clifford, James, and George E. Marcus, eds. *Writing Culture: The Poetics and Politics of Ethnography*. Berkeley: University of California Press, 1986.

Coburn, Elaine, Aileen Moreton-Robinson, George Sefa Dei, and Makere Stewart-Harawira. "Unspeakable Things: Indigenous Research and Social Science." *Socio* 2 (2013): 331–48. https://doi.org/10.4000/socio.524.

Colchester, Marcus, and Sophie Chao, eds. *Conflict or Consent? The Palm Oil Sector at a Crossroads*. Moreton-in-Marsh: Forest Peoples Programme, Sawit Watch, and TUK-Indonesia, 2013.

Coté, Charlotte. "'Indigenizing' Food Sovereignty: Revitalizing Indigenous Food Practices and Ecological Knowledges in Canada and the United States." *Humanities* 5, no. 3 (2016): 57. https://doi.org/10.3390/h5030057.

Cousins, Thomas. "Antiretroviral Therapy and Nutrition in Southern Africa: Citizenship and the Grammar of Hunger." *Medical Anthropology* 35, no. 5 (September–October 2016): 433–46. https://doi.org/10.1080/01459740.2016.1141409.

Coveney, John. "In Praise of Hunger: Public Health and the Problem of Excess." In *Alcohol, Tobacco and Obesity: Morality, Mortality and the New Public Health*, edited by Kirsten Bell, Darlene McNaughton, and Amy Salmon, 146–60. New York: Routledge, 2011.

Crenshaw, Kimberlé. "Demarginalizing the Intersection of Race and Sex: A Black Feminist Critique of Antidiscrimination Doctrine, Feminist Theory and Antiracist Politics." *University of Chicago Legal Forum* 1, article 8 (1989): 139–67. https://chicagounbound.uchicago.edu/cgi/viewcontent.cgi?article =1052&context=uclf.

Das, Veena. *Life and Words: Violence and the Descent into the Ordinary*. Berkeley: University of California Press, 2007.

Davis, Janae, Alex A. Moulton, Levi van Sant, and Bryan Williams. "Anthropocene, Capitalocene, . . . Plantationocene? A Manifesto for Ecological Justice in an Age of Global Crises." *Geography Compass* 13, no. 5 (May 2019): e12438. https://doi.org/10.1111/gec3.12438.

de Boeck, Filip. "'When Hunger Goes Around the Land': Hunger and Food among the Aluund of Zaire." *Man* 29, no. 2 (June 1994): 257–82. https://doi .org/10.2307/2804474.

de Castro, Josué. *Geografia da Fome*. Rio de Janeiro: O Cruzeiro, 1946.

Deer, Sarah, Jodi A. Byrd, Durba Mitra, and Sarah Haley. "Rage, Indigenous Feminisms, and the Politics of Survival." *Signs: Journal of Women in Culture and Society* 46, no. 4 (Summer 2021): 1057–71. https://doi.org/10.1086/713294.

Derrida, Jacques. "'Eating Well,' or the Calculation of the Subject: An Interview with Jacques Derrida." In *Who Comes after the Subject?*, edited by Eduardo Cadava, Jean-Luc Nancy, and Peter Connor, 96–119. New York: Routledge, 1991.

Derrida, Jacques. *The Gift of Death*. Translated by David Wills. Chicago: University of Chicago Press, 1996.

Despret, Vinciane. *What Would Animals Say If We Asked the Right Questions?* Translated by Brett Buchanan. Minneapolis: University of Minnesota Press, 2016.

Despret, Vinciane, and Michel Meuret. "Cosmoecological Sheep and the Arts of Living on a Damaged Planet." *Environmental Humanities* 8, no. 1 (May 2016): 24–36. https://doi.org/10.1215/22011919-3527704.

Devereux, George. *Theories of Famine*. New York: Harvester Wheatsheaf, 1993.

de Waal, Alexander. *Famine That Kills: Darfur, Sudan*. Oxford: Oxford University Press, 2005.

Dhamoon, Rita. "A Feminist Approach to Decolonizing Antiracism: Rethinking Transnationalism, Intersectionality, and Settler Colonialism." *Feral Feminisms* 4 (Summer 2015): 20–37. https://feralfeminisms.com/rita-dhamoon/.

Diaz, Vicente M., and J. Kēhaulani Kauanui. "Native Pacific Cultural Studies on the Edge." *Contemporary Pacific* 13, no. 2 (Fall 2001): 315–42. https://www.jstor .org/stable/23717595.

Dickinson, Maggie. *Feeding the Crisis: Care and Abandonment in America's Food Safety Net*. Berkeley: University of California Press, 2019.

Dillon, Grace. "Foreword." In *Dangerous Spirits: The Windigo in Myth and History*, edited by Shawn C. Smallman and Grace Dillon, 15–19. Toronto: Heritage House, 2014.

Douglas-Jones, Rachel, Nayanika Mathur, Catherine Trundle, and Tarapuhi Vaeau. "Trial by Fire: Trauma, Vulnerability and the Heroics of Fieldwork." *Commoning Ethnography* 3, no. 1 (2020): 91–116. https://doi.org/10.26686/ce.v3i1.6650.

Drèze, Jean, and Amartya Sen, eds. *The Political Economy of Hunger: Selected Essays*. New York: Oxford University Press, 2007.

DuBois, Cora. *The People of Alor: A Social-Psychological Study of an East Indian Island*. Minneapolis: University of Minnesota Press, 1944.

Dundon, Alison. "DNA, Israel and the Ancestors—Substantiating Connections through Christianity in Papua New Guinea." *Asia Pacific Journal of Anthropology* 12, no. 1 (2011): 29–43.

Durutalo, Simione. "Anthropology and Authoritarianism in the Pacific Islands." In *Confronting the Margaret Mead Legacy: Scholarship, Empire, and the South Pacific*, edited by Lenora Foerstel and Angela M. Gilliam, 205–32. Philadelphia: Temple University Press, 1992.

Dyer, Michelle. "Eating Money: Narratives of Equality on Customary Land in the Context of Natural Resource Extraction in the Solomon Islands." *Australian Journal of Anthropology* 28 (2017): 88–103. https://doi.org/10.1111/taja.12213.

Edelman, Marc, Tony Weis, Amita Baviskar, et al. "Introduction: Critical Perspectives on Food Sovereignty." *Journal of Peasant Studies* 41, no. 6 (2014): 911–31. https://doi.org/10.1080/03066150.2014.963568.

Edkins, Jenny. *Whose Hunger? Concepts of Famine, Practices of Aid*. Minneapolis: University of Minnesota Press, 2000.

Eichhorn, Stephen J. "Resource Extraction as a Tool of Racism in West Papua." *International Journal of Human Rights* 27, no. 6 (2022): 994–1016. https://doi.org/10.1080/13642987.2022.2036722.

Elmslie, Jim. "The Great Divide: West Papuan Demographics Revisited; Settlers Dominate Coastal Regions but the Highlands Still Overwhelmingly Papuan." *Asia-Pacific Journal* 15, no. 2 (2017): 1–11. https://apjjf.org/wp-content/uploads/2023/11/article-1385.pdf.

Elmslie, Jim, and Camellia Webb-Gannon. "A Slow-Motion Genocide: Indonesian Rule in West Papua." *Griffith Journal of Law and Human Dignity* 1, no. 2 (2013): 142–66. https://ro.uow.edu.au/sspapers/4021/.

Eräsaari, Matti. "'Wasting Time' the Veratan Way: Conspicuous Leisure and the Value of Waiting in Fiji." *HAU: Journal of Ethnographic Theory* 7, no. 2 (Autumn 2017): 309–29. https://doi.org/10.14318/hau7.2.029.

Errington, Frederick, and Deborah Gewertz. "Pacific Island Gastrologies: Following the Flaps." *Journal of the Royal Anthropological Institute* 14 (2008): 590–608. https://www.jstor.org/stable/20203687.

Essex, James. "Idle Hands Are the Devil's Tools: The Geopolitics and Geoeconomics of Hunger." *Annals of the Association of American Geographers* 102, no. 1 (January 2012): 191–207. https://www.jstor.org/stable/41412761.

Eves, Richard. *The Magical Body: Power, Fame, and Meaning in a Melanesian Society*. Amsterdam: Harwood Academic Publishers, 1998.

Eves, Richard. "Remembrance of Things Passed: Memory, Body and the Politics of Feasting in New Ireland, Papua New Guinea." *Oceania* 66, no. 4 (June 1966): 266–77. https://www.jstor.org/stable/40332135.

Fairbairn-Dunlop, Peggy. "Gender, Culture and Sustainable Development—The Pacific Way." In *Culture and Sustainable Development in the Pacific*, edited by Antony Hooper, 62–75. Canberra: Australian National University E-Press and Asia Pacific Press, 2005.

Fajans, Jane. "Shame, Social Action, and the Person among the Baining." *Ethos* 11, no. 3 (Autumn 1983): 166–80. https://www.jstor.org/stable/639971.

Fajans, Jane. *They Make Themselves: Work and Play among the Baining of Papua New Guinea*. Chicago: University of Chicago Press, 1997.

Farmer, Paul. *AIDS and Accusation: Haiti and the Geography of Blame*. Berkeley: University of California Press, 2006.

Farrelly, Trisia A., and Unaisi Nabobo-Baba. "Talanoa as Empathic Apprenticeship." *Asia Pacific Viewpoint* 55, no. 3 (2014): 319–30. https://doi.org/10.1111/apv.12060.

Fassin, Didier. "The Public Afterlife of Ethnography." *American Ethnologist* 42, no. 4 (2015): 592–609.

Firth, Raymond. *Social Change in Tikopia: Re-study of a Polynesian Community after a Generation*. New York: Macmillan, 1960.

Fischler, Claude. "Gastro-nomie et gastro-anomie: Sagesse du corps et crise bioculturelle de l'alimentation moderne." *Communications* 31 (1979): 189–210. https://www.persee.fr/doc/comm_0588-8018_1979_num_31_1_1477.

Flowers, Rachel. "Refusal to Forgive: Indigenous Women's Love and Rage." *Decolonization: Indigeneity, Education and Society* 4, no. 2 (2015): 32–49. https://jps.library.utoronto.ca/index.php/des/article/view/22829/19320.

Food and Agriculture Organization. *Food Security*. Policy brief. Rome: Food and Agriculture Organization, 2006.

Food Security Council, Ministry of Agriculture, and World Food Programme. *Food Security and Vulnerability Atlas of Indonesia, 2015*. Jakarta: Food Security Council, Ministry of Agriculture, and World Food Programme, 2015. https://wfp.tind.io/record/126674?ln=en&v=pdf.

Forbes, Jack. *Columbus and Other Cannibals: The Wetiko Disease of Exploitation, Imperialism, and Terrorism*. New York: Seven Stories Press, 2011.

Forest Peoples Programme. "Request for Consideration of the Situation of Indigenous Peoples in Merauke, Papua Province, Indonesia, under the United Nations

Committee on the Elimination of Racial Discrimination's Urgent Action and Early Warning Procedures." July 31, 2011. http://www.forestpeoples.org/sites/fpp /files/news/2011/08/EW_UA Indigenous Peoples Merauke Indonesia July 31 2011 Final.pdf.

Forest Peoples Programme. "Request for Further Consideration of the Situation of the Indigenous Peoples of Merauke, Papua Province, Indonesia, and Indigenous Peoples in Indonesia in General, under the Committee on the Elimination of Racial Discrimination's Urgent Action and Early Warning Procedures." February 6, 2012. http://www.forestpeoples.org/sites/fpp/files/publication/2012 /02/2012-cerd-80th-session-ua-update-final.pdf.

Forest Peoples Programme. "Request for Further Consideration of the Situation of the Indigenous Peoples of Merauke, Papua Province, Indonesia, under the Committee on the Elimination of Racial Discrimination's Urgent Action and Early Warning Procedures." July 25, 2013. https://www.forestpeoples. org/en/topics/un-human-rights-system/publication/2013/request-further -consideration-situation-indigenous-pe.

Forest Peoples Programme, PUSAKA, and Sawit Watch. *"A Sweetness Like unto Death": Voices of the Indigenous Malind of Merauke, Papua*. Moreton-in-Marsh: Forest Peoples Programme, Sawit Watch, PUSAKA, and Rights and Resources Institute. 2013. https://www.forestpeoples.org/fr/topics/secteur -prive-autres/publication/2013/sweetness-unto-death-voices-indigenous -malind-merauke-p.

Fresno-Calleja, Paloma. "Fighting Gastrocolonialism in Indigenous Pacific Writing." *Interventions: International Journal of Postcolonial Studies* 19, no. 7 (2017): 1041–55. https://doi.org/10.1080/1369801X.2017.1401938.

Fujikane, Candace. *Mapping Abundance for a Planetary Future: Kanaka Maoli and Critical Settler Cartographies in Hawai'i*. Durham, NC: Duke University Press, 2021.

Galudra, G., M. van Noordwijk, S. Suyanto, I. Sardi, U. Pradhan, and D. Catacutan. "Hot Spots of Confusion: Contested Policies and Competing Carbon Claims in the Peatlands of Central Kalimantan, Indonesia." *International Forestry Review* 13, no. 4 (2011): 431–41. https://www.jstor.org/stable/24310765.

Garthwaite, Kayleigh. *Hunger Pains: Life Inside Foodbank Britain*. Bristol: Polity Press, 2016.

Gay y Blasco, Paloma. "Uncertainty, Failure and Reciprocal Ethnography." In *Gender and Genre in Ethnographic Writing*, edited by Elisabeth Tauber and Dorothy L. Zinn, 133–61. London: Palgrave Macmillan, 2021.

Gegeo, David W. "Indigenous Knowledge and Empowerment: Rural Development Examined from Within." *Contemporary Pacific* 10, no. 2 (Fall 1998): 289–315. https://www.jstor.org/stable/23706891.

Gegeo, David W., and Karen A. Watson-Gegeo. "'How We Know': Kwara'ae Rural Villagers Doing Indigenous Epistemology." *Contemporary Pacific* 13, no. 1 (Spring 2001): 55–88. https://www.jstor.org/stable/23718509.

Gegeo, David W., and Karen A. Watson-Gegeo. "Whose Knowledge? Epistemological Collisions in Solomon Islands Community Development." *Contemporary Pacific* 14, no. 2 (Fall 2002): 377–409. http://hdl.handle.net/10125/13653.

Giay, Benny. "Zakheus Pakage and His Communities: Indigenous Religious Discourse, Socio-political Resistance, and Ethnohistory of the Me of Irian Jaya." PhD diss., Vrije Universiteit, 1995.

Giffort, Danielle. "Show or Tell? Feminist Dilemmas and Implicit Feminism at Girls' Rock Camp." *Gender and Society* 25, no. 5 (October 2011): 569–88. https://www.jstor.org/stable/23044173.

Ginn, Franklin, Uli Beisel, and Maan Barua. "Flourishing with Awkward Creatures: Togetherness, Vulnerability, Killing." *Environmental Humanities* 4 (2014): 113–24.

Ginoza, Ayano. "Archipelagic Feminisms: Critical Interventions into the Gendered Coloniality of Okinawa." *Critical Ethnic Studies* 7, no. 2 (2021). https://manifold.umn.edu/read/ces0702-07/section/1f30ad41-550a-4df2-9448-4b84f160090a.

Giraud, Eva H. *What Comes after Entanglement? Activism, Anthropocentrism, and an Ethics of Exclusion.* Durham, NC: Duke University Press, 2019.

Githire, Njeri. *Cannibal Writes: Eating Others in Caribbean and Indian Ocean Women's Writing.* Urbana: University of Illinois Press, 2014.

Glazebrook, Diana. *Permissive Residents: West Papuan Refugees Living in Papua New Guinea.* Canberra: Australian National University Press, 2008.

Goffe, Rachel. "Reproducing the Plot: Making Life in the Shadow of Premature Death." *Antipode* 55, no. 4 (2022): 1024–46. https://doi.org/10.1111/anti.12812.

Goldman, Laurence C., and Chris Ballard. *Fluid Ontologies: Myth, Ritual, and Philosophy in the Highlands of Papua New Guinea.* Westport, CT: Bergin and Garvey, 1998.

Goldstein, Alyosha. "The Ground Not Given: Colonial Dispositions of Land, Race, and Hunger." *Social Text* 36, no. 2 (2018): 83–106. https://doi.org/10.1215/01642472-4362373.

Gómez-Barris, Macarena. "Mapuche Hunger Acts: Epistemology of the Decolonial." *Transmodernity* 1, no. 3 (Spring 2012): 120–32. https://escholarship.org/uc/item/6305p8vr.

Goodyear-Ka'ōpua, Noelani. "Indigenous and Decolonizing Studies in Education." In *Indigenous and Decolonizing Studies in Education*, edited by Eve Tuck and K. Wayne Yang, 82–102. New York: Routledge, 2018.

Gordillo, Gastón R. "The Breath of the Devils: Memories and Places of an Experience of Terror." *American Ethnologist* 29, no. 1 (February 2002): 33–57. https://www.jstor.org/stable/3095020.

Gould, Jeffrey. *To Lead as Equals: Rural Protest and Political Consciousness in Chinandenga, Nicaragua, 1912–1979.* Chapel Hill: University of North Carolina Press, 1990.

Govindrajan, Radhika. *Animal Intimacies: Interspecies Relatedness in India's Central Himalayas.* Chicago: University of Chicago Press, 2018.

Grant, Kevin. *Last Weapons: Hunger Strikes and Fasts in the British Empire, 1890–1948*. Berkeley: University of California Press, 2019.

Green, Joyce. "Introduction—Indigenous Feminism: From Symposium to Book." In *Making Space for Indigenous Feminism*, edited by Joyce Green, 14–19. London: Zed Books, 2007.

Gregory, Chris. "Skinship: Touchability as Virtue in East-Central India." *HAU: Journal of Ethnographic Theory* 1, no. 1 (Fall 2011): 179–209. https://doi.org/10.14318/hau1.1.007.

Gribaldo, Alessandra. *Unexpected Subjects: Intimate Partner Violence, Testimony, and the Law*. Chicago: HAU Books, 2021.

Guthman, Julie. *Weighing In: Obesity, Food Justice, and the Limits of Capitalism*. Berkeley: University of California Press, 2011.

Haddon, Alfred C. *The Tugeri Head-Hunters of New Guinea*. Leiden: E. G. Brill, 1891.

Hadiprayitno, Irene I. "Behind Transformation: The Right to Food, Agricultural Modernisation and Indigenous Peoples in Papua, Indonesia." *Human Rights Review* 16 (2015): 123–41. https://doi.org/10.1007/s12142-015-0353-7.

Halapua, Sitiveni. "Talanoa in Building Democracy and Governance." Paper presented at the conference "Future Leaders of the Pacific," Pago Pago, American Samoa, February 4–7, 2013. http://talanoa.org/Home_files/Talanoa in Building Democracy and Governance.pdf.

Halvaksz, Jamon A., II. "The Taste of Public Places: *Terroir* in Papua New Guinea's Emerging Nation." *Anthropological Forum* 23, no. 2 (2013): 142–57. https://doi.org/10.1080/00664677.2012.753868.

Haraway, Donna J. *When Species Meet*. Minneapolis: University of Minnesota Press, 2008.

Hardin, Jessica. *Faith and the Pursuit of Health: Cardiometabolic Disorders in Samoa*. New Brunswick, NJ: Rutgers University Press, 2018.

Hastrup, Kirsten. "Hunger and the Hardness of Facts." *Man* 28, no. 4 (December 1993): 727–39. https://www.jstor.org/stable/2803994.

Hatch, Anthony R., Sonya Sternlieb, and Julia Gordon. "Sugar Ecologies: Their Metabolic and Racial Effects." *Food, Culture, and Society* 22, no. 5 (2019): 595–607. https://doi.org/0.1080/15528014.2019.1638123.

Hatley, James. "Blood Intimacies and Biodicy: Keeping Faith with Ticks." *Australian Humanities Review* 50 (May 2011): 63–76. https://australianhumanitiesreview.org/2011/05/01/blood-intimacies-and-biodicy-keeping-faith-with-ticks/.

Hau'ofa, Epeli. *We Are the Ocean: Selected Works*. Honolulu: University of Hawai'i Press, 2008.

Henritze, Evan, Sonora Goldman, Sarah Simon, and Adam D. Brown. "Moral Injury as an Inclusive Mental Health Framework for Addressing Climate Change Distress and Promoting Justice-Oriented Care." *The Lancet* 7, no. 3 (2023): E238–E241. https://doi.org/10.1016/S2542-5196(22)00335-7.

Hernawan, Budi J., and Anthony van den Broek. "Dialog Nasional Papua: Sebuah Kisah Memoria Passionis." *Tifa Irian*, March 1999.

Herrmann, Rachel B. *To Feast on Us as Their Prey: Cannibalism and the Early Modern Atlantic*. Fayetteville: University of Arkansas Press, 2019.

Hinkson, Melinda. *See How We Roll: Enduring Exile between Desert and Urban Australia*. Durham, NC: Duke University Press, 2021.

Hobart, Hi'ilei J. K. "Food, Work, and Radical Care." Keynote presented at the conference "Food Matters and Materialities: Critical Understandings of Food Cultures," Carleton University, September 24, 2021.

Hobart, Hi'ilei J. K., and Tamara Kneese. "Radical Care: Survival Strategies for Uncertain Times." *Social Text* 38, no. 1 (March 2020): 1–16. https://doi.org/10.1215/01642472-7971067.

Holland, Sharon P., Marcia Ochoa, and Kyla Wazana Tompkins. "On the Visceral: An Introduction." *GLQ: A Journal of Lesbian and Gay Studies* 20, no. 4 (2014): 391–406. https://www.muse.jhu.edu/article/556200.

Holmberg, Allan R. *Nomads of the Longbow*. New York: Natural History Press, 1969.

Holtzman, Jon D. "Food and Memory." *Annual Review of Anthropology* 35 (2007): 361–78. https://doi.org/10.1146/annurev.anthro.35.081705.123220.

hooks, bell. *Ain't I a Woman. Black Women and Feminism*. London: Pluto Press, 1982.

hooks, bell. *Black Looks: Race and Representation*. New York: Routledge, 2014.

hooks, bell. *Talking Back: Thinking Feminist, Thinking Black*. Toronto: Between the Lines, 1989.

hooks, bell. *Teaching to Transgress: Education as the Practice to Freedom*. London: Routledge, 1994.

Howard, Mary, and Ann V. Millard. *Hunger and Shame: Child Malnutrition and Poverty on Mount Kilimanjaro*. London: Routledge, 1997.

Huhndorf, Shari M., and Cheryl Suzack. "Indigenous Feminism: Theorizing the Issues." In *Indigenous Women and Feminism: Politics, Activism, Culture*, edited by Cheryl Suzack, Shari M. Huhndorf, Jeanne Perrault, and Jean Barman, 1–20. Vancouver: University of British Columbia Press, 2010.

Ishiyama, Noriko, and Kim TallBear. "Nuclear Waste and Relational Accountability in Indian Country." In *The Promise of Multispecies Justice*, edited by Sophie Chao, Karin Bolender, and Eben S. Kirksey, 185–203. Durham, NC: Duke University Press, 2022.

Ito, Takeshi, Noer F. Rachman, and Laksmi Savitri. "Power to Make Land Dispossession Acceptable: A Policy Discourse Analysis of the Merauke Integrated Food and Energy Estate (MIFEE), Papua, Indonesia." *Journal of Peasant Studies* 41, no. 1 (2014): 29–50. https://doi.org/10.1080/03066150.2013.873029.

Jacka, Jerry K. *Alchemy in the Rainforest: Politics, Ecology, and Resilience in a New Guinea Mining Area*. Durham, NC: Duke University Press, 2015.

Jaimes Guerrero, M. A. "'Patriarchal Colonialism' and Indigenism: Implications for Native Feminist Spirituality and Native Womanism." *Hypatia* 18, no. 2 (Spring 2003): 58–69. https://www.jstor.org/stable/3811011.

Jeffries, Marshall. "Re-membering Our Own Power: Occaneechi Activism, Feminism, and Political Action Theories." *Frontiers: A Journal of Women Studies* 36, no. 1 (2015): 160–95. https://doi.org/10.5250/fronjwomestud.36.1.0160.

joannemariebarker and Teresia K. Teaiwa. "Native Information." *Inscriptions* 7 (1994): 16–41. https://culturalstudies.ucsc.edu/inscriptions/volume-7/joannemariebarker-teresia-teaiwa/.

Jobson, Ryan C. "The Case for Letting Anthropology Burn: Sociocultural Anthropology in 2019." *American Anthropologist* 122, no. 2 (2020): 259–71. https://doi.org/10.1111/aman.13398.

Jolly, Margaret. "Beyond the Horizon? Nationalisms, Feminisms, and Globalization in the Pacific." *Ethnohistory* 52, no. 1 (Winter 2005): 137–66. https://doi.org/10.1215/00141801-52-1-137.

Jolly, Margaret. "Gifts, Commodities and Corporeality: Food and Gender in South Pentecost, Vanuatu." *Canberra Anthropology* 14, no. 1 (1991): 45–66. https://doi.org/10.1080/03149099109508475.

Jolly, Margaret, and Martha Macintyre, eds. *Family and Gender in the Pacific: Domestic Contradictions and the Colonial Impact.* Cambridge: Cambridge University Press, 2011.

Kabutaulaka, Tarcisius T. "Re-presenting Melanesia: Ignoble Savages and Melanesian Alter-Natives." *Contemporary Pacific* 27, no. 1 (2015): 110–45. https://www.jstor.org/stable/24809815.

Kabutaulaka, Tarcisius T. "Rumble in the Jungle: Land, Culture and (Un)sustainable Logging in Solomon Islands." In *Culture and Sustainable Development in the Pacific,* edited by Antony Hooper, 88–97. Canberra: Australian National University E-Press and Asia Pacific Press, 2005.

Kadir, Hatib A. "Women's Grievances and Land Dispossession: Reading Landscapes through Papuan Independent Films." *eTropic: electronic journal of studies in the Tropics* 21, no. 1 (2022): 143–64. https://doi.org/10.25120/etropic.21.1.2022.3843.

Kahaleole Hall, Lisa. "Navigating Our Own 'Sea of Islands': Remapping a Theoretical Space for Hawaiian Women and Indigenous Feminism." *Wicazo Sa Review* 24, no. 2 (Fall 2009): 15–38. https://www.jstor.org/stable/40587779.

Kahaleole Hall, Lisa. "Strategies of Erasure: U.S. Colonialism and Native Hawaiian Feminism." *American Quarterly* 60, no. 2 (June 2008): 273–80. https://www.jstor.org/stable/40068535.

Kahn, Miriam. *Always Hungry, Never Greedy: Food and the Expression of Gender in a Melanesian Society.* Long Grove, IL: Waveland Press, 1994.

Kahn, Miriam. "'Men Are Taro' (They Cannot Be Rice): Political Aspects of Food Choices in Wamira, Papua New Guinea." *Food and Foodways* 3, no. 1–2 (1988): 41–57. https://doi.org/10.1080/07409710.1988.9961936.

Kahn, Miriam, and Lorraine Sexton. "The Fresh and the Canned: Food Choices in the Pacific." *Food and Foodways* 3, no. 1–2 (1988): 1–18. https://doi.org/10.1080/07409710.1988.9961934.

Kalofonos, Ippolytos A. "'All I Eat Is ARVs': The Paradox of AIDS Treatment Interventions in Central Mozambique." *Medical Anthropology Quarterly* 24, no. 3 (September 2010): 363–80. https://doi.org/10.1111/j.1548-1387.2010.01109.x.

Kamma, Freerk. *Koreri-Messianic Movements in the Biak-Numfor Culture Area.* The Hague: Martinus Nijhoff, 1972.

Kanem, Veronika T., and Adele N. Norris. "An Examination of the Noken and Indigenous Cultural Identity: Voices of Papuan Women." *Journal of Cultural Analysis and Social Change* 3, no. 1 (2018): 1–11. https://doi.org/10.20897/jcasc/86189.

Kanem, Veronika T., and Adele N. Norris. "Indigenous Women, Traditional Goods, and Identity: Voices of Papuan Women from the Merauke Regency of Papua Province." *Women Talking Politics*, no. 1 (November 2016): 7–9.

Karides, Marina. "Why Island Feminism?" *Shima* 11, no. 1 (2017): 30–39. https://doi.org/10.21463/shima.11.1.06.

Karma, Filep. *Seakan Kitorang Setengah Binatang: Rasialisme Indonesia di Tanah Papua.* Deiyai: Cetakan Pertama, 2014.

Kēhaulani Kauanui, J. "Native Hawaiian Decolonization and the Politics of Gender." *American Quarterly* 60, no. 2 (June 2008): 281–87. https://www.jstor.org/stable/40068536.

Kēhaulani Kauanui, J. *Paradoxes of Hawaiian Sovereignty: Land, Sex, and the Colonial Politics of State Nationalism.* Durham, NC: Duke University Press, 2018.

Kelleher, Margaret. *The Feminization of Famine: Expressions of the Inexpressible?* Durham, NC: Duke University Press, 1997.

Kelley, Lindsay. *After Eating: Metabolizing the Arts.* Cambridge: Massachusetts Institute of Technology Press, 2023.

Kemal, Anwar. "UN CERD Formal Communication to the Permanent Mission of Indonesia regarding Allegations of Threatening and Imminent Irreparable Harm for Indigenous Peoples in Merauke District Related to the MIFEE Project." Geneva: Chairperson of the Committee on the Elimination of Racial Discrimination, September 2, 2011. http://www.forestpeoples.org/sites/fpp/files/publication/2011/09/cerduaindonesiao2092011fm.pdf.

Kimura, Aya H. *Hidden Hunger: Gender and the Politics of Smarter Foods.* Ithaca, NY: Cornell University Press, 2013.

Kirksey, Eben S., and Sophie Chao. "Introduction: Who Benefits from Multispecies Justice?" In *The Promise of Multispecies Justice*, edited by Sophie Chao, Karin Bolender, and Eben S. Kirksey, 1–20. Durham, NC: Duke University Press, 2022.

Kirsch, Stuart. *Engaged Anthropology: Politics beyond the Text.* Berkeley: University of California Press, 2018.

Kirsch, Stuart. "Rumour and Other Narratives of Political Violence in West Papua." *Critique of Anthropology* 22, no. 1 (2002): 53–79. https://doi.org/10.1177/0308275X020220010301.

Kluge, Emma. "West Papua and the International History of Decolonization, 1961–69." *International History Review* 42, no. 6 (2020): 1155–72. https://doi .org/10.1080/07075332.2019.1694052.

Knauft, Bruce M. *South Coast New Guinea Cultures: History, Comparison, Dialectic.* Cambridge: Cambridge University Press, 1993.

Koentjaraningrat, Kanjeng P. H., and Daniel C. Ajamiseba. "Reaksi Penduduk Asli Terhadap Pembangunan dan Perubahan." In *Irian Jaya: Membangun Masyarakat Majemuk*, edited by R. M. Koentjaraningrat, 433–52. Jakarta: Djambatan, 1994.

Koentjaraningrat, Kanjeng P. H., and Harsja W. Bachtiar. *Penduduk Irian Barat.* Jakarta: Penerbitan Universitas Jakarta, 1963.

Kompas. "Merauke Diharapkan Jadi Lumbung Padi Nasional." April 6, 2006. Accessed January 3, 2010, http://www.depdagri.go.id/news/2006/04/06/merauke -diharapkan-jadi-lumbung-padi-nasional.

Koshy, Susan, Lisa M. Cacho, Jodi A. Byrd, and Jordan Jefferson, eds. *Colonial Racial Capitalism.* Durham, NC: Duke University Press, 2022.

Kulick, Don. *A Death in the Rainforest: How a Language and a Way of Life Came to an End in Papua New Guinea.* Chapel Hill, NC: Algonquin Books, 2019.

Kuokkanen, Rauna. "From Indigenous Economies to Market-Based Self-Governance: A Feminist Political Economic Analysis." *Canadian Journal of Political Science* 44, no. 2 (June 2011): 275–97. https://www.jstor.org/stable/41300542.

Kuokkanen, Rauna. *Restructuring Relations: Indigenous Self-Determination, Governance, and Gender.* New York: Oxford University Press, 2019.

Kusumaryati, Veronika. "The Great Colonial Roads." *Landscape Architecture Frontiers* 5, no. 2 (2017): 137–45. https://doi.org/10.15302/J-LAF-20170211.

Kwiatkowski, Lynn M. *Struggling with Development: The Politics of Hunger and Gender in the Philippines.* Boulder, CO: Westview Press, 1998.

Landecker, Hannah. "Food as Exposure: Nutritional Epigenetics and the New Metabolism." *BioSocieties* 6, no. 2 (June 2011): 167–94. https://doi.org/10.1057/ biosoc.2011.1.

LaRocque, Emma. "The Colonization of a Native Woman Scholar." In *Women of the First Nations: Power, Wisdom, and Strength*, edited by Christine Miller and Patricia M. Chuchryk, 11–18. Winnipeg: University of Manitoba Press, 1996.

Lattas, Andrew. "Sorcery and Colonialism: Illness, Dreams and Death as Political Languages in West New Britain." *Man* 28, no. 1 (March 1993): 51–77. https:// doi.org/10.2307/2804436.

La Via Campesina. "Food Sovereignty | Explained." January 15, 2003. https:// viacampesina.org/en/food-sovereignty/.

Lawrence, Peter. *Road Belong Cargo: A Study of the Cargo Movement in the Southern Madang District, New Guinea.* Manchester: Manchester University Press, 1964.

Leach, James. *Creative Land: Place and Procreation on the Rai Coast of Papua New Guinea.* New York: Berghahn, 2003.

Lefebvre, Henri. "Conspicuous Consumption: The Figure of the Serial Killer as Cannibal in the Age of Capitalism." *Theory, Culture, and Society* 22, no. 3 (June 2005): 43–62. https://doi.org/10.1177/0263276405053719.

Leith, Denise. *The Politics of Power: Freeport in Suharto's Indonesia.* Honolulu: University of Hawai'i Press, 2003.

Leon-Quijano, Camilo. "Why Do 'Good' Pictures Matter in Anthropology?" *Cultural Anthropology* 37, no. 3 (August 2022): 572–98. https://doi.org/10.14506/ca37.3.11.

Li, Tanya M., and Pujo Semedi. *Plantation Life: Corporate Occupation in Indonesia's Oil Palm Zone.* Durham, NC: Duke University Press, 2023.

Liboiron, Max. *Pollution Is Colonialism.* Durham, NC: Duke University Press, 2021.

Lin, Yi-Chun Tricia. "An Introduction: "Indigenous Feminisms: Why Transnational? Why Now?" *Lectora*, no. 22 (2016): 9–12. https://doi.org/10.1344/Lectora2016.22.1.

Lindenbaum, Shirley. *Kuru Sorcery: Disease and Danger in the New Guinea Highlands.* Palo Alto, CA: Mayfield, 1979.

Lindstrom, Lamont. *Cargo Cult: Strange Stories of Desire from Melanesia and Beyond.* Honolulu: University of Hawai'i Press, 1993.

Litz, Brett T., Nathan Stein, Eileen Delaney, et al. "Moral Injury and Moral Repair in War Veterans: A Preliminary Model and Intervention Strategy." *Clinical Psychology Review* 29, no. 8 (December 2009): 695–706. https://doi.org/10.1016/j.cpr.2009.07.003.

Livingston, Julie. *Self-Devouring Growth: A Planetary Parable as Told from Southern Africa.* Durham, NC: Duke University Press, 2019.

Loichot, Valérie. *The Tropics Bite Back: Culinary Coups in Caribbean Literature.* Minneapolis: University of Minnesota Press, 2013.

Lorde, Audre. "The Uses of Anger." *Women's Studies Quarterly* 9, no. 3 (Fall 1981): 7–10.

MacCarthy, Michelle. "Playing Politics with Yams: Food Security in the Trobriand Islands of Papua New Guinea." *Culture, Agriculture, Food, and Environment* 34, no. 2 (December 2012): 136–47. https://doi.org/10.1111/j.2153-9561.2012.01073.x.

MacClancy, Jeremy, ed. *Exotic No More: Anthropology for the Contemporary World.* 2nd ed. Chicago: University of Chicago Press, 2019.

Macintyre, Martha, and Simon Foale. "Global Imperatives and Local Desires: Competing Economic and Environmental Interests in Melanesian Communities." In *Globalisation and Culture Change in the Pacific*, edited by Victoria S. Lockwood, 149–64. Upper Saddle River, NJ: Pearson Prentice Hall, 2004.

Macintyre, Martha, and Ceridwen Spark. *Transformations of Gender in Melanesia.* Acton: Australian National University Press, 2017.

MacRae, Graeme, and Thomas Reuter. "Lumbung Nation: Metaphors of Food Security in Indonesia." *Indonesia and the Malay World* 48, no. 142 (2020): 338–58. https://doi.org/10.1080/13639811.2020.1830535.

Macura-Nnamdi, Ewa. "The Alimentary Life of Power." GLQ: *A Journal of Lesbian and Gay Studies* 21, no. 1 (January 2015): 95–120. https://www.muse.jhu.edu/article/566790.

Manufandu, Septer. "Land Grabbing and Human Rights Issues in Food and Energy Estates in Papua." In *Human Rights and Agribusiness: Plural Legal Approaches to Conflict Resolution, Institutional Strengthening and Legal Reform*, edited by Marcus Colchester and Sophie Chao, 130–44. Bogor: Forest Peoples Programme and Asia Indigenous Peoples Network, 2011.

Marcus, George E., and Michael M. J. Fischer. *Anthropology as Cultural Critique: An Experimental Moment in the Human Sciences*. Chicago: University of Chicago Press, 1986.

Martinkus, John. *The Road: Uprising in West Papua*. Collingwood, Australia: Black Inc., 2020.

Martuwarra RiverofLife, Anne Poelina, Donna Bagnall, and Michelle Lim. "Recognizing the Martuwarra's First Law Right to Life as a Living Ancestral Being." *Transnational Environmental Law* 9, no. 3 (2020): 541–68. https://doi.org /10.1017/S2047102520000163.

Matapo, Jacoba, and Dion Enari. "Re-imagining the Dialogic Spaces of Talanoa through Samoan Onto-Epistemology." *Waikato Journal of Education* 26 (2021): 79–88. https://doi.org/10.15663/wje.v26i1.770.

Maulia, Erwida. "Indonesia Pledges to 'Feed the World.'" *Jakarta Post*. January 30, 2010. https://www.thejakartapost.com/news/2010/01/30/indonesia-pledges -feed-world039.html.

Mbembe, Achille. *On the Postcolony*. Berkeley: University of California Press, 2001.

McCarthy, John F. "Tenure and Transformation in Central Kalimantan: After the 'Million Hectare' Project." In *Land for the People: The State and Agrarian Conflict in Indonesia*, edited by Anton Lucas and Carol Warren, 183–214. Athens: Ohio University Press, 2013.

McCarthy, John F., Jacqueline A. C. Vel, and Suraya Afiff. "Trajectories of Land Acquisition and Enclosure: Development Schemes, Virtual Land Grabs, and Green Acquisitions in Indonesia's Outer Islands." *Journal of Peasant Studies* 39, no. 2 (2012): 521–49. https://doi.org/10.1080/03066150.2012.671768.

McClaurin, Irma. "Walking in Zora's Shoes or 'Seek[ing] Out de Inside Meanin' of Words': The Intersections of Anthropology, Ethnography, Identity, and Writing." In *Anthropology Off the Shelf: Anthropologists on Writing*, edited by Alisse Waterston and Maria D. Vesperi, 119–33. London: Blackwell, 2009.

McDonnell, Siobhan. "'The Land Will Eat You': Land and Sorcery in North Efate, Vanuatu." In *Talking It Through: Responses to Sorcery and Witchcraft Beliefs and Practices in Melanesia*, edited by Miranda Forsyth and Richard Eves, 137–60. Canberra: Australian National University Press, 2015.

McGranahan, Carole. "Theory as Ethics." *American Ethnologist* 49, no. 3 (August 2022): 289–301. https://doi.org/10.1111/amet.13087.

McGranahan, Carole, ed. *Writing Anthropology: Essays on Craft and Commitment*. Durham, NC: Duke University Press, 2020.

McLennan, Amy K., M. Shimonovich, Stanley J. Ulijaszek, and M. Wilson. "The Problem with Relying on Dietary Surveys: Sociocultural Correctives to

Theories of Dietary Change in the Pacific islands." *Annals of Human Biology* 45, no. 3 (May 2018): 272–84. https://doi.org/10.1080/03014460.2018.1469668.

McNamara, Karen E., and Carol Farbotko. "Resisting a 'Doomed' Fate: An Analysis of the Pacific Climate Warriors." *Australian Geographer* 48, no. 1 (2017): 17–26. https://doi.org/10.1080/00049182.2016.1266631.

Mendenhall, Emily. *Rethinking Diabetes: Entanglements with Trauma, Poverty, and HIV*. Ithaca, NY: Cornell University Press, 2019.

Messer, Ellen. "Anthropological Perspectives on Diet." *Annual Reviews in Anthropology* 13 (1984): 205–50. https://www.jstor.org/stable/2155668.

Messer, Ellen, and Parker Shipton. "Hunger in Africa: Untangling Its Human Roots." In *Exotic No More: Anthropology on the Front Lines*, edited by Jeremy MacClancy, 227–50. Chicago: University of Chicago Press, 2002.

Milne, Sarah. *Corporate Nature: An Insider's Ethnography of Global Conservation*. Tucson: University of Arizona Press, 2022.

Mimica, Jadran. *Of Humans, Pigs, and Souls: An Essay on the Yagwoia Womba Complex*. Chicago: HAU Books, 2020.

Miner, Joshua D. "Consuming the Wiindigoo: Native Figurations of Hunger and Food Bureaucracy." In *The Aesthetics and Politics of Global Hunger*, edited by Anastasia Ulanowicz and Manisha Basu, 229–58. London: Palgrave Macmillan, 2015.

Miyarrka Media. *Phone and Spear: A Yuta Anthropology*. London: Goldsmiths, 2019.

Mohanty, Chandra Talpade. "Under Western Eyes: Feminist Scholarship and Colonial Discourses." *Feminist Review* 30 (Autumn 1988): 61–88. https://doi.org/10.2307/1395054.

Mol, AnneMarie. *Eating in Theory*. Durham, NC: Duke University Press, 2021.

Monson, Rebecca. "The Politics of Property: Gender, Land and Political Authority in Solomon Islands." In *Kastom, Property, and Ideology: Land Transformations in Melanesia*, edited by Siobhan McDonnell, Matthew G. Allen, and Colin Filer, 383–404. Canberra: Australian National University Press, 2017.

Montagu, Ashley. *Touching: The Human Significance of the Skin*. New York: Columbia University Press, 1971.

Moore, Sally Falk. *Comparing Impossibilities: Selected Essays of Sally Falk Moore*. Chicago: University of Chicago Press, 2016.

Morauta, Louise, Ann Chowning, Current Issues Collective (B. Kaspou and Others), et al. "Indigenous Anthropology in Papua New Guinea [and Comments and Reply]." *Current Anthropology* 20, no. 3 (September 1979): 561–76. https://www.jstor.org/stable/2742112.

Morell-Hart, Shanti. "Foodways and Resilience under Apocalyptic Conditions." *Culture, Agriculture, Food and Environment* 34, no. 2 (December 2012): 161–71. https://doi.org/10.1111/j.2153-9561.2012.01075.x.

Moreton-Robinson, Aileen. *Talkin' Up to the White Woman: Indigenous Women and Feminism*. Minneapolis: University of Minnesota Press, 2021.

Mosko, Mark S. *Ways of Baloma*. Chicago: HAU Books, 2017.

Mote, Okto, and Danilyn Rutherford. "From Irian Jaya to Papua: The Limits of Primordialism in Indonesia's Troubled East." *Indonesia*, no. 72 (October 2001): 115–40. https://doi.org/10.2307/3351483.

Moura-Koçoğlu, Michaela. "Decolonizing Gender Roles in Pacific Women's Writing: Indigenous Feminist Theories and the Reconceptualization of Women's Authority." *Contemporary Women's Writing* 11, no. 2 (July 2017): 239–58. https://doi.org/10.1093/cww/vpx015.

Mrázek, Rudolf. *Engineers of Happy Land: Technology and Nationalism in a Colony*. Princeton, NJ: Princeton University Press, 2002.

Munro, Jenny. "Global HIV Interventions and Technocratic Racism in a West Papuan NGO." *Medical Anthropology* 39, no. 8 (November–December 2020): 704–19. https://doi.org/10.1080/01459740.2020.1739036.

Munro, Jenny. "Indigenous Masculinities and the 'Refined Politics' of Alcohol and Racialization in West Papua." *Contemporary Pacific* 31, no. 1 (2019): 36–63. https://doi.org/10.1353/cp.2019.0005.

Munro, Jenny. "'Now We Know Shame': Malu and Stigma among Highlanders in the Papuan Diaspora." In *From 'Stone Age' to 'Real-Time': Exploring Papuan Temporalities, Mobilities and Religiosities*, edited by Martin Slama and Jenny Munro, 169–94. Canberra: Australian National University Press, 2015.

Munro, Jenny, and Yohana Baransano. "From Saving to Survivance: Rethinking Indigenous Papuan Women's Vulnerabilities in Jayapura, Indonesia." *Asia Pacific Viewpoint* 64, no. 2 (August 2023): 209–21. https://doi.org/10.1111/apv.12367.

Myrttinen, Henri. "Under Two Flags: Encounters with Israel, Merdeka and the Promised Land in Tanah Papua." In *From 'Stone Age' to 'Real-Time': Exploring Papuan Temporalities, Mobilities and Religiosities*, edited by Martin Slama and Jenny Munro, 125–44. Canberra: Australian National University Press, 2015.

Nabobo-Baba, Unaisi. *Knowing and Learning: An Indigenous Fijian Approach*. Suva, Fiji: University of the South Pacific, 2006.

Nabobo-Baba, Unaisi. "Research and Pacific Indigenous Peoples: Silenced Pasts and Challenged Futures." In *Researching Pacific and Indigenous Peoples: Issues and Perspectives*, edited by Tupeni L. Baba, 'Okusitino Māhina, Nuhisifa Williangs, and Unaisi Nabobo-Baba, 17–31. Auckland: University of Auckland Press, 2004.

Nally, David. "Against Food Security: On Forms of Care and Fields of Violence." *Global Society* 30, no. 4 (2016): 558–82. https://doi.org/10.1080/13600826.2016.1158700.

Nally, David. *Human Encumbrances: Political Violence and the Great Irish Famine*. Notre Dame, IN: University of Notre Dame Press, 2011.

Narayan, Kirin. *Alive in the Writing: Crafting Ethnography in the Company of Chekhov*. Chicago: University of Chicago Press, 2012.

Narokobi, Bernard Mullu. "Art and Nationalism." *Gigibori* 3, no. 1 (1976): 12–15.

Nash, June. *We Eat the Mines and the Mines Eat Us: Dependency and Exploitation in Bolivian Tin Mines*. New York: Columbia University Press, 1993.

Naupa, Anna. "Making the Invisible Seen: Putting Women's Rights on Vanuatu's Land Reform Agenda." In *Kastom, Property and Ideology: Land Transformations in Melanesia*, edited by Siobhan McDonnell, Matthew G. Allen, and Colin Filer, 305–26. Canberra: Australian National University Press, 2017.

Neilson, Jeff, and Josephine Wright. "The State and Food Security Discourses of Indonesia: Feeding the *Bangsa.*" *Geographical Research* 55, no. 2 (May 2017): 131–43. https://doi.org/10.1111/1745-5871.12210.

Neitch, Kenna. "Indigenous Persistence: Challenging the Rhetoric of Anti-colonial Resistance." *Feminist Studies* 45, no. 2–3 (2019): 426–54. https://doi.org/10.15767/feministstudies.45.2-3.0426.

Nerenberg, Jacob. "Terminal Economy: Politics of Distribution in Highland Papua, Indonesia." PhD diss., University of Toronto, 2018.

Newland, Lynda. "The Lost Tribes of Israel—and the Genesis of Christianity in Fiji: Missionary Notions of Fijian Origin from 1835 to Cession and Beyond." *Oceania* 85, no. 3 (November 2015): 256–70. https://www.jstor.org/stable/44161347.

Nichter, Mark. "Idioms of Distress Revisited." *Culture, Medicine, and Psychiatry* 34, no. 2 (June 2010): 401–16. https://doi.org/10.1007/s11013-010-9179-6.

Nickel, Sarah A. "'I Am Not a Women's Libber Although Sometimes I Sound Like One': Indigenous Feminism and Politicized Motherhood." *American Indian Quarterly* 41, no. 4 (Fall 2017): 299–335. https://doi.org/10.1353/aiq.2017.a679037.

Nickel, Sarah A. "Introduction." In *In Good Relation: History, Gender, and Kinship in Indigenous Feminisms*, edited by Sarah A. Nickel and Amanda Fehr, 1–19. Manitoba: University of Manitoba Press, 2020.

Nott, John. "'How Little Progress'? A Political Economy of Postcolonial Nutrition." *Population and Development Review* 44, no. 4 (December 2018): 771–91. https://www.jstor.org/stable/45174456.

Nurhasan, Mulia, Agus M. Maulana, Desy L. Ariesta, et al. "Toward a Sustainable Food System in West Papua, Indonesia: Exploring the Links between Dietary Transition, Food Security, and Forests." *Frontiers in Sustainable Food Systems* 5 (2022): 1–20. https://doi.org/10.3389/fsufs.2021.789186.

Obeyesekere, Gananath. *Cannibal Talk: The Man-Eating Myth and Human Sacrifice in the South Seas.* Berkeley: University of California Press, 2005.

Office of the United Nations High Commissioner for Human Rights. "South-East Asia/Agrofuel: UN Rights Experts Raise Alarm on Land Development Mega-projects." May 23, 2012. http://www.srfood.org/en/south-east-asia-agrofuel-un-rights-experts-raise-alarm-on-land-development-mega-projects.

Ogoye-Ndegwa, Charles, and Jens Aagaard-Hansen. "Famines and Famished Bodies in a Food Deficit Locality among the Luo of Kenya." *Food and Foodways* 14, no. 3–4 (2006): 231–47. https://doi.org/10.1080/07409710600962019.

Ondawame, Otto J. *One People, One Soul: West Papuan Nationalism and the Organisasi Papua Merdeka.* Belair, Australia: Crawford House, 2009.

Ondawame, Otto J. "West Papua: The Discourse of Cultural Genocide and Conflict Resolution." In *Cultural Genocide and Asian State Peripheries*, edited by Barry Sautman, 103–38. New York: Palgrave Macmillan, 2006.

Oosterwal, Gottfried. "A Cargo Cult in the Mamberamo Area." *Ethnology* 2, no. 1 (January 1963): 1–14. https://doi.org/10.2307/3772964.

Pandian, Anand. *A Possible Anthropology: Methods for Uneasy Times*. Durham, NC: Duke University Press, 2019.

Pandian, Anand, and Stuart J. McLean, eds. *Crumpled Paper Boat: Experiments in Ethnographic Writing*. Durham, NC: Duke University Press, 2017.

Paper Boat Collective. "Introduction: Archipelagos, a Voyage in Writing." In *Crumpled Paper Boat: Experiments in Ethnographic Writing*, edited by Anand Pandian and Stuart J. McLean, 1–28. Durham, NC: Duke University Press, 2017.

Parreñas, Juno Salazar. "Ethnography after Anthropology: Become Moles, Not Mining Corporations." *American Ethnologist* 50, no. 3 (August 2023): 453–61. https://doi.org/10.1111/amet.13201.

Paxson, Heather, ed. *Eating beside Ourselves: Thresholds of Foods and Bodies*. Durham, NC: Duke University Press, 2022.

Pelluchon, Corine. *Nourishment: A Philosophy of the Political Body*. Translated by Justin E. H. Smith. London: Bloomsbury, 2019.

Peña, Devon. *The Terror in the Machine: Technology, Work, Gender, and Ecology on the US-Mexico Border*. Austin: University of Texas Press, 1997.

Phillips, Kristin D. *An Ethnography of Hunger: Politics, Subsistence, and the Unpredictable Grace of the Sun*. Bloomington: Indiana University Press, 2018.

Pictou, Sherry. "Decolonizing Decolonization: An Indigenous Feminist Perspective on the Recognition and Rights Framework." *South Atlantic Quarterly* 119, no. 2 (April 2020): 371–91. https://doi.org/10.1215/00382876-8177809.

Plumwood, Val. "Tasteless: Towards a Food-Based Approach to Death." *Environmental Values* 17, no. 3 (August 2008): 323–30. https://www.jstor.org/stable/30302203.

Pollock, Nancy J. *These Roots Remain: Food Habits in Islands of the Central and Eastern Pacific*. Laie: Institute of Polynesian Studies, 1992.

Povinelli, Elizabeth A. *The Cunning of Recognition: Indigenous Alterities and the Making of Australian Multiculturalism*. Durham, NC: Duke University Press, 2002.

Prasetyo, Erwin Edhi, and Timbuktu Harthana. "Suku Marind Hidup di Antara Busur Dan Pacul." *Kompas*, April 17, 2011. http://regional.kompas.com/read/2011/04/17/15110830/Suku.Marind.Hidup.di.Antara.Busur.dan.Pacul.

Pratt, Susanne. "Care, Toxics and Being Prey: I Want to Be Good Food for Others." *Australian Feminist Studies* 34, no. 102 (2019): 437–53. https://doi.org/10.1080/08164649.2019.1702873.

Price, Catherine, and Sophie Chao. "Multispecies, More-Than-Human, Non-human, Other-Than-Human: Reimagining Idioms of Animacy in an Age of Planetary Unmaking." *Exchanges: The Interdisciplinary Research Journal* 10, no. 2 (2022): 177–93. https://doi.org/10.31273/eirj.v10i2.1166.

Probyn, Elspeth. *Carnal Appetites: Foodsexidentities*. London: Routledge, 2000.

Probyn, Elspeth. *Eating the Ocean*. Durham, NC: Duke University Press, 2016.

Purwestri, Ratna C., Bronwen Powell, Dominic Rowland, et al. *From Growing Food to Growing Cash: Understanding the Drivers of Food Choice in the Context of Rapid Agrarian Change in Indonesia*. Info Brief no. 263 (July 2019). Center for International Forestry Research. https://doi.org/10.17528/cifor/007360.

Ravuvu, Asesela. *Vaka i Taukei: The Fijian Way of Life*. Suva: University of the South Pacific, 1983.

Razaki, Ardi. "Delapan Kasus Gizi Buruk Ditemukan di Merauke." *Radio Republik Indonesia*, June 3, 2018.

Redvers, Nicole, Michael Yellow Bird, Diana Quinn, Tyson Yunkaporta, and Kerry Arabena. "Molecular Decolonization: An Indigenous Microcosm Perspective of Planetary Health." *International Journal of Environmental Research and Public Health* 17, no. 12 (June 2020): 4586. https://doi.org/10.3390/ijerph17124586.

Richards, Audrey. *Hunger and Work in a Savage Tribe: A Functional Study of Nutrition among the Southern Bantu*. London: Routledge, 1932.

Richards, Audrey. *Land, Labor, and Diet in Northern Rhodesia: An Economic Study of the Bemba Tribe*. Oxford: Oxford University Press, 1939.

Richens, John. *Tik Merauke: An Epidemic Like No Other*. Melbourne: Melbourne University Press, 2021.

Rival, Laura. "Androgynous Parents and Guest Children: The Huaorani Couvade." *Journal of the Royal Anthropological Institute* 4, no. 4 (December 1998): 619–42. https://doi.org/10.2307/3034825.

Robbins, Joel. "Beyond the Suffering Subject: Toward an Anthropology of the Good." *Journal of the Royal Anthropological Institute* 19, no. 3 (September 2013): 447–62. https://www.jstor.org/stable/42001631.

Robbins, Joel. "Secrecy and the Sense of an Ending: Narrative, Time, and Everyday Millenarianism in Papua New Guinea and in Christian Fundamentalism." *Comparative Studies in History and Society* 43, no. 3 (July 2001): 525–51. https://www.jstor.org/stable/2696680.

Rose, Deborah Bird. "Multispecies Knots of Ethical Time." *Environmental Philosophy* 9, no. 1 (Spring 2012): 127–40. https://www.jstor.org/stable/26169399.

Rose, Deborah Bird. *Nourishing Terrains: Australian Aboriginal Views of Landscape and Wilderness*. Canberra: Australian Heritage Commission, 1996.

Rose, Deborah Bird. "Slowly ~ Writing into the Anthropocene." *TEXT* 17, no. 20 (October 2013): 1–14. https://doi.org/10.52086/001c.28826.

Ross, Luana. "From the 'F' Word to Indigenous/Feminisms." *Wicazo Sa Review* 24, no. 2 (Fall 2009): 39–52. https://www.jstor.org/stable/40587780.

Roy, Parama. *Alimentary Tracts: Appetites, Aversions, and the Postcolonial*. Durham, NC: Duke University Press, 2010.

Rudiak-Gould, Peter. *Climate Change and Tradition in a Small Island State: The Rising Tide*. London: Routledge, 2015.

Runtuboi, Yubelince Y., Dwiko B. Permadi, Muhammad Alif K. Sahide, and Ahmad Maryudi. "Oil Palm Plantations, Forest Conservation and Indigenous Peoples in West Papua Province: What Lies Ahead?" *Forest and Society* 5, no. 1 (April 2021): 23–31. https://doi.org/0.24259/fs.v5i1.11343.

Rutherford, Danilyn. "Book Review: *In the Shadow of the Palms: More-Than-Human Becomings in West Papua.*" *Journal of Asian Studies* 83, no. 1 (February 2023): 198–200. https://doi.org/10.1215/00219118-10872680.

Rutherford, Danilyn. "Kinky Empiricism." In *Writing Culture and the Life of Anthropology*, edited by Orin Starn, 105–18. Durham, NC: Duke University Press, 2015.

Rutherford, Danilyn. *Laughing at Leviathan: Sovereignty and Audience in West Papua*. Chicago: University of Chicago Press, 2012.

Rutherford, Danilyn. "Nationalism and Millenarianism in West Papua: Institutional Power, Interpretive Practice, and the Pursuit of Christian Truth." In *The Limits of Meaning: Case Studies in the Anthropology of Christianity*, edited by Matthew Engelke and Matt Tomlinson, 105–27. New York: Berghahn, 2006.

Rutherford, Danilyn. *Raiding the Land of the Foreigners: The Limits of the Nation on an Indonesian Frontier*. Princeton, NJ: Princeton University Press, 2003.

Sahlins, Marshall. "What Kinship Is (Part One)." *Journal of the Royal Anthropological Institute* 17, no. 1 (March 2011): 2–19. https://www.jstor.org/stable/23011568.

Sanabria, Emilia, and Emily Yates-Doerr. "Alimentary Uncertainties: From Contested Evidence to Policy." *BioSocieties* 10 (June 2015): 117–24. https://doi.org/10.1057/biosoc.2015.17.

Santos Perez, Craig. "Facing Hawaiʻi's Future." *Kenyon Review*, July 10, 2013. https://www.kenyonreview.org/2013/07/facing-hawaiʻi's-future-book-review/.

Santos Perez, Craig. *Navigating CHamoru Poetry: Indigeneity, Aesthetics, and Decolonization*. Tucson: University of Arizona Press, 2022.

Sapp Moore, Sophie. "Between the State and the Yard: Gender and Political Space in Haiti." *Gender, Place and Culture* 28, no. 9 (2021): 1306–26. https://doi.org/10.1080/0966369X.2020.1846500.

Sarwono, Sarlito W. *Teori-Teori Psikologi Sosial*. Jakarta: Raja Grafindo Persada, 1998.

Sawit Watch and Forest Peoples Programme. "Joint Statement at the Asia Regional Consultation with the UN Special Rapporteur on the Rights of Indigenous Peoples on the Situation of Indigenous Peoples in Asia." Kuala Lumpur, Malaysia, March 12, 2013. http://www.forestpeoples.org/sites/fpp/files/publication/2013/03/fppsawitwatch-statementmarch2013.pdf.

Schaeffer, Felicity A. *Unsettled Borders: The Militarized Science of Surveillance on Sacred Indigenous Land*. Durham, NC: Duke University Press, 2022.

Schanbacher, William D. *The Politics of Food: The Global Conflict between Food Security and Food Sovereignty*. Santa Barbara, CA: Praeger Security International, 2010.

Scheper-Hughes, Nancy. *Death without Weeping: The Violence of Everyday Life in Brazil*. Berkeley: University of California Press, 1993.

Scheper-Hughes, Nancy. "Hungry Bodies, Medicine, and the State: Toward a Critical Psychological Anthropology." In *New Directions in the Study of Psychological Anthropology*, edited by Theodore Schwartz, Geoffrey M. White, and Catherine A. Lutz, 221–48. Chapel Hill: University of North Carolina Press, 1992.

Scheper-Hughes, Nancy. "The Madness of Hunger: Sickness, Delirium, and Human Needs." *Culture, Medicine, and Psychiatry* 12, no. 4 (December 1988): 429–58. https://doi.org/10.1007/BF00054497.

Schieffelin, Edward L. *The Sorrow of the Lonely and the Burning of the Dancers.* New York: St. Martin's Press, 1976.

Scott, James C. *Domination and the Arts of Resistance: Hidden Transcripts.* New Haven, CT: Yale University Press, 1990.

Scott-Smith, Tom. *On an Empty Stomach: Two Hundred Years of Hunger Relief.* Ithaca, NY: Cornell University Press, 2020.

Scrinis, Gyorgy. *Nutritionism: The Science and Politics of Dietary Advice.* London: Allen and Unwin, 2013.

Semali, Ladislaus M., and Joe K. Kincheloe. *What Is Indigenous Knowledge? Voices from the Academy.* London: Routledge, 1999.

Sen, Amartya. *Poverty and Famines: An Essay on Entitlement and Deprivation.* London: Oxford University Press, 1981.

Seputar Papua. "2021, Kasus Stunting di Merauke Meningkat 21,4 persen." July 16, 2021. https://seputarpapua.com/view/2021-kasus-stunting-di-merauke -meningkat-214-persen.html.

Serpenti, Laurentius M. *Cultivators in the Swamps: Social Structure and Horticulture in a New Guinea Society (Frederik-Hendrik Island, West New Guinea).* Assen: Van Gorcum, 1965.

Sexton, Lorraine. "'Eating' Money in Highland Papua New Guinea." *Food and Foodways* 3, no. 1–2 (1988): 119–42. https://doi.org/10.1080/07409710.1988.9961940.

Shack, William A. "Hunger, Anxiety, and Ritual: Deprivation and Spirit Possession among the Gurage of Ethiopia." *Man* 6, no. 1 (1971): 30–43. https://doi.org /10.2307/2798425.

Shanahan, Mike. "Palm Oil: The Pros and Cons of a Controversial Commodity." *Dialogue Earth*, June 13, 2023. https://dialogue.earth/en/food/11627-palm-oil -the-pros-and-cons-of-a-controversial-commodity/.

Shanley, Kate. "Thoughts on Indian Feminism." In *A Gathering of Spirit: Writing and Art by North American Indian Women*, edited by Beth Brant, 213–15. Ithaca, NY: Firebrand, 1984.

Shipton, Parker. "African Famines and Food Security: Anthropological Perspectives." *Annual Review of Anthropology* 19 (1990): 353–94. https://www.jstor.org/stable/2155970.

Shotwell, Alexis. *Against Purity.* Minneapolis: University of Minnesota Press, 2016.

Simpson, Audra. "On Ethnographic Refusal: Indigeneity, 'Voice' and Colonial Citizenship." *Junctures* 9 (December 2007): 67–80. https://junctures.org/index.php/junctures/article/view/66/60.

Simpson, Audra, and Andrea Smith. "Introduction." In *Theorizing Native Studies*, edited by Audra Simpson and Andrea Smith, 1–30. Durham, NC: Duke University Press, 2014.

Simpson, Leanne B. *As We Have Always Done: Indigenous Freedom through Radical Resistance*. Minneapolis: University of Minnesota Press, 2017.

Simpson, Leanne B. "Indigenous Resurgence and Co-resistance." *Journal of the Critical Ethnic Studies Association* 2, no. 2 (Fall 2016): 19–34. https://doi.org/10.5749/jcritethnstud.2.2.0019.

Singh, Bhrigupati. "Hunger and Thirst: Crises at Varying Thresholds of Life." In *Living and Dying in the Contemporary World*, edited by Veena Das and Clara Han, 576–98. Oakland: University of California Press, 2016.

Slama, Martin. "Papua as an Islamic Frontier: Preaching in 'the Jungle' and the Multiplicity of Spatio-temporal Hierarchisations." In *From 'Stone Age' to 'Real-Time': Exploring Papuan Temporalities, Mobilities and Religiosities*, edited by Martin Slama and Jenny Munro, 243–67. Canberra: Australian National University Press, 2015.

Smith, Will. *Mountains of Blame: Climate and Culpability in the Philippine Uplands*. Seattle: University of Washington Press, 2020.

Smythe, Julian. "The Laughter That Knows the Darkness: The Mamas' Resistance to Annihilative Violence in West Papua." In *Routledge Handbook of Peacebuilding and Ethnic Conflict*, edited by Jessica Senehi, Imani M. Scott, Sean Byrne, and Thomas G. Matyók, 164–73. London: Routledge, 2022.

Solomon, Harris. *Metabolic Living: Food, Fat, and the Absorption of Illness in India*. Durham, NC: Duke University Press, 2016.

Sontag, Susan. *Illness as Metaphor & AIDS and Its Metaphors*. New York: Penguin, 2014.

Souder, Laura. "Feminism and Women's Studies on Guam." *National Women's Studies Association Journal* 3, no. 3 (Autumn 1991): 442–46. https://www.jstor.org/stable/4316157.

Spark, Ceridwen. "'Food Is Life': Documenting the Politics of Food in Melanesia." *Pacific Journalism Review* 21, no. 1 (2015): 77–85. https://doi.org/10.24135/pjr.v21i2.119.

Spark, Ceridwen, John Cox, and John Corbett. "'Keeping an Eye Out for Women': Implicit Feminism, Political Leadership, and Social Change in the Pacific Islands." *Contemporary Pacific* 33, no. 1 (2021): 64–95. https://doi.org/10.1353/cp.2021.0003.

Spivak, Gayatri Chakravorty. "Can the Subaltern Speak?" In *Marxism and the Interpretation of Culture*, edited by Carl Nelson and Lawrence Grossberg, 271–313. Urbana: University of Illinois Press, 1989.

Spivak, Gayatri Chakravorty. "Subaltern Studies: Deconstructing Historiography." In *Selected Subaltern Studies*, edited by Ranajit Guha and Gayatri C. Spivak, 3–32. New York: Oxford University Press, 1988.

Starblanket, Gina. "Being Indigenous Feminists: Resurgence against Contemporary Patriarchy." In *Making Space for Indigenous Feminism*, edited by Joyce Green, 21–41. Halifax: Fernwood, 2017.

Starn, Orin. "Introduction." In *Writing Culture and the Life of Anthropology*, edited by Orin Starn, 1–24. Durham, NC: Duke University Press, 2015.

Starn, Orin, ed. *Writing Culture and the Life of Anthropology*. Durham, NC: Duke University Press, 2015.

Stasch, Rupert. "Giving Up Homicide: Korowai Experience of Witches and Police (West Papua)." *Oceania* 72, no. 1 (September 2001): 33–52. https://www.jstor.org/stable/40332094.

Stasch, Rupert. "Singapore, Big Village of the Dead: Cities as Figures of Desire, Domination, and Rupture among Korowai of Indonesian Papua." *American Anthropologist* 118, no. 2 (June 2016): 258–69. https://doi.org/10.1111/aman.12525.

Stasch, Rupert. *Society of Others: Kinship and Mourning in a West Papuan Place*. Berkeley: University of California Press, 2009.

Stengers, Isabelle. "The Cosmopolitical Proposal." In *Making Things Public: Atmospheres of Democracy*, edited by Bruno Latour and Peter Weibel, 994–1003. Cambridge: Massachusetts Institute of Technology Press, 2005.

Stewart, Kathleen. *Ordinary Affects*. Durham, NC: Duke University Press, 2007.

Stewart, Pamela J., and Andrew J. Strathern. *Humors and Substances: Ideas of the Body in New Guinea*. Westport, CT: Bergin and Garvey, 2001.

Stewart-Harawira, Makere. "Practicing Indigenous Feminism: Resistance to Imperialism." In *Making Space for Indigenous Feminism*, edited by Joyce Green, 124–39. London: Zed Books, 2007.

Stewart-Harawira, Makere. "Returning the Sacred: Indigenous Ontologies in Perilous Times." In *Radical Human Ecology: Intercultural and Indigenous Approaches*, edited by Rose Roberts and Lewis Williams, 94–109. New York: Taylor and Francis, 2012.

Stoler, Ann L. *Capitalism and Confrontation in Sumatra's Plantation Belt, 1879–1979*. New Haven, CT: Yale University Press, 1985.

Strangio, Sebastian. "Protests Greet Indonesia's Renewal of Papuan Autonomy Law." *The Diplomat*, July 19, 2021. https://thediplomat.com/2021/07/protests-greet-indonesias-renewal-of-papuan-autonomy-law/.

Strathern, Andrew J. "Melpa Food-Names as an Expression of Ideas on Identity and Substance." *Journal of the Polynesian Society* 86, no. 4 (December 1977): 503–11. https://www.jstor.org/stable/20705296.

Street, Alice. *Biomedicine in an Unstable Place: Infrastructure and Personhood in a Papua New Guinean Hospital*. Durham, NC: Duke University Press, 2014.

Suriyanto. "20 Persen Balita Merauke Kurang Gizi." *CNN Indonesia*, June 30, 2016. https://www.cnnindonesia.com/nasional/20160630104359-20-142030 /20-persen-balita-merauke-kurang-gizi.

Syah, Abdel. "Ini Kata Bupati Merauke Soal Anak Kurang Gizi." *Kabar Papua*, July 12, 2018. https://kabarpapua.co/ini-kata-bupati-merauke-soal-adanya -anak-kurang-gizi/.

TallBear, Kim. "An Indigenous Reflection on Working beyond the Human/Not Human." *GLQ: A Journal of Lesbian and Gay Studies* 21, no. 2–3 (June 2015): 230–35. https://www.muse.jhu.edu/article/582037.

TallBear, Kim. "Standing with and Speaking as Faith: A Feminist-Indigenous Approach to Inquiry." *Journal of Research Practice* 10, no. 2 (2014): 1–7. https://jrp. icaap.org/index.php/jrp/article/view/405.html.

TallBear, Kim. "Why Interspecies Thinking Needs Indigenous Standpoints." *Fieldsights*, November 18, 2011. https://culanth.org/fieldsights/why-interspecies -thinking-needs-indigenous-standpoints.

Tallis, Raymond. *Hunger*. New York: Routledge, 2014.

Tappan, Jennifer. *The Riddle of Malnutrition: The Long Arc of Biomedical and Public Health Interventions in Uganda*. Athens: Ohio State University Press, 2017.

Taussig, Michael. *The Corn Wolf*. Chicago: University of Chicago Press, 2015.

Teaiwa, Katerina M. *Consuming Ocean Island: Stories of People and Phosphate from Banaba*. Bloomington: Indiana University Press, 2014.

Teaiwa, Teresia K. "The Ancestors We Get to Choose: White Influences I Won't Deny." In *Theorizing Native Studies*, edited by Audra Simpson and Andrea Smith, 43–55. Durham, NC: Duke University Press, 2014.

Teaiwa, Teresia K. "On Analogies: Rethinking the Pacific in a Global Context." *Contemporary Pacific Studies* 18, no. 1 (2006): 71–87. https://www.jstor.org /stable/23721899.

Thomas, Deborah A., and Kamari M. Clarke. "Can Anthropology Be Decolonized?" *SAPIENS*, January 24, 2023. https://www.sapiens.org/culture/can -anthropology-be-decolonized/.

Thompson, Janna. "Being in Time: Ethics and Temporal Vulnerability." In *Vulnerability: New Essays in Ethics and Feminist Philosophy*, edited by Catriona Mackenzie, Wendy Rogers, and Susan Dodds, 162–79. Oxford: Oxford University Press, 2014.

Throop, Jason. "Sacred Suffering: A Phenomenological Anthropological Perspective." In *Phenomenology in Anthropology: A Sense of Perspective*, edited by Kalpana Ram and Chris Houston, 68–89. Bloomington: Indiana University Press, 2015.

Ticktin, Miriam. "A World without Innocence." *American Ethnologist* 44, no. 4 (2017): 577–90.

Timmer, Jaap. "Papua Coming of Age: The Cycle of Man's Civilization and Two Other Papuan Histories." In *From 'Stone Age' to 'Real-Time': Exploring Papuan*

Temporalities, Mobilities and Religiosities, edited by Martin Slama and Jenny Munro, 95–124. Canberra: Australian National University Press, 2015.

Timmer, Jaap. "The Return of the Kingdom: Agama and the Millennium among the Imyan of Irian Jaya, Indonesia." *Ethnohistory* 47, no. 1 (Winter 2000): 29–65. https://www.muse.jhu.edu/article/11645.

Timmer, Jaap. "Straightening the Path from the Ends of the Earth: The Deep Sea Canoe Movement in Solomon Island." In *Flows of Faith: Religious Reach and Community in Asia and the Pacific*, edited by Lenore Manderson, William Smith, and Matt Tomlinson, 201–14. Dordrecht: Springer, 2012.

Tompkins, Kyla Wazana. *Racial Indigestion: Eating Bodies in the 19th Century*. New York: New York University Press, 2012.

Trask, Haunani-Kay. "Feminism and Indigenous Hawaiian Nationalism." *Feminist Theory and Practice* 21, no. 4 (Summer 1996): 906–16. https://www.jstor.org/stable/3175028.

Trnka, Susanna, Jesse Hession Grayman, and Lisa L. Wynn. "Decolonizing Anthropology: Global Perspectives." *American Ethnologist* 50, no. 3 (August 2023): 345–461. https://anthrosource.onlinelibrary.wiley.com/toc/15481425/2023/50/3.

Trnka, Susanna, Jesse Hession Grayman, and Lisa L. Wynn, eds. "What Good Is Anthropology? Celebrating 50 Years of *American Ethnologist*." Special issue, *American Ethnologist* 51, no. 1 (February 2024). https://americanethnologist.org/journal/issues/volume-51-issue-1-february-2024/.

Trouillot, Michel-Rolph. "Culture on the Edges: Caribbean Creolization in Historical Context." In *From the Margins: Historical Anthropology and Its Futures*, edited by Brian K. Axel, 189–210. Durham, NC: Duke University Press, 2002.

Tuana, Nancy. "Viscous Porosity: Witnessing Katrina." In *Material Feminisms*, edited by Stacy Alaimo and Susan J. Hekman, 188–210. Bloomington: Indiana University Press, 2008.

Tuck, Eve, and K. Wayne Yang. "Decolonization Is Not a Metaphor." *Decolonization: Indigeneity, Education and Society* 1, no. 1 (2012): 1–40.

Tuhiwai Smith, Linda. *Decolonizing Methodologies: Research and Indigenous Peoples*. New York: Zed Books, 2012.

Turnbull, Colin. *The Mountain People*. New York: Touchstone, 1972.

Tynan, Lauren. "What Is Relationality? Indigenous Knowledges, Practices and Responsibilities with Kin." *Cultural Geographies* 28, no. 4 (2021): 597–610. https://doi.org/10.1177/14744740211029287.

Ulijaszek, Stanley J., Neil Mann, and Sarah Elton. *Evolving Human Nutrition: Implications for Public Health*. Cambridge: Cambridge University Press, 2012.

Underhill-Sem, Yvonne. "Contract Scholars, Friendly Philanthropists and Feminist Activists: New Development Subjects in the Pacific." *Third World Quarterly* 33, no. 6 (2012): 1095–112. https://doi.org/10.1080/01436597.2012.681499.

van Baal, Jan. *Dema: Description and Analysis of Marind-Anim Culture (South New Guinea)*. The Hague: Martinus Nijhoff, 1966.

van Eeuwijk, Brigit O. *Small but Strong: Cultural Contexts of (Mal-)Nutrition among the Northern Kwanga (East Sepik Province, Papua New Guinea)*. Basel: Wepf, 1992.

van Houten, Christina. "Gendered Political Economies and the Feminization of Hunger: M. F. K. Fisher and the Cold War Culture Wars." In *The Aesthetics and Politics of Global Hunger*, edited by Anastasia Ulanowicz and Manisha Basu, 115–34. London: Palgrave Macmillan, 2015.

van Oosterhout, Dianne. "The Scent of Sweat: Notions of Witchcraft and Morality in Inanwatan." In *Humors and Substances: Ideas of the Body in New Guinea*, edited by Pamela J. Stewart and Andrew J. Strathern, 23–50. Westport, CT: Bergin and Garvey, 2001.

Vaughan, Megan. *The Story of an African Famine: Gender and Famine in Twentieth-Century Malawi*. London: Cambridge University Press, 2009.

Vernon, James. *Hunger: A Modern History*. Cambridge, MA: Harvard University Press, 2007.

Vesperi, Maria D., and Alice Waterston. "Introduction: The Writer in the Anthropologist." In *Anthropology Off the Shelf: Anthropologists on Writing*, edited by Alice Waterston and Maria D. Vesperi, 1–11. London: Blackwell, 2011.

Vilaça, Aparecida. "Making Kin Out of Others in Amazonia." *Journal of the Royal Anthropological Institute* 8, no. 2 (June 2002): 347–65. https://www.jstor.org/stable/3134479.

Visweswaran, Kamala. *Fictions of Feminist Ethnography*. Minneapolis: University of Minnesota Press, 1994.

Vizenor, Gerald R. *Manifest Manners: Narratives on Postindian Survivance*. Lincoln: University of Nebraska Press, 1999.

Vogel, L. C., and John Richens. "Donovanosis in Dutch South New Guinea: History, Evolution of the Epidemic and Control." *Papua and New Guinea Medical Journal* 32, no. 3 (September 1989): 203–18. https://pubmed.ncbi.nlm.nih.gov/2683480/.

von Poser, Anita. "Bosmun Foodways: Emotional Reasoning in a Papua New Guinea Lifeworld." In *The Anthropology of Empathy: Experiencing the Lives of Others in Pacific Societies*, edited by Douglas W. Hollan and Jason C. Throop, 169–94. New York: Berghahn, 2011.

von Poser, Anita. *Foodways and Empathy: Relatedness in a Ramu River Society, Papua New Guinea*. New York: Berghahn, 2013.

Vunibola, Suliasi, and Matthew Scobie. "Islands of Indigenous Innovation: Reclaiming and Reconceptualising Innovation within, against and beyond Colonial-Capitalism." *Journal of the Royal Society of New Zealand* 52, supp. 1 (2022): 4–17. https://doi.org/10.1080/03036758.2022.2056618.

Wāhpāsiw, Omeasoo, and Louise Halfe. "Conversations on Indigenous Feminism." In *In Good Relation: History, Gender, and Kinship in Indigenous Feminisms*, edited by Sarah A. Nickel and Amanda Fehr, 207–29. Manitoba: University of Manitoba Press, 2020.

Waiko, John. "Komge Oro: Land and Culture or Nothing." *Gigibori* 3, no. 1 (1976): 16–19.

WALHI Papua, GRAIN, PUSAKA, et al. *Swallowing Indonesia's Forests*. March 2021. https://awasmifee.potager.org/uploads/2021/03/Swallowing-Indonesias-Forests.pdf.

Wardlow, Holly. *Wayward Women: Sexuality and Agency in a New Guinea Society*. Berkeley: University of California Press, 2006.

Warin, Megan. *Abject Relations: Everyday Worlds of Anorexia*. New Brunswick, NJ: Rutgers University Press, 2009.

Warin, Megan J., and Tanya Zivkovic. *Fatness, Obesity, and Disadvantage in the Australian Suburbs: Unpalatable Politics*. Cham: Springer International, 2019.

Washburn, Kathleen. "'No Page Is Ever Truly Blank': An Interview with Craig Santos Perez." *Postcolonial Text* 10, no. 1 (2015): 1–13. https://www.postcolonial.org/index.php/pct/article/view/1879/1785.

Waterston, Alice, and Maria D. Vesperi, eds. *Anthropology Off the Shelf: Anthropologists on Writing*. London: Blackwell, 2011.

Watts, Michael. *Silent Violence: Food, Famine and Peasantry in Northern Nigeria*. Berkeley: University of California Press, 1983.

Webb-Gannon, Camellia. *Morning Star Rising: The Politics of Decolonization in West Papua*. Honolulu: University of Hawai'i Press, 2021.

Webb-Gannon, Camellia. "#Papuanlivesmatter: How a Narrative of Racism Has Elevated West Papua's Decolonisation Movement." *International Journal of Human Rights* 27, no. 6 (2023): 1050–73. https://doi.org/10.1080/13642987.2022.2057959.

Weiner, Annette B. *Inalienable Possessions: The Paradox of Keeping-While-Giving*. Berkeley: University of California Press, 1992.

Weiner, Annette B. *Women of Value, Men of Renown*. Austin: University of Texas Press, 1976.

Weismantel, Mary J. *Food, Gender, and Poverty in the Ecuadorian Andes*. Long Grove, IL: Waveland Press, 1988.

Weiss, Erica, and Carole McGranahan. "Rethinking Pseudonyms in Ethnography: An Introduction." In "Rethinking Pseudonyms in Ethnography," edited by Carole McGranahan and Erica Weiss, *American Ethnologist*, December 13, 2021. https://americanethnologist.org/features/collections/rethinking-pseudonyms-in-ethnography/rethinking-pseudonyms-in-ethnography-an-introduction.

Wentworth, Chelsea. "Public Eating, Private Pain: Children, Feasting, and Food Security in Vanuatu." *Food and Foodways* 24, no. 3–4 (2016): 136–52. https://doi.org/10.1080/07409710.2016.1210888.

West, Paige. *Conservation Is Our Government Now: The Politics of Ecology in Papua New Guinea*. Durham, NC: Duke University Press, 2006.

West, Paige. "Translation, Value, and Space: Theorizing an Ethnographic and Engaged Environmental Anthropology." *American Anthropologist* 107, no. 4 (December 2005): 632–42. https://www.jstor.org/stable/3567381.

Whyte, Kyle P. "Food Sovereignty, Justice and Indigenous Peoples: An Essay on Settler Colonialism and Collective Continuance." In *The Oxford Handbook of Food Ethics*, edited by Anne Barnhill, Mark Budolfson, and Tyler Doggett, 1–24. New York: Oxford University Press, 2018.

Widjojo, Muridan S. *Papua Road Map: Negotiating the Past, Improving the Present, and Securing the Future*. Jakarta: Indonesian Institute of Sciences, 2010.

Wilbur, Rachel E., and Joseph B. Gone. "Beyond Resilience: A Scoping Review of Indigenous *Survivance* in the Health Literature." *Development and Psychopathology* 35, no. 5 (December 2023): 2226–40. https://doi.org/10.1017/S0954579423000706.

Willerslev, Rane, and Lotte Meinert. "Understanding Hunger with Ik Elders and Turnbull's *The Mountain People*." *Ethnos* 82, no. 5 (2017): 820–45. https://doi.org/10.1080/00141844.2016.1138984.

Wilson, Marisa, ed. *Postcolonialism, Indigeneity and Struggles for Food Sovereignty: Alternative Food Networks in Subaltern Spaces*. London: Routledge, 2014.

Winchester, Simon. *Land: How the Hunger for Ownership Shaped the Modern World*. London: HarperCollins, 2011.

Wing, John R., and Peter King. *Genocide in West Papua? The Role of the Indonesian State Apparatus and a Current Needs Assessment of the Papuan People*. Broadway, New South Wales: Breakout Design and Print, 2005.

Winter, Christine. "Sand as Subject of Multispecies Justice." In *Beyond Bios: The Life of Matter and the Matter of Life*, edited by Sophie Chao, Christine Winter, and David Schlosberg. Durham, NC: Duke University Press, forthcoming.

Winter, Christine. "A Seat at the Table: Te Awa Tupua, Te Urewera, Taranaki Maunga and Political Representation." *Borderlands* 20, no. 1 (April 2021): 116–39. https://link.gale.com/apps/doc/A682026252/AONE?u=anon~5b6eb5c4&sid=googleScholar&xid=f22fe4b8.

Winter, Christine. "Unearthing the Time/Space/Matter of Multispecies Justice." *Cultural Politics* 18, no. 2 (March 2023): 39–56. https://doi.org/10.1215/17432197-10232459.

Wooltorton, Sandra, Anne Poelina, and Len Collard. "River Relationships: For the Love of Rivers." *River Research and Applications* 38, no. 3 (March 2022): 393–403. https://doi.org/10.1002/rra.3854.

Worsley, Peter. *The Trumpet Shall Sound: A Study of "Cargo" Cults in Melanesia*. New York: Schocken, 1968.

Wospakrik, Josina O. "Transculturation and Indigenous Amungme Women of Papua, Indonesia." PhD diss., University of New South Wales, 2019.

Wulff, Helena, ed. *The Anthropologist as Writer: Genres and Contexts in the Twenty-First Century*. New York: Berghahn, 2016.

Wynter, Sylvia. "Novel and History, Plot and Plantation." *Savacou*, no. 5 (1971): 95–102.

Yates-Doerr, Emily. "Intervals of Confidence: Uncertain Accounts of Global Hunger." *BioSocieties* 10 (2015): 229–46. https://doi.org/10.1057/biosoc.2015.9.

Yates-Doerr, Emily. "The Opacity of Reduction: Nutritional Black-Boxing and the Meanings of Nourishment." *Food, Culture and Society* 15, no. 2 (2012): 293–313. https://doi.org/10.2752/175174412X13233545145381.

Yates-Doerr, Emily. *The Weight of Obesity: Hunger and Global Health in Postwar Guatemala*. Berkeley: University of California Press, 2015.

Yoneyama, Lisa. "Liberation under Siege: U.S. Military Occupation and Japanese Women's Enfranchisement." *American Quarterly* 57, no. 3 (September 2005): 885–910.

Young, Michael W. *Fighting with Food: Leadership, Value, and Social Control in a Massim Society*. Cambridge: Cambridge University Press, 1971.

Young, Michael W. "'The Worst Disease': The Cultural Definition of Hunger in Kalauna." In *Shared Wealth and Symbol: Food, Culture, and Society in Oceania and Southeast Asia*, edited by Lenore Manderson, 111–26. Cambridge: Cambridge University Press, 1986.

Yunkaporta, Tyson. "All Our Landscapes Are Broken: Right Story and the Law of the Land." *Griffith Review Online*, April 1, 2020. https://www.griffithreview.com/articles/all-our-landscapes-are-broken/.

Yunkaporta, Tyson. *Sand Talk: How Indigenous Thinking Can Save the World*. Melbourne: Text Publishing, 2019.

Zelenietz, Marty. "Sorcery and Social Change: An Introduction." In *Sorcery and Social Change in Melanesia*, edited by Marty Zelenietz and Shirley Lindenbaum, 3–14. Adelaide: University of Adelaide Press, 1981.

Zinn, Howard. "Speaking Truth to Power with Books." In *Anthropology Off the Shelf: Anthropologists on Writing*, edited by Alice Waterston and Maria D. Vesperi, 15–20. London: Blackwell, 2011.

autonomy, 91, 124, 189n15
autophagy, 168

Baal, Jan van, 117, 156
babies, 64, 113, 115
bad hunger (*kelaparan buruk*), 49–50, 52, 196n35
bagi sama dunia ("share with the world"), 143
Baining, 72
Barker, Joanne, 181n24
Barnabus, 136
Basic Agrarian Law (1960), 125
Basik-Basik (pig) clan, 29, 86, 87
Bateson, Gregory, 121
Bayau, West Papua, 1, 30
bekas luka (scars), 101
Bendita, 130, 131, *131*, 135
Bernardina, 154
Betasamosake Simpson, Leanne, 31
Bian River, *39*, 118, 119
biodiversity, 4
biofortification, 64, 113, 193n11
biofuel policies, 146
biomedical institutions, 73, 195n28
bird-hunting expeditions, 58–59
birds of paradise, 58–59
Blaney, Fay, 205n24
boan. *See* clans
bodily permeability, 52
Boeck, Filip de, 199n7
Boelaars, Jan, 156
Boscacci, Louise, 203n10
breath (*nafas*), 31
Brenton, Barrett, 187n5
Briggs, Charles, 146
brothels, 82. *See also* sex workers
burial, 47, 98
Byrd, Jodi, 204n21

capitalism, 3, 7, 21, 23, 70, 116; colonialism and, 146, 150, 167; colonial racial, 15, 16, 20, 57, 165–66, 171; logics of, 8–9, 133–35; metabolic justice relation to, 169–70; techno, 97–98, 170; violence and, 118, 142
capitalist modernity, 8–9
Caritas, 58–59, 60–62

Carlotta, 81, 84
Carmelita, 76–77
cassowary, 40, 51
Castro, Josué de, 179n9
Catholic Church, 80
Catholicism, 47, 130, 131
Cendrawasih University, 155–56
cerita (story), 44–45
Césaire, Aimé, 110
Cesarina, 123–24
Chamoiseau, Patrick, 110
chemical pesticides, 72
children, *13*, 42–43; enculturation of, 50–51; gender relation to, 199n1
Choudhury, Athia, 69
Christianity, settler-colonial rule relation to, 131–32. *See also* Jesus Christ
Circia, 68, 73
Cistina, 123, 124
citational methodology, 179n10
cities (*kota*), 99, 101–4; plastic foods in, 100, 118; sorcery/witchcraft relation to, 107. *See also* Merauke City
clans (*boan*), 187n4; Basik-Basik (pig), 29, 86–87; Kaize (cassowary), 1, 30, 55; Kavzum (eel), 118, 119–20; Mahuze (dog), 29; Ndiken (white stork), 25; Sami (snake), 93
clinical gaze, 67, 193n13
clinics, 54, 57, 73, 113. *See also* medical facilities
Coburn, Elaine, 19
collective metabolism, 52–53
colonialism, 17, 22, 90, 101, 156; capitalism and, 146, 150, 167; gastro, 8, 75, 165–66
colonial racial capitalism, 15, 16, 20, 171; gender relation to, 165–66; oil palm plantations and, 57
colonization, 6–7, 21; Dutch, 59–60, 105, 107, 117; Indonesian, 60–61, 62; of West Papua, 23, 186n53
colonized-colonizer divide, 75
colostrum, 45, 46
commodified foodways, 167
communicative justice, 146
community, 38, 50, 125–26, 128; *semangat* relation to, 36–37; skin relation to, 34

masculinity, 15, 17, 195n33
Massim, 190n31
material fulfillment, 147
material wealth, 118. *See also* money, hunger for
Matthias, 112–13
McClaurin, Irma, 159
McGranahan, Carole, 150
meaning-making, 134–35, 140–41
Media, Miyarrka, 208n48
media representation, 19–20
medical facilities, 66–68
medicalization, 6
medicine men (messav anim), 106, 117, 122
meditation, 40
Mega Rice Project, 192n7
memoria passionis ("passionate remembrance"), 129
memories (*ingatan*), 40–41, 78, 153–54, 197n7
men, 57, 82–84, 162, 195n33, 205n25; agribusiness relation to, 15, 22, 80, 81, 116, 148–49; ancestor spirits relation to, 121; bird-hunting expeditions relation to, 58; cities relation to, 102; decisions by, 65, 118, 123, 129; forest foodways relation to, 29; as hunters, 41–42; Indonesian colonization relation to, 60–61; moral injury of, 110–11; oil palm corporations relation to, 80, 144; roads relation to, 91; sexually transmitted disease and, 104; shame of, 152–53; sorcery relation to, 108; structural inequalities and, 142
mental manipulation, 107–8, 109–10. *See also* sorcery/witchcraft
Merauke City, 82, 90, 99, *100*, 101, 118
Merauke Integrated Food and Energy Estate (MIFEE), 3, 62, 192n7, 200n15
Merauke regency, Papua province, Indonesia, *xv*, 3–4
messav anim (medicine men), 106, 117, 122
metabolic justice, 7, 47, 73, 167–68, 171; capitalism relation to, 169–70; ethnographic writing relation to, 172
metaphors, 207n43

MIFEE. *See* Merauke Integrated Food and Energy Estate
Mikaela, 1
military, 92, 104, 106–7, 125–26
Millard, Ann, 199n8
mill effluents, 64
millenarianism, 131–32, 133–34
Mina, 24, 137, *138*, 139–40, 151, 175–76
Ministry of Research and Technology, of Indonesia, 181n27
Mirabela, 55–56, 84, 148–49; on hunger for money, 81–82, 83; on women, 150
miras (hard liquor), 82
miscarriages, 13, 112
misrepresentation, 154, 155–56, 160–61
missionization, 23, 59, 107, 117
modernity, 8–9, 148, 165
Mohanty, Chandra Talpade, 15–16
money, hunger for (*lapar uang*), 22, 80, 84–85, 196n34; men relation to, 81–84; pollution relation to, 110
monocrops, 3, 27, 56, 71, 90, 169
monsoon hunger (*kelaparan angin musim*), 49
Moore, Sally Falk, 18
moral economies, 27–28, 48
moral injury, 110–11, 198n21
more-than-human kinships, 28, 29, 47, 165, 177n3; freedom and, 33, 34; relationality and, 57
mourning, 98–99
multiculturalism, 125
Munro, Jenny, 134, 193n13
Muslims, 132

Nabobo-Baba, Unaisi, 39, 144, 150
nafas (breath), 31
names, 149–50
Narayan, Kirin, 162–63
Narokobi, Bernard Mullu, 156
narrative plotting, 157, 207n34
Naupa, Anna, 195n33
Ndiken (white stork) clan, 25
Neitch, Kenna, 186n49
New Britain Island, 72
New Guinea, 60, 62, 126, 132
new hunger (*kelaparan baru*), 58, 69–70

NGOs. *See* nongovernmental
organizations
Nickel, Sarah, 14–15
nonbiodegradable waste, 74
nongovernmental organizations (NGOs),
4, 80
non-innocence: of ethnographic writing,
18–19, 23, 141–43, 160–62, 163–64;
hesitation relation to, 172
nonverbal realities, writing relation to, 159
Nora, 136–37, 143, 146, 149–50, 173
nourishment, 32, 44, 45, 96, 133–34,
171–72; environment relation to,
188n9; in forest foodways, 37, 56–57,
70–71, 72–73
Nusa Tenggara Timur, 4
nutritional black-boxing, 69
nutritional structural violence, 6–7

Obeyesekere, Gananath, 147
oil palm corporations (*perusahaan
sawit*), 14, 56, 84, 126–27, 152; ancestor spirits compared to, 122; government relation to, 104–5; hunger
for money relation to, 81–82; men
relation to, 80, 144; mental manipulation by, 107–8, 109–10; paternalism
of, 145; social welfare schemes of, 56,
74–77
"Oil Palm Expansion in West Papua,"
181n29
oil palm plantations, 55, 57, 62, *81*, 90;
freedom and, 196n36; irrigation
systems for, *109*; men on, 83–84;
sorcery/witchcraft relation to, 107
oil palms, 3–4, *63*, 85, 123, 177n1; ancestor
spirits relation to, 117; in dreams,
197n5; forest foodways relation to,
22; violence relation to, 57
Oktavia, 97
Olivia, 68–69, 147–48, 170
orang tua (elders), 43
Oskar, 112–13
Otsus, 124, 200n16
overconsumption, 50–51

pain, 168
palm oil, 9, 11, 14, 126, 169, 177n1

Paola, 54–55
Paolina, 129–30
Papuan Customary Council, 200n16
Papuan Democracy Forum, 200n16
Papuan Voices, 204n18
Papua province, Indonesia, Merauke regency, xv, 3–4
Parreñas, Juno Salazar, 10
"passionate remembrance" (*memoria
passionis*), 129
paternalism, 145, 147, 154
patriarchy, 129, 150, 205n24
Patricia, 73, 74, 77, 79
Paulina, 139–40, 151, 157, 158
peace (*damai*), 38, 39, 71–72, 100–101
Pelluchon, Corine, 188n9
PEM. *See* protein energy malnutrition
pemerintah. *See* government
pendatang (settlers), 77
pengorbanan diri ("self-sacrifice"), 130
Perpetua, 118, *119*, 119–20
persistence, 186n49
perusahaan sawit. *See* oil palm
corporations
Phone and Spear (Media), 208n48
Pia, 104
Pictou, Sherry, 195n33
Pius, 107–8
placenta, 46
plant and animal kin (amai), 33, 61–62,
69, 72, 92–93, 177n3
plantation labor force, 61
plastic foods (*lapar makanan plastik*),
73, *74*, 83, 110, 170; in cities, 100, 118;
decisions relation to, 108, 109; infrastructure of, 77–78; sago compared
to, 79; social welfare schemes and,
74–77
plume trade, 58, 62, 105
Plumwood, Val, 47
pneumonia, 66–67
pollution, 109–10, 118, 119
Pollution Is Colonialism (Liboiron), 179n10
Poser, Anita von, 37
positionality, 7, 9, 17, 47, 142, 207n43;
of anthropologists, 10–11; in forest
foodways, 28–29
Povinelli, Elizabeth, 125

power asymmetries, 64–65, 125, 162
power dynamics, 10, 15
pregnancy, 112, 191n33
premastication, 36, 46
prey, positionality of, 47
primitivism, paternalism relation to, 154
privatization, 60–61, 126
privilege, 163, 168
processed foods, 56, 64, 113, 193n11
progress (*kemajuan*), 75
protein energy malnutrition (PEM), 64
protests, 180n21
pseudonyms, 149–50, 152, 204n19
punishment, by ancestor spirits, 23, 48, 51, 113, 116–18, 135

racial slurs, 103
racist tropes, 156, 203n16
radical care, 98–99
Rafaela, 33
ramai (liveliness), 37–38, 51, 59, 71
Redvers, Nicole, 191n39
Regulation No. 40 of 1996 on Business Use Permits, 124–25
Regulation of the Ministry of Agriculture No. 26 on Guidance on Plantation Business Permits, 125
relationality, 6, 49, 51–52, 57
representation, 19–20, 154, 155–56, 160–61
reproductive health, 185n48
researcher-researched dynamic, 9
resistance, 186n49, 206n32
resource extraction, colonization for, 6–7
responsibility, 171, 185n46; anthropology and, 209n14; knowledge relation to, 144–45
restrained care, 188n10
rice barn (*lumbung padi*), 62
Richards, Audrey, 190n28
ritual codes, 29, 48
ritualized etiquette, 46
ritualized practice, 117, 181n27
roadkill, 13, 14, 87–88, 93, 96, 97–98
roads (*jalan*), 90–93, 107
Robbins, Joel, 157

romanticization, 19, 27–28, 185n45
Rose, Deborah Bird, 96–97, 184n44
Ross, Luana, 205n25
Roundtable on Sustainable Palm Oil, 126
Roy, Parama, 8
Rubina, 92

"sacredscience," 31, 187n6
sago (<u>dahk</u>), 1, 25–27, 32, 44–45, 70–73, 199n4; biomedical institutions relation to, 195n28; interpersonal disputes relation to, 30–31; plastic foods compared to, 79; wetness and, 26–27, 35; women relation to, 42–43
sago-processing structure, 35
Sami (snake) clan, 93
Santos Perez, Craig, 75, 171
Sarwono, Sarlito, 156
satiety (*kekenyangan*), 22, 60, 70, 134, 147–48, 170; forest foodways and, 27–29, 32, 36; nourishment relation to, 45; plastic foods relation to, 74, 78, 79; *semangat* relation to, 37; sharing relation to, 30–31
scars (*bekas luka*), 101
Schaeffer, Felicity, 31, 187n6
Scheper-Hughes, Nancy, 6
scientification, of hunger, 69, 166
Scobie, Matthew, 20
Scott, James, 184n43
Scott-Smith, Tom, 166
sedenterization policies, 59–60, 71–72
Selena, 130, 131, *131*, 132
self-determination, 166, 183n38, 200n16, 205n24
"self-sacrifice" (*pengorbanan diri*), 130
semangat (energy/vitality), 29, 36–37, 49, 71
sentient ecology, 31
Serafina, 106
settler-colonial rule, 15, 92, 102, 131–32
settlers (*pendatang*), 77
sexually transmitted disease, 67, 82, 89, 103–4
sexual violence, 89, 198n15, 205n25
sex workers, 82, 103–4